Silicon Valley: Planet Startup

D0921672

Silicon Valley: Planet Startup

Disruptive Innovation, Passionate Entrepreneurship &
Hightech Startups

Peter Ester
Arne Maas

Rotterdam Business School
Research Center Entrepreneurship and Business Innovation
Amsterdam University Press

Cover design: Klaas Wijnberg
Lay-out: Crius Group, Hulshout

Amsterdam University Press English-language titles are distributed in the US and Canada by
the University of Chicago Press.

ISBN	978 94 6298 280 2
e-ISBN	978 90 4853 283 4
DOI	10.5117/9789462982802
NUR	782

Silicon Valley is a mindset, not a location
Reid Hoffman, co-founder LinkedIn

To our partners:

Amelia Román, born and raised in Silicon Valley, working and living in the Netherlands

Sabine Dessart, Arne's favorite cook, and a successful entrepreneur herself

Contents

Foreword

Success in the StartupDelta

"You don't have to be big to do great things," I once heard an entrepreneur say. And he was right. Silicon Valley is the perfect example.

Covering an area of only 1,800 square miles, the Silicon Valley region is home to some of the largest and fastest-growing companies of our time. Companies like Google, eBay, and of course Apple. Which leads to the intriguing question of how? How did this region become the birthplace of so many successful startups? What is its secret? And what lessons can we draw from Silicon Valley's success?

These are questions that not only I, but also businesses, entrepreneurs, and governments all over the world are trying to answer. In this book, Dutch professors Peter Ester and Arne Maas unravel the mystery of Silicon Valley, showing us what is needed to foster a productive environment for startups – and what should be avoided. They offer insights we will take to heart.

Since 2014, we have been developing our own Silicon Valley in the Netherlands, the 'StartupDelta'. The Netherlands has a lot to offer budding startups: hightech knowledge, an innovative mindset, and a large dose of enterprising spirit. More and more Dutch people, most of them young, are taking the risk of starting their own business. That's a sound basis. This book shows us the importance of combining the passion of young entrepreneurs with practical elements like adequate financing, excellent education, and a good network.

And that is exactly what we are doing with the Dutch StartupDelta. This initiative brings together public administrators, scientists, investors, and entrepreneurs around a shared goal: making the Netherlands an ideal location for startups, where young entrepreneurs with futuristic ideas can turn their dreams into reality. It is fantastic to see what a stimulating effect this is having. Today the Dutch startup ecosystem ranks fourth in Europe. And for us, of course, the sky is the limit.

As Steve Jobs once said: "Great things are never done by one person, they're done by a team of people." This book is both a guide and a source of inspiration. So let us continue working together to make the Dutch StartupDelta a great success.

Mark Rutte
Prime Minister of the Netherlands

Acknowledgements

We would like to thank the twenty-three startup founders who participated in this study and who generously took the time to talk to us about their business adventures, their passion and ambition, and their enthusiasm and dedication. It was a pleasure interviewing such gifted and committed entrepreneurs. We wish them all the success in the world in developing ventures that make a distinctive impact in their respective markets. Thank you: Faruk Ateş (Presentate), Neal Blaak (ZappoTV), Thijs Boekhoff (Ingen-Housz), Ruben Daniëls (Cloud9 IDE), Edial Dekker (Eventbrite), Jan Grotenbreg (SiliconValleyLink), Pieter Hoff, (Groasis), Arthur van Hoff (Jaunt), Jurriaan Kamp (The Intelligent Optimist), Salar al Khafaji (Silk), Dirk de Kok (Mobtest), Eric-Jan van Leeuwen (Login VSI), Pieter Bas Leezenberg (SkyGeo), Ronald Mannak (JumpCam), David Mayer (RENDLE), Pieter Noordam (RFIsoft), Marieke van der Poel (Proef), Vincent van de Poll (GROM), Rip Pruisken (Rip van Wafels), Adrie Reinders (EFactor), Maarten Sierhuis (Ejenta), Valentin Smirnoff (Incubator Wells Fargo R&D), and Harm TenHoff (BayLink).

In order to fully understand Silicon Valley as an ecosystem, we also interviewed a number of startup stakeholders in the Bay Area. These experts helped us to frame Silicon Valley as an intricate web of actors, agencies, and entrepreneurs that constitutes the innovativeness of the region. We are grateful to Sean Randolph, President Bay Area Council Economic Institute, San Francisco, for sharing his insights about trends in entrepreneurship in Silicon Valley. We thank Oscar Garcia, Director Mountain View Chamber of Commerce, and Ken Rosenberg, Chair of the Mountain View Chamber of Commerce, for their perspectives on the startup culture and the impact of hightech icons such as Google on local communities.

We are much indebted to Ian Patrick Sobieski, Managing Director Band of Angels, Menlo Park, for explaining the role of venture capital in funding hightech startups in Silicon Valley and for allowing us to be present at one of the Angels' pitch events; a truly remarkable experience. Many thanks also to Cees Jan Koomen, a seasoned Venture Capitalist (Silicon Valley & High Tech Campus Eindhoven), initiator of Point One Innovation Fund, for sharing his unique experience with supporting startups on both sides of the ocean. We thank Tom Beck and Scott Gardner, President and CEO of R2integrated and Liquid, respectively. As leaders of their marketing agencies they explained us how marketing works in the Valley. Curtis Mo, Partner at DLA Piper, provided us useful insights in his work as a lawyer focusing on dealmaking for startups. Vish Mishra, a very energetic and seasoned venture capitalist, mentor at incubator The Hive, and Venture Director of Clearstone, shared with us many ideas about investing in the Valley. So did Bill Reichert and Marco ten Vaanholt. Bill as managing director of Garage Technology Ventures, sharing with us his expertise and experience around early stage investments. Marco as managing partner of BootUp Ventures, sharing his expertise and experience with investing and accelerating international startups. Duncan Logan, founder and CEO of RocketSpace, explained his unique way of accelerating startups, among which are Spotify and Uber. Elizabeth Yin, partner at 500 Startups, clarified the workings of an accelerator with a strong focus on customer acquisition and fundraising. Last but not least, we thank Quirijn Kleppe, Philipp Schubert, Waad Jaradat, and Alexandre Gallardo, students at San Jose State University, who shared their career dreams and startup attitudes with us. They made clear that their careers will be very much steered by their learning experience at SJSU and their exposure to the Silicon Valley startup vibe.

Universities play a vital role in Silicon Valley, both in terms of R&D and in having launched thousands of startups. We express our thanks to Marguerite Gong Hancock, Stanford University, Associate Director of the Stanford Program on Regions of Innovation and Entrepreneurship (SPRIE) and leading expert on immigrant entrepreneurship. We greatly acknowledge the collaboration by the Lucas Graduate School of Business, San Jose State University: David Steele, Dean; Steve Kwan, Associate Dean; Malu Roldan, Associate Dean; Curt Anderson, Director Marketing & Communications; and Anuradha Basu, Director Silicon Valley Center for Entrepreneurship. We are looking forward to extending our co-operation through joint student exchange projects, case competitions, and cross-cultural research on entrepreneurship.

Furthermore, we are grateful to Edwin Tan and Allen Chiu, Deputy District Director and Congressional Aide of US Congressman Mike Honda respectively, for their vision on the role of government in advancing innovation and entrepreneurship, and for their outlook on the rapidly increasing inequality in Silicon Valley.

A number of Belgian government agencies active in the Bay Area enlarged our Dutch perspective on Silicon Valley. Many thanks to Baudouin de Hemptinne, Belgian Trade Commission; Nathalie Delrue-McGuire, Honorary Consul Belgium; Eric Gabrys, Brussels Invest & Export and Audra Martyn, Belgian Trade Commission.

Dutch policymakers were also interviewed in order to learn the details of Dutch economic and international policy in promoting startups, both in the Netherlands and in Silicon Valley. We acknowledge the input of Bianca Oudshoff, Coos Santing, and Pieter Waasdorp, Ministry of Economic Affairs, and of Nora Dessing, Ministry of Foreign Affairs.

The Dutch Consulate in San Francisco has been very helpful in various stages of our research project. We are impressed by its vital role as a liaison between the Netherlands and the Bay area. We are grateful to Hugo van Meijenfeldt, Consul-General and his staff members Ard van der Vorst (Head of Economic Affairs), Anne Donker, Jasper Smit, and Robert Thijssen. Special thanks also to Peter Laanen, former International Trade Director of the Netherlands Business Support Office, Consulate-General of the Netherlands, San Francisco. His help was very instrumental in involving Dutch entrepreneurs in this study. His network is impressive.

Our Research Associate Tim van Duren participated in all phases of the project. We highly value his assistance and efforts. We also thank our colleague and cross-cultural expert Pieter van Nispen tot Pannerden for his input on the topic of cultural diversity and innovation.

Many thanks to Helen J. van Oosten and Amelia Román for their professional English language correction of the book.

Finally, we greatly acknowledge Cees van der Kraan, Dean of Rotterdam Business School, and Guy Bauwen, Director of the Research Center Entrepreneurship and Business Innovation of Rotterdam University. They both share a stimulating sensitivity for innovative forms of international entrepreneurship. Thank you for supporting this study, both financially and substantively.

Peter Ester
Arne Maas
Rotterdam/Silicon Valley, November 2015

Business Focus of Participating Startup Founders & CEOs

In order to get a better understandings of the startup entrepreneurs that we talked to in writing this book – both in the personal interviews and in the group interview sessions – and to add some local flavor, this chapter will present concise descriptions of these startups and its founders.

Faruk Ateş, Co-founder of Presentate. A new tool for creating presentations and other visual content. On line sharing. Serves all platforms and devices. Fast, with professionally designed templates, and a speed-optimized interface. Focus on effective presentations, audience-oriented.

Neal Blaak, Co-founder of ZappoTV. Serial entrepreneur. ZappoTV is a next generation TV service. With a hybrid set-top box, it combines off air digital TV, with internet video, social networking, music, and photos. At home and on the go, for iOS and Android. Offices in Silicon Valley and the Netherlands.

Thijs Boekhoff, Founder and CEO of Ingen-Housz. A startup with a focus on disruptive innovation in healthcare. Integrated healthcare technology and solutions for medical cost reduction and process improvement. Providing greater self-management and extended independent living. Target groups: elderly and chronically ill.

Ruben Daniëls, CEO and Co-founder of Cloud9 IDE. First-ever commercial cloud-based integrated development environment (IDE) for JavaScript developers incorporating HTML5, and supporting Python, Ruby, and PHP. Developers can access, edit, and share projects anywhere, to build, test, debug, and deploy web and mobile applications in as little as half the time, with fewer technical skills. Next-generation technology.

Edial Dekker, former CEO and Co-founder of the Berlin-based startup Gidsey. Now Senior Product Manager at Eventbrite, San Francisco. Eventbrite is a global marketplace for live experiences that lets people find and create events in 180+ countries.

Jan Grotenbreg, CEO and founder of Silicon Valley Link. Provides strategic marketing and business development services for transatlantic companies that see Silicon Valley as a strategic place to expand their business. Focus on ICT, Telecom, CleanTech, and Semiconductors.

Pieter Hoff, CEO and Founder of Groasis. Inventor of the anti-desertification Groasis Waterboxx. His invention supports plant and tree survival in dry areas (deserts, mountains) without using groundwater or electricity. It collects water by catching rainwater and by producing and catching water from condensation. No irrigation needed. The Waterboxx won *Popular Science*'s Best 2010 Invention award, beating even the iPad.

Arthur van Hoff, most successful Dutch serial entrepreneur in Silicon Valley. Founder and CTO of Jaunt VR. Provides end-to-end solution for creating cinematic VR experiences. Arthur was on the pioneering developers team of the Java programming language at Sun Microsystems. Started and sold several highly successful companies including Marimba, Strangeberry, ZING, and Ellerdale. Advisor to many startups.

Jurriaan Kamp, Co-founder of The Intelligent Optimist: an independent international media platform focused on solutions, possibilities, and inspiration. Optimism is believed to be the most effective and efficient strategy to drive the innovation and creativity that are necessary to solve the problems that people and society face.

Salar al Khafaji, CEO and Co-founder of Silk, a cloud-based (big) data publishing platform. Allows users to create visualizations from their data sources and offers an application programming interface (API) to help developers instantly create Web pages with embedded visualizations. Silk delivers its service without the need for any hardware or software installation, everything is performed directly in the user's browser.

Dirk de Kok is CEO and Founder of Mobtest. His company helps mobile developers to improve their apps via user testing. The Mobtest platform lets developers distribute their apps, select testers, and gather implicit and explicit feedback. With this feedback developers know how to improve their apps.

Eric-Jan van Leeuwen, CEO Login VSI. Provides proactive performance management solutions for virtualized desktop and server environments. Helps clients with more predictable performance, higher availability, and a more consistent end user experience. Offices in Silicon Valley and Amsterdam.

Pieter Bas Leezenberg, CEO and Co-founder of SkyGeo. Supports managers of large-scale infrastructure monitor their assets. Technology based on satellite radar imaging. Tracking with millimeter-accuracy deformation in levees, railroads, storage tanks, pipelines, dams, and other critical infrastructure.

Ronald Mannak, serial entrepreneur, JumpCam lead iOS engineer. JumpCam is a collaborative video app for iPhone and Android. It enables people to create joint videos by piecing together shots into mini-movies that can grow and evolve over time. Named *Time Magazine*'s top 100 apps of 2013.

David Mayer, Founder and Chief Product Officer, Rendle, Inc. Provides analytics to help employers measure the effectiveness of their wellness efforts and provide employees with tools to help raise awareness and educate about the importance of lifestyle to a healthy life. The goal is to reduce medical expenditures and to increase productivity and company morale.

Pieter Noordam, Founder and CEO of RFIsoft. Markets and develops products for workflow management and data analytics. Focus on HW/SW systems integration, energy monitoring management, vision system data analysis, smart consumables in the biotech industry, and product marking.

Marieke van der Poel. Chief Creative Officer of Proef Trend Forecasting. Strategic partner in translating consumer needs into brand capabilities. From brainstorming to macro trend mapping. From trends to tangible product and design direction. Offices in San Francisco, New York City, and Los Angeles.

Vincent van de Poll, CEO and Co-owner of GROM. Personalized 3D printed protective smartphone cases. B2B: easy to use customization software, affordable customer oriented 3D printed product solution. Offices in San Francisco and Hong Kong. One of the leading global accelerators, 500 Startups, located in Mountain View, decided to invest in GROM.

Rip Pruisken, co-founded Rip van Wafels together with Marco De Leon. The company's mission is to enable the increasingly busy population in the US to savor the time they spend eating convenient foods. Their first product, a multi-purpose snack wafel, is a better for you indulgence that can be eaten as a breakfast topped with yogurt, as an energy boost for sport, or as a mid-afternoon snack with your hot drink. A perfectly suitable snack for the busy Silicon Valley lifestyle.

Adrie Reinders, serial entrepreneur, CEO and Co-founder of EFactor. Offers online and face-to-face matching to relevant parties that can help grow a member's business such as investors, mentors, and peers to bring out and nurture today's new business ideas. EFactor is the world's largest niche Entrepreneurial Network.

Maarten Sierhuis, Founder of Ejenta and director of Nissan Research Center Silicon Valley. Ejenta applies artificial intelligence, agent technology, and sensor technology to the development of intelligent personal assistants for daily living, healthcare, and space. Ejenta's platform is based on exclusively licensed NASA technology.

Valentin Smirnoff, former startup founder (Tinypay, Linger), now Mobile UX Designer at incubator within Wells Fargo, R&D/Emerging Technologies Group. Creating UX and graphic design for native iOS and Android applications. Implementing emerging technologies in payments, e-commerce, location-based, security, and authentication services.

Harm TenHoff, CEO Baylink, conducting and advancing intercontinental business between Silicon Valley and Europe. Focus on hightech medical devices in early stage innovation that may revolutionize clinical practice and patient care. Medical device incubator & business accelerator. Has been awarded 20 US patents for medical devices.

1. Introduction: The Silicon Valley Saga

This book was written out of fascination about how Silicon Valley became and continues to be the absolute world leader in innovative entrepreneurship and pioneering hightech startups. The Valley gave birth to a number of amazingly successful companies that changed the world and changed our lifestyle. And continues to do so. Apple, Google, Oracle, Yahoo, eBay, Facebook, LinkedIn, WhatsApp, Twitter, Instagram, all immensely impacted our societies, our economies, our workplaces, and our personal lives. Their impact is felt across generations, cultures, and nations. The power of social media that is generated by the widely adopted ICT products, services, and networks of these hightech giants is unparalleled and even spans continents. The rise of the smartphone led to a mobile apps revolution that created a phenomenal boost in startups which will – again – change the way we do business, the way we work, the way we travel, and the way we communicate. New and equally innovative ventures eagerly entered the perpetually competitive Silicon Valley arena such as Dropbox, Uber, Airbnb, SpaceX, Tesla, and many others. These new ventures also penetrated new sectors including health, biomedical technology, artificial intelligence, cleantech, sustainable transportation, space, drones and robots, machine learning, cloud computing and big data, self-driving cars, and the Internet of Things. The Silicon Valley technology portfolio is impressive and manages to renew itself constantly.

With the highest concentration of startups in the world, Silicon Valley is Planet Startup. A corridor of about sixty miles between San Francisco and San Jose, squeezed in between Interstate 280 and Highway 101. An area of about 1,800 square miles (0.05% of the USA) and a population of almost 3 million (almost 1% of the USA). Located in the San Mateo and Santa Clara counties in the Bay Area, the Valley links towns such as Palo Alto, Menlo Park, Mountain View, Cupertino, Sunnyvale, and Santa Clara that house the headquarters of iconic hightech companies and thousands of startups who dream of reaching the same echelon.[1] Not a particularly nice region, at least not with respect to architecture, history or nature as it is dominated by long strips of typically American shopping centers and offices, connected by a crowded El Camino Real.[2] Since its pioneering start in semiconductors, computer networks, personal computers, programming, and the Internet, Silicon Valley has become the global hotspot of hightech innovation and entrepreneurship. It has made the area into one of the most prosperous and successful regions in the world. The Bay Area – with Silicon Valley as its technological epicenter – has a GDP which compared to national economies would rank it as the 19th economy in the world, only two places below the Netherlands.[3] It is home to more US and Global Fortune 500 companies than anywhere in the nation except New York. Half of the top 100 private cleantech companies and the vast majority of the most influential social media companies are located in this region.[4] The 25 largest technology companies employ over one million workers, counting a large share of highly qualified software programmers and engineers. Success breeds success, so the Valley formula shows. In 2014, Silicon Valley hightech firms had nearly a third of the entire cash reserves held by US companies, and showed record profits of over $103 billion.[5] These phenomenal profits equal 85% of the Netherlands' annual budget for Health and Education. Forty percent of total US venture capital is invested in Silicon Valley. It witnessed 23 IPOs in 2014, 8% of the total US IPOs. The Valley's share of US patents is about 13%, reaching almost 16,000 in 2013 (1,910 more than in the year before).[6] Apple and Google, the two most innovative global companies according to the Global Innovation 1000 Study, together spent over $12.5 billion on R&D.[7] Silicon Valley has a highly educated population which it needs in order to stay innovative. The educational attainment of its workforce is far above the US average: almost half of the Valley's adult population has a bachelor degree or higher. The educational system is outstanding with the best private and public universities in the area. Silicon Valley's talent flows and diversity are reflected in a large share of foreign born migrants: more than one out of three residents was born outside the United States. Immigrants have contributed greatly to the entrepreneurial landscape of Silicon Valley: more than four out of ten startups are founded by first-generation immigrants (particularly from India and China). Some of the immigrant entrepreneurs have become extraordinarily successful. Think Sergey Brin (Google), Andrew Grove (Intel), Vinod Khosla (Sun Microsystems), or Jan Koum (WhatsApp). The contribution of immigrant entrepreneurship to Silicon Valley's thriving economy is generally applauded. Compared to the European debate it has created much more favorable social frames on the role of immigrants and immigration in making economies more entrepreneurial.

Hightech industries have brought Silicon Valley great prosperity. With average annual earnings over $116,033[8], the Valley is one of the most affluent areas in the US. But there is a high price to pay: its wealth is very unevenly distributed, the income gap is widening and social inequality is increasing. The Valley's middle class is disappearing. They are priced out due to the rapidly rising cost of living caused by, among other things, the overheated housing market. Silicon Valley, as we will see, is witnessing a growing social divide based on income, class, and ethnicity. It is a region of contradictory societal developments.

All the major Silicon Valley hardware and software industries began their march to fame and fortune as small but eager startups, as new ventures that wanted to shake markets and challenge existing technologies. The combination of mature hightech companies and the satellite ring of thousands of startups going for gold too, is what makes Silicon Valley such an exciting place. The entrepreneurial energy of new businesses is almost contagious and signifies the culture of the Valley. Startups are what the area is all about. It symbolizes the dominant entrepreneurial spirit and reflects the willingness to compete and to be different. The continuous rise and fall of numerous startups echoes a resilient culture of innovative entrepreneurship that sets Silicon Valley apart. It has somehow succeeded in creating a culture that is both competitive and open, both inner and outer oriented, both focused at winning and at sharing. In establishing a culture that does not condemn business failure but embraces a determining attitude of "stand up and try again." A culture that celebrates serial entrepreneurship.

For decades the Valley attracted loads of passionate and committed entrepreneurs who all shared one goal: to build a successful business. To start and grow a company that will change the world. Among them many hightech nerds & nomads who firmly believe that their innovation is truly disruptive and will make the cut. Ambitious entrepreneurs who are dedicated to be successful even if it takes tremendous perseverance and dealing with misfortunes.

And misfortunes there are. Most startups fail, but that is seen as part of a Darwinian business logic: new ventures are locked in an ongoing "survival of the fittest". Some will make it, most will not. To fail is okay, but it has to be done quickly. "Fail fast" is probably the chief Silicon Valley mantra. But there is more to the Silicon Valley story than the mere number of startups, the pro-innovation culture, the huge share of venture capital that the Valley captures, and the highly skilled labor force. Part of the intriguing puzzle is a widely branched support system of incubators and accelerators, of lawyers and advisors, of new venture schools and campuses that all aim at making startups successful and helping them grow. All these interrelated elements constitute what we call the 'Silicon Valley Innovation & Startup Model': the institutions and culture that shape this exceptional region. Outlining and understanding this model is the leitmotiv of this book. More specifically, we want to sketch and analyze the Silicon Valley story for a European audience of students, scholars, entrepreneurs, and policymakers. We strongly believe that Europe – and our home country the Netherlands – can learn solid lessons from Silicon Valley's unique position as Planet Startup. The main questions that will be raised are: what can Europe do to become more competitive in terms of innovation and entrepreneurship?; how can it stimulate a vibrant startup economy?; what does this require with respect to institutional reform and cultural renewal, and regarding elementary support structures? Europe, so we hold, needs to renew, rejuvenate, and revitalize its global economic position. A paradigmatic change towards an advanced and innovative European startup economy is necessary. The Silicon Valley startup narrative, so we will argue, points at major ecosystem preconditions that need to be met in order to realize this fundamental economic shift.

We want to tell the Silicon Valley story both from the outside and from the inside. The outside story draws the broader picture of the institutional and cultural basics of the 'Silicon Valley Innovation & Startup Model'. The inside story takes a different perspective: the view from Dutch entrepreneurs with a startup venture in Silicon Valley. By letting them speak, we hear their personal business experiences and adventures, and find out how doing business in the Valley energized and impacted their startup. Their transatlantic startup undertakings are a connecting theme throughout this book.

Why Dutch startups?

A new business needs a clear focus, and so does a book on startups. We decided to center our study on Dutch startup businesses in Silicon Valley. Not because of misplaced ethnocentrism, but because the study is part of a larger research program on the role of startups and startup regions in which we participate at the Rotterdam Business School and the Research Center Entrepreneurship and Business Innovation of Rotterdam University, University of Applied Sciences. Empirical insights into the push and pull factors of Dutch entrepreneurs who have located their new business in Silicon Valley will hopefully generate important know-how, which may in turn empower the startup community and culture in the Netherlands. A strong and innovative startup economy is vital for the Netherlands to remain competitive on the European and global market. What can we learn from the Silicon Valley experience of Dutch startups in this respect? How can their business stories provide helpful feedback for the strengthening and acceleration of startup developments in the Netherlands?

There are also other reasons why we choose to focus on new Dutch ventures in the Valley. There are strong economic ties between the Netherlands and the United States that are important as contextual country-level factors. These bilateral ties are reflected in a number of strategic financial parameters, marking four centuries of intensive trade relations between the two countries. The United States, which is the fifth most important import country for the Netherlands, imports amounted to €26.6 billion in 2012; 12% more than in 2011. The 2012 export to the United States was €19.8 billion. The Netherlands is the third largest foreign investor in the United States, after the United Kingdom and Japan.[9] Dutch businesses achieved a cumulative direct investment in the American economy of almost $30 billion in 2012. In the same year, American companies increased their investment in the Dutch economy by $53 billion to $723 billion. For the fifth consecutive year, the Netherlands ranks as the United States' largest foreign investment outbound country.[10] More than 2,100 US companies have their headquarters in the Netherlands. American exports to the Netherlands supported over 285,000 jobs in 2012. Some 250 Dutch companies are settled in the United States. The European business presence in the Bay Area is considerable: fifth place in terms of European firms with affiliates in the region.[11] The Netherlands, furthermore, ranks as the sixth European country with respect to number of patents with Bay Area and European co-inventors. The Netherlands Embassy in Washington, DC, calculated that the economic ties between the United States and the Netherlands are supporting 685,000 American jobs. California – Silicon Valley included – is good for almost 60,000 jobs and $4.3 billion of export to the Netherlands.[12]

In summary, the focus of this book will be on Dutch startups based on our targeted research program, the strong economic trade relations between the two countries with Silicon Valley as our niche region, and some pragmatic reasons.

Target groups

This book aims to disclose the Silicon Valley unique innovation and startup story, by outlining its exceptional ecosystem, by picturing its alluring entrepreneurial culture, and by listening to the business adventures of Dutch startups in the Valley. In doing so, we want to help entrepreneurs who dream of starting a business in this hightech startup Valhalla. Furthermore, we want to enrich students and scholars of entrepreneurship & innovation, international business, marketing, finance & new business models, human capital & HRM, and cultural diversity by showing how ambitious, competitive, and challenging business environments can make the difference. Finally, we hope that European and Dutch policymakers will be inspired to seriously invest in creating infrastructures, supportive laws, and facilities for a booming startup economy.

The way we worked

A brief outline of our methodology used in collecting data and background information for this book clarifies the different ways in which we operated in understanding the big picture of Silicon Valley's ecosystem of innovation, entrepreneurship, and startup community. Triangulation of methods was the main research approach, both of primary and secondary data sources.[13] In more plain English: a variety of investigation methods were used. We studied the literature, both scholarly books and popular accounts, we interviewed startup founders and CEOs in Silicon Valley, talked to policymakers and stakeholders on both sides of the ocean, and participated in Valley startup events. In tracing Dutch startups in the area a snowball sampling procedure was used.[14] We defined a Dutch startup as a relatively young business (up to three years) with a Dutch founder and/or Dutch CEO that specifically settled in Silicon Valley (San Francisco included). Some businesses were older but they were instrumental in developing longer term perspectives. The Dutch Ministry of Economic Affairs and the Consulate General of the Netherlands in San Francisco provided us with lists of Dutch startups. And startups were asked for names of other Dutch startups as well. This non-probability sample technique worked well. The Consulate is in standing contact with quite a number of Dutch startups and organizes network events on a regular basis. From 2014 onwards, we made several carefully prepared research trips to Silicon Valley during which we interviewed twenty-three Dutch startup entrepreneurs (see Appendix 1), thirteen Silicon Valley stakeholders and policymakers, and six Dutch policymakers and stakeholders (see Appendix 2). In order to get a more dynamic and interactive discussion on the startup community in the Valley, we also organized and chaired two group sessions (with 4-5 Dutch startup entrepreneurs each) at the Dutch Consulate in San Francisco. Apart from two cross-Atlantic talks via Skype, all interviews were face-to-face. The questionnaires for the startup entrepreneurs and group interviews were thematically structured (see Appendix 3 & 4); the stakeholder questionnaires were targeted at the specific stakeholder organization. The themes addressed in the personal and group interviews with startup founders and CEOs followed the main micro, meso, and macro dimensions of the conceptual representation of the 'Silicon Valley Innovation & Startup Model', and are outlined in the next chapter. These themes relate to the chief push and pull factors in the entrepreneurs' decision-making process to settle their business in Silicon Valley; the innovativeness of their startups' main product or service; their definition of the market and the competition; their startup stories and business experiences; the access to VC and angel startup funding; the role of leading universities and private research institutes in the Valley; the job market situation and the pool of talent; the role of government; the advanced support structure; and, last but not least, the pro-innovation attitude and thriving startup community culture in Silicon Valley.

The interview response rates turned out to be very satisfactory: nearly all entrepreneurs that we approached agreed to an interview. The nature of the personal and group interviews was generally pleasant, lively, informative, and open. All interviews – apart from the Dutch stakeholders – were in English and (with the respondent's permission) were recorded digitally. Transcripts were made by a specialized transcription service, Flatworld Solutions based in Bangalore, India. Interviews were analyzed with Atlas.ti, professional software for research on qualitative data. Interview quotes reported in this book were agreed to by the respondents. Our initial conclusions from the interview sessions were discussed in two feedback sessions with the staff of the General Consulate.

Furthermore, we made several local field trips to a.o. RocketSpace, the high-quality technology campus in downtown San Francisco that offers an entire ecosystem custom-focused on accelerating startup growth; to 500 Startups, a premium accelerator in Palo Alto; to Hacker Dojo, an open community of hackers and startups in Mountain View; to the Band of Angels in Menlo Park, the oldest startup seed funding organization in the Valley; and to the opening of WhatsApp's new headquarters in Mountain View. We visited the campuses of Google, Apple, and Facebook, and had meetings at Stanford University and San Jose State University. After our return to the Netherlands we stayed in contact with respondents and stakeholders for follow-up conversations and in several cases for joint research and education (e.g. student exchange) projects.

Book overview

The book is structured as follows. In Chapter 2 we briefly sketch some of the decisive factors in the history of Silicon Valley that made it into the world capital of innovation, entrepreneurship, and high tech startups. These factors are the main ingredients of what we have introduced above as the 'Silicon Valley Innovation & Startup Model' that will be used throughout this book. In essence, this proposed conceptual model represents the Valley's ecosystem that is assumed to be the core foundation of the success story of this hightech hotspot. Its main elements, as we see it, are: thinking big and product innovativeness, defining market needs and timely pivoting, building strong teams and access to talent, ample funding opportunities, strong innovation culture, excellent institutes of higher learning, distinctive role of government, and professional support structure. The model will be validated in our interviews among startup founders and stakeholders. Chapters 3 to 10 examine the separate dimensions of the 'Silicon Valley Innovation & Startup Model' in more detail. Chapter 3 looks at why startup entrepreneurs came to Silicon Valley with their particular product or service. What was their drive and how important is the underlying Big Idea? Understanding one's target group and the need for flexible customer response is the subject of Chapter 4. Creating a winning team and hiring gifted employees is analyzed in Chapter 5, and Chapter 6 describes the unique angel and venture capital funding networks in Silicon Valley. The competitive but open innovation culture of the Valley's startup community is the main focus of Chapter 7. This innovation mindset, as Chapter 8 argues, is reinforced by outstanding universities, colleges, and research institutes in the area. Chapter 9 focuses on the role of the US government in facilitating innovation, e.g. by funding research and by issuing visas to non-US hightech talent, and Chapter 10 outlines the professional startup support structure in Silicon Valley. The innovation and entrepreneurial success story of Silicon Valley may not obscure its darker sides: growing social inequality and the hightech industry's lack of gender and ethnic diversity. Chapter 11 analyzes a number of painful social issues: widening income gaps, tech boom gentrification, exploding housing prices, and the diversity problem. Chapter 12 presents our view on what Europe and the Netherlands can learn from the Silicon Valley innovation experience and how we can improve and accelerate the startup communities in our part of the world. The main conclusion will be that we need to seriously upgrade our innovation and startup ecosystem combined with a true boost of our entrepreneurial culture. Institutional reform and cultural reform is the secret. We need an ambitious agenda for ambitious entrepreneurship. Education, entrepreneurs, and government should work closely together to advance this agenda. The book finishes with twelve practical guidelines in Chapter 13 for entrepreneurs who are thinking of beginning a startup in Silicon Valley. Should they stay or should they go? That is the question.

2. The Silicon Valley Innovation & Startup Model

Path-dependency of transformational technologies

It would be historically naïve to suggest that the present status of Silicon Valley as a technologically unrivalled region was the intended result of an instant process of industrialization and innovation. Technological hotspots do not originate overnight but are rooted in longer geographic and economic developments.[1] In this chapter, we will argue that the growth of the hightech industry in Silicon Valley has to be understood from (much) earlier technological (and industrial) developments in this formerly agricultural region, some of which go back to the beginning of the 20th century. There is a certain pattern of path-dependency in successive (upstream and downstream) cutting edge innovation waves that made Silicon Valley into the number one innovation area in the world.[2] Earlier vacuum tube radio technology was a fruitful breeding ground for later technologies such as microwave tubes, semiconductors, and integrated circuits. These later technologies, in turn, paved the way for the more recent hardware and software revolution which now brings about a non-stop stream of smart phone and other mobile devices apps.

The Valley's success has obvious historical antecedents that need to be highlighted in order to grasp its full meaning. We cannot understand the hightech revolution that the Valley witnessed in the past decades without looking at technological developments and innovations that fed this revolution. Silicon Valley has a geographic and economic history that is region-specific and therefore its innovation achievements are unlikely to be copied successfully by other areas. Replication of the Silicon Valley success story is not an option: history cannot be repeated. This in itself is an important policy lesson for regions elsewhere in the world that have grand innovation and growth ambitions. Advanced technological regions do not start from scratch but have to build on the available resources and circumstances, on elementary forms of existing ecosystems of innovation, entrepreneurship, and culture. There is no such thing as an innovation master plan, no one-size-fits-all approach.

But the argument of the need for historic sophistication goes further, much further even. The developments that helped to transform Silicon Valley into the innovation champion it is today, also foreshadowed basic elements of its entrepreneurial economy, its startup culture, its talent pool, its outstanding research universities, its VC funding agencies, its public and private R&D investments, and its support system and networks. Together these basic elements constitute the Valley's ecosystem, or in our words the 'Silicon Valley Innovation & Startup Model'. This chapter will introduce the model in general terms which subsequently will be elaborated and tested in the following chapters. As such, the model structures the book and offers a frame of reference for lessons to be learned from the Silicon Valley innovation and startup experience. We will start the chapter by briefly (and selectively) outlining the historic antecedents of the different underlying technology waves. The analysis will cover the 1910-1970 period, thus up to the personal computer and the later Internet and communication software revolution. This delimitation is somewhat arbitrary, but the main reason is to show how this hardware and software revolution is rooted in the Valley's innovation legacy.

A little history

Silicon Valley was not an accident. The fast and explosive growth of the personal computer industry in the 1970s was not an isolated stand-alone development. It was made possible, according to science historian Christophe Lécuyer, "by practices, skills, and competencies that had accumulated in the area for more than 40 years."[3] It all started in the radio era shortly after the turn of the 20th century. Given its geography and maritime business, the Bay Area was a known US region of radio amateurs. A vibrant community of radio enthusiasts with a distinct culture that valued openness, sharing, and experimentation. They had a strong technical and often entrepreneurial bent, were trained in radio technology, metalworking, and mechanics, and had a keen eye for innovation in their field. In retrospect, the Bay Area community of self-made engineers marked the start of a booming radio transmission industry that would be of great strategic relevance to the military sector, maritime business, and in a more general sense to the broadcasting and entertainment sector. According to Piero Scaruffi, "radio engineering created two worlds in the Bay Area that would greatly influence its future: a hightech industry and a community of hightech amateurs."[4]

A pressing technological challenge in the early radio years was the need to keep signal strength over longer distances. The customary spark-gap transmitters were weak and unreliable. Better and stronger receiver amplifiers could do the trick. The Federal Telegraph Corporation (FTC)

in Palo Alto, a "startup" founded in 1909 by Stanford alumnus Cyril El-
well, was the first Silicon Valley company to develop and commercialize
vacuum tube technology that enabled one to restore and amplify radio
signals enormously.[5] This eventually led FTC to develop the first global
wireless communication system. Having the lead technology, the company
played a crucial role in the advancement and go-to-market of this new
radio transmission technology. But its significance goes further. Many
future electronics entrepreneurs started their career at FTC, founded their
own startups, and further developed the vacuum tube technology.[6] The
startups that FTC produced represent the early emphasis of the Silicon
Valley innovation model on firm spinoffs. The Silicon Valley radio era also
showed that it were engineers who started the electronic companies, not
businessmen. This too would become a defining trademark of the Valley
and its startup culture.

World War I had a major impact on the demand for radio technology.
The US navy needed powerful shipboard transmitters for its war fleet and
FTC was awarded large orders for ever larger power transmitter stations.
Contracts were substantial. The end of the war, however, abruptly stopped
the military demand, orders were cancelled, and FTC needed to refocus its
core activities. The war impact, nevertheless, illustrates the leading role
of government as a key market actor in the early Silicon Valley innovation
era. This role would, contrary to popular belief, not be lost in the following
decades.

Vacuum tubes became more advanced, improving both the transmission,
reception, and signal amplification, and would soon dominate the electronics industry. Comparable to the post-World War II role of the transistor,
vacuum tubes in the pre-War period increased electronic systems reliability,
decreased costs, power requirements, and size.[7] The market potential of
commercial radio broadcasting was huge: between 1920 and 1924 the
number of in-home radio receivers increased from five thousand units to
twenty-five million units. Radio became big and vacuum tubes too. But
the competition did not stand still either. The setting up in 1919 of the East
Coast company RCA, the Radio Corporation of America, by GE and Western
Electric, would soon take over the long-distance radio industry with its exclusive cross-licensing agreements and patent controls.[8] Its aggressive policy
also demonstrated the rapidly growing importance of intellectual property
rights in Silicon Valley in these early days of technological innovation.

Stanford University has been a strong and consistent player in building
and progressing Silicon Valley's ecosystem. From its beginning in 1891,
this renowned institute of higher learning underlined the importance of

applied research with a firm focus on innovative engineering. Although its policy of actively promoting startups as applied research spinoffs dated from later years, Stanford ardently committed itself to building partnerships with existing companies in the area. Frederick Terman, Stanford's visionary dean of engineering and later provost, pioneered the creation of a symbiotic university-industry collaboration.[9] Academia and industry, in his view, ought to be strong partners sharing a mutual interest in designing and the bringing to market of inventive and potentially profitable products. This adage would become the pillar of Silicon Valley's innovation model. Terman, a brilliant scholar, vigorously encouraged and trained entrepreneurship among his students, helping them to start their own companies. This was also a way to stop the brain drain to the East Coast where engineering graduates could more easily find employment.[10] Today's startups are tomorrow's employers, so his philosophy ran. Two legendary Stanford startup examples under Terman's inspiring leadership were Varian Associates and Hewlett-Packard. Varian developed the klystron tube, the first generator of microwaves, which revolutionized radar technology. In fact, microwave technology would be the Next Big Thing in Silicon Valley. Moreover, the Varian group experimented with new organization and work principles such as a cooperative business model ("association of equals"), an employee-oriented culture, and non-hierarchical work teams.[11] The company also introduced employee profit-sharing. Hewlett-Packard started by building resistance-tuned oscillators, particularly for the film industry. Walt Disney Studios became their first customer. HP initiated the idea of employee participation by giving workers stock options. Later these would become pretty standard fringe benefits in the Valley. The company also pioneered the practice of treating employees as an organization's human capital, stressing the need for continuous training. It introduced concepts such as "management by objectives", "walk around management", "flexibilization and quality circles".[12] HP flattened the management hierarchy and introduced stock options for personnel.[13] Eventually, HP grew into an electronics mammoth with over 300,000 employees and revenues of more than $110 billion. Besides their roles in technological innovation, Varian and HP are interesting examples of early leadership in social innovations. A key to innovation was the combination of creative geniuses such as William Shockley and Steve Jobs with collaborative teamwork.[14] Principles that would mold Silicon Valley's later management and organization style. Many other companies would later follow in Stanford's rich startup legacy including Google, Gap, Cisco, Yahoo, Netflix, and Tesla.

As indicated, microwave technology became the new cutting edge technology. Litton Industries was a pioneering manufacturer of large high-powered microwave vacuum tubes for ground-based radar systems. World War II and the Korean War led to a rush for microwave tubes by the military, from which Litton greatly benefitted. As a flourishing startup it set the stage for many other new ventures that entered the microwave business. We already mentioned Varian Associates which became a major contractor for the US Department of Defense, making it the largest microwave tube company in the country. Its expertise of klystrons in creating a fuse for atomic bombs enabled them to secure lucrative government contracts in this war period. During World War II, the US government became the leading agency for commissioning military research and development contracts, not only on the East but also on the West Coast. Defense spending increased tremendously from 4% of America's GDP in 1948 to 13% in 1953.[15] The Japanese air attack on Pearl Harbor led the US Army and Navy to a quick development of high-frequency radar and the building of a worldwide network of radio communication systems. Advanced radio technologies were needed to bypass the enemy's radar system. The demand for transmitting tubes grew to millions of tubes per year. Companies such as Eitel-McCullough, ICE, and Heintz & Kaufman greatly benefited from this huge growth in demand for transmitting tubes. In 1943, Eitel-McCullough produced 150,000 tubes per month, which made it the largest electronics company in the Bay Area. Its novel production methods and quality controls set the standard for the power tube industry.

The burgeoning demand of the military sector for advanced and applied electronics expertise, gave a formidable boost to the founding of many research centers including the Electronics Defense Laboratory (EDL), General Electric Microwave Laboratory, Microwave Physics Laboratory, Microwave Engineering Laboratories, to name but a few. All these new research institutes sought the proximity of Stanford University. Dean Frederick Terman started the Electronics Research Laboratories (ERL), conducting basic research in microwave tubes, heavily funded by defense money.[16] The military's role became even more pronounced during the Cold War which created two antagonistic global power blocks: the Soviet Union and the United States and its allies.[17] It resulted in an unprecedented competitive technological battle between the two blocks. The launching by the Soviets of the Sputnik satellite was the beginning of a ferocious space race in the late 1950s. The Pentagon reacted by creating DARPA, the Defense Advanced Research Projects Agency, whose mission was to establish the US superiority in the field of military technology and defense.[18] The new agency played a very prominent role in funding major innovative technology projects in topical areas such as space, ballistic missile defense, and nuclear testing. DARPA is still active, concentrating on innovative hightech defense technologies, with a budget of about $3 billion. The aggressive space race between the USSR and the US, and the funding that became available through DARPA, among others, for basic and applied research, led Silicon Valley to enter a new sector of innovation: aerospace and missiles. Lockheed Corporation became the chief player in Silicon Valley in entering this market. It won the navy contract for developing the Polaris submarine ballistic missile, the Minuteman missile systems, and the first reconnaissance and surveillance contracts from the CIA and the air force. By 1964, Lockheed Missiles and Space would become the largest employer in Silicon Valley with 25,000 employees. Historian Stuart Leslie is quite right in labeling the military "the biggest 'Angel' of them all" in the making of Silicon Valley.[19] Without the massive Cold War defense spending, Silicon Valley would not be what it is now: "For better and for worse, Silicon Valley owes its present configuration to patterns of federal spending, corporate strategies, industry-university relationships, and technological innovation shaped by the assumptions and priorities of Cold War defense policy."[20]

Stanford Dean Terman – sometimes nicknamed "the father of Silicon Valley" – was also the genius behind Stanford Industrial Park (now Stanford Research Park) which opened in 1951.[21] The Park was initiated to attract hightech businesses to the university's campus in order to promote collaboration with innovative companies, both in terms of research and education. To stimulate cross-fertilization between academic and industrial research and to provide students with a challenging entrepreneurial environment. An additional prime goal was to enhance university revenues from bringing innovations to the market, also through the founding of startups. Science parks were not new in the US at that time, but the explicit focus on innovations and startups was.[22] Terman granted Stanford professors one day per week release time for consulting work. Furthermore, he introduced salary splitting, where faculties were urged to find a sponsor, the government in particular, to fund up to 50% of their salary. This stimulated entrepreneurship among professors and generated extra income for the university. Getting external funding for its research projects became a main faculty target. Terman, in his own words, built "steeples of excellence" to gain world renown for Stanford University. "When you formed a track team (...) you did not go after two men who could jump three feet high; you went for one man who could jump six feet."[23] Stanford Industrial Park became home to many successful startups and companies – besides Varian Associates and

Hewlett-Packard – such as Eastman Kodak, Zenith, General Electric, and Lockheed Corporation. Under Terman's leadership, Industrial Park earned the reputation of being a nexus of innovation and entrepreneurship. In retrospect, Stanford University was an early example of an incubator, a startup facilitator that would later become an indispensable new venture support agency in Silicon Valley's innovation model.[24]

The technological developments in Silicon Valley in the pre-War and early post-World War II years helped to build and enrich its innovation infrastructure which cleared the way for the semiconductor revolution in the late 1950s. A revolution that transformed the Valley into the main center in the US for the manufacturing of silicon devices and gave it its name: Silicon Valley.[25] A revolution, moreover, that led the Valley into the nascent computer era.

This new technological breakthrough centered around Fairchild Semiconductor, which was founded in Palo Alto in 1957. Fairchild was an early split-off of Shockley Semiconductor whose founder William Shockley was the co-inventor of the semiconductor at Bell Laboratories, for which he later was awarded the Nobel Prize in Physics. The Fairchild startup, which probably was the first Bay Area venture-funded startup, focused on the development and production of diffused silicon transistors. The startup consisted of a strong and passionate team of dedicated engineers under the inspiring leadership of Robert Noyce (the later co-founder of Intel). In a short time, Fairchild became a highly successful firm, growing from 180 employees in 1959 to 1,400 employees a year later, to about 10,000 in 1965. Its sales grew in just two years from $500,000 in 1958 to $21 million in 1960. The innovative semiconductor manufacturer – "the darling of the semiconductor business" according to VC Floyd Kwamme – became the leading producer in the US of advanced silicon devices. IBM and the military were the first customers.[26] Part of its success was the revolutionary planar technology, which enabled the production of extremely reliable transistors and diodes as well as the invention of the integrated circuit, another groundbreaking innovation, which could incorporate an entire electronic circuit into the silicon crystal.[27] Soon these would become standard for the rapidly growing semiconductor industry. The young company, according to Martin Kenny and Urs von Burg, "quickly became a technological leader in the transistor industry and spearheaded the transition to the integrated circuit."[28] Fairchild excelled in standardizing rigid reliability requirements for its production processes and systems. Its perfection of reliability practices, testing procedures, and process controls impressed the world of military avionics which continuously pressed for ultra-reliability. Fairchild's participation in the Minuteman development – the intercontinental nuclear ballistic missile – proved and sanctioned its quality standards.

Fairchild Semiconductors also successfully experimented with in-company social innovations. It gave substantial freedom and autonomy to work teams, encouraged collective decision-making, promoted a participatory, egalitarian, and informal management style, and provided employee benefits such as stock options. Varian Associates served as a role model. The need for a highly skilled workforce (and to keep the unions away) sharpened and modernized the company's human resource policy. Moreover, Fairchild introduced new marketing concepts such as giving strong technical support to its customers, an early version of modern webcare. It innovated the sales approach by not approaching the CEOs of potential client firms but its design engineers responsible for product development.

The market for silicon semiconductors was booming. Silicon was cheap and ubiquitous. Manufacturers of consumer electronics and computers (still mostly for large business applications) eagerly adopted semiconductors and integrated circuits. Fairchild was in the middle of this thriving business and the commercial opportunities inspired many of its engineers to launch their own startups. Numerous semiconductor startups can be traced as spinoffs from Fairchild. According to Dado Banato and Kevin Fong, between 1966 and 1969, 27 new chip companies were formed by ex-Fairchild employees.[29] Silicon Valley biographer Christophe Lécuyer rightfully concludes that "Fairchild transformed the San Francisco Peninsula into a major center of expertise for the processing and design of advanced silicon components (...). At the same time, the formation of Fairchild Semiconductor introduced new attitudes toward entrepreneurship."[30]

But the importance of Fairchild even goes beyond its technological reshaping of the electronics industry and its trendsetting management-employee practices. The company played a pioneering role in shaping Silicon Valley's remarkable history of startup venture capital. The initial capital raisers for Fairchild and several ex-Fairchild partners and associates became prominent venture capitalists. Some of them created venture capital funds that presently are among the most influential VC firms in Silicon Valley. Arthur Rock, the most important capital raiser for Fairchild, is generally seen as the builder of venture capital, originally called "adventure capital".[31] Nowadays, Sequoia Capital, and Kleiner Perkins Caufield & Byers are prime examples. The success of Fairchild's many spinoffs (the so-called "Fairchildren"), with Intel as the most famous one, and the fast growth of the semiconductor industry attracted many venture capitalist to invest in Silicon Valley startups. It marked the beginning of Silicon Valley as venture capital center and as a funding model for new innovative ventures. The acceleration of the importance of VC funding was strongly reinforced by the federal Small Business Investment Company Act (1958) of the Eisenhower administration which provided up to $300,000 in government matching money for $150,000 investment money by a private partner wishing to establish a small business investment corporation.[32] There was also a spiraling effect: startups that went public or that were acquired by others generated a lot of capital gains for VCs through high rates of return, which in turn were invested in new startups. In short: a vicious circle of investment. Martin Kenney and Richard Florida underline the broader significance of the rise of Silicon Valley venture capital: "Venture capital evolved with Silicon Valley's technology base, drawing from it and nurturing it by providing the funds for new initiatives. In this process it became integral to the entire region's dynamism and fueled the creation of an economy based on new firm formation."[33]

The booming of the Silicon Valley new venture economy also brought a lot of law firms to the area specialized in the setting up of new businesses, investment contracts, patents and intellectual property rights, and IPOs (initial public stock offerings). The most prominent and largest law firms included Wilson, Sonsini, Goodrich and Rosati, Ware and Freidenrich, and Fenwick, Davis and West. Business advice was as important as legal advice. A conclusion that still holds today. The business advisory role is an essential part of the Silicon Valley law community. Sociologist Mark Suchman distinguishes two main roles of the Valley's law firms: dealmaking and counseling, and three additional roles: gatekeeper, proselytizer, and matchmaker.[34] The specific development of the law community and law practice in Silicon Valley since the 1960s has created a strong support network that helps startups in all stages of their new venture, a network of broad business advice that transcends the classic boundaries of legal advice. Often law firms work with deferred payments for pre-funded startups: they will charge once they receive capital. If the company never raises funds, the obligation goes down with the company. The importance of law firms was stressed in 2011: Apple and Google both spent more on patents and lawsuits than they did on R&D that year.[35]

The 1960s also saw the renewal of US immigration laws, which would greatly affect Silicon Valley's prime business. In 1965, President Johnson signed the Hart-Cellar Immigration Bill that allowed higher quotas of immigrants with skills in high demand. The new law created new opportunities for foreign-born engineers, which led to a substantial influx in Silicon Valley of skilled hardware and software specialists, particularly from Asia. It would also mark the beginning of a rich tradition of successful immigrant entrepreneurship in the Valley. In fact, as regional technology expert AnnaLee Saxenian states: "The growth of immigrant entrepreneurship is one of the most dramatic changes in Silicon Valley in recent years. (…) These new immigrant entrepreneurs are a growing presence in the most technologically dynamic and globally competitive sectors of the Silicon Valley economy."[36]

The 1960s were an extraordinary era in another respect too in the Bay Area, particularly in San Francisco and Berkeley. It witnessed the birth of the hippie movement which would have a major cultural impact that also affected the startup culture in Silicon Valley, both directly and indirectly. Its nonconformist philosophy and alternative lifestyle were inspired by values such as the importance of creativity, experimentation, independent thinking, and being critical of tradition and authority. The hippie community stressed the need for sharing and openness, and heralded a culture of health. Experimenting with mind-expanding music and drugs were part of this new youth culture. The countercultural movement was very much change-oriented, idealistic, and anti-establishment, challenging the status quo.[37] Provocative, utopian, eccentric, and sometimes subversive. Perhaps not at face value, but these alternative and rebellious values of the new hippie generation resemble many of the values that would shape the Silicon Valley culture of innovation. Certainly not all of them, e.g. the Valley's overt materialism, but the overlap is telling.[38] For many people, Steve Jobs ("put a dent in the universe") was the Silicon Valley hippie par excellence. Eva de Valk, a Dutch Silicon Valley watcher, speaks of Silicon Valley as the "Nerdy" version of the hippie culture aiming to make the world a better place through technology and innovation.[39] Present Valley examples are the hacker culture, the maker movement, the Burning Man festival, and the digital civil rights movement. No Silicon Valley, so the argument goes, without its peculiar tradition of techno weirdos. It was a tradition of not merely nonconformists, but of extremely committed and technology-focused nonconformists which definitely triggered Silicon Valley's culture and state of mind.

The mid-seventies heralded a new technological metamorphosis which would radically transform our way of living: the coming of the personal computer and, somewhat later, the Internet, followed next by the software and (more recently) the social media explosion. Silicon Valley, again, was the cradle of this global revolution. A revolution that would generate social, economic, and cultural changes beyond imagination. Once again, Silicon Valley was well equipped to play a pioneering and visionary role in this technological paradigm shift. The post-Cold War drastic decrease in US defense spending forced Silicon Valley's electronics businesses to redefine its core activities. This need for refocus led many of them to enter the civilian market and to shift to consumer goods and products. The development of the personal computer perfectly matched this market and marketing change. Silicon Valley had the transistor and integrated circuit expertise, the entrepreneurial spirit to blaze new trails, intensive collaboration with top class universities and R&D labs, a supportive network of business counseling, an eager and well-educated workforce, and the skills to manage high growth startups. The major breakthrough of the personal computer in the 1980s (such as Apple's Macintosh), and the coming of the Internet in the 1990s, would accelerate Silicon Valley's hightech reorientation and establish its worldwide reputation in the consumer computer market. The number of startups exploded. The Valley, according to author Michael Lewis in his book on Netscape co-founder Jim Clark, "had given engineers a place where they could make their living outside the enormous gray corporations that expected them to conform. It tended to attract the technologists who value their freedom and want to live on the edge."[40] The Valley would become the global engine for innovation that launched the main technological dynasties of our digital age.

This short historical overview shows that Silicon Valley has built a solid reputation in innovation over the preceding fifty years and has played a dominant role in bringing about fundamental technological changes. Its latest shift towards silicon transistors and integrated circuits prepared it well for leading the digital era. Over the years, Silicon Valley developed an infrastructure of venture capital, research centers, and support networks that provides outstanding support for innovative startups to go into business. Social innovations such as employee stock options and profit sharing helped to attract and keep talent. And so did the emphasis on flat organizations, team work, and the creation of a meritocratic business culture. The Silicon Valley's institutions and culture were a great breeding ground for dot-com startups and innovative hightech entrepreneurship. Silicon Valley, so our hypothesis runs, seemed the right place at the right time for the digital revolution. The right place and time because of its resilient startup economy and energetic startup culture. Because it could benefit from a remarkable ecosystem and a challenging culture that highlights creative entrepreneurship, disruption, and excellence. A matured ecosystem and culture that were built in over half a century and that have shown an amazing ability to reinvent themselves. This would create the right conditions for the new heroes of the digital age, that all began as struggling but passionate startups: Apple, Sun Microsystems, Intel, Google, Netscape, Oracle, Facebook, Twitter, eBay, WhatsApp, and many others.

Global engine of innovation

The genesis of Silicon Valley as the world capital of innovation mirrored the historical antecedents that shaped its unique habitat. It showed that technological developments are interrelated and path-dependent. The whole is more than the sum of its parts. An almost organic, prototypical clustering of innovation as Silicon Valley connoisseur Tapan Munroe argues.[41] Our analysis, hopefully, demonstrates that Silicon Valley's excellence in innovative entrepreneurship is built on a distinctive and well-founded combination of institutional and cultural factors. It created a track record of innovation successes that is unrivalled. A booming startup economy that many other regions in the world are eager to learn from. In this section, we want to combine these institutional and cultural factors into a heuristic overarching model that we think helps in understanding and explaining Silicon Valley's success story. The so-called 'Silicon Valley Innovation & Startup Model' will be elaborated in the following chapters and tested in our interviews with Silicon Valley startup entrepreneurs. The 'Silicon Valley Innovation & Startup Model' structured our data analysis and will guide the interpretation of the main results.

The model distinguishes three interacting levels of the Silicon Valley innovation and startup ecosystem. The micro level specifies three main factors that relate to how expected startup success is framed in the Valley: the startup must be based on a Big Idea that will really shake and change the market (product); the new venture must be headed by a strong team that succeeds in hiring the best and most gifted talents available (team & talent); and the founders need to be capable of timely pivoting their original startup business strategy when circumstances change rapidly (pivot & perseverance). The meso level identifies four institutions that have been decisive in building Silicon Valley's startup infrastructure: access to ample VC new business funding; a government that invests in innovation and believes in a startup economy, is a launching customer of innovative products, and a setter of market rules; high caliber universities and research centers that excel in innovation, work closely with industry, and actively promote new ventures; and the presence of a strong network system of startup support agencies. Finally, the macro level points at the typical Silicon Valley culture that celebrates entrepreneurship and shares innovation, favors the passionate pursuit of big dreams, emphasizes openness and learning, is risk prone and tolerates failure, and has the right startup mindset.[42] A culture, evidently, that impacts both other levels as well. The figure below outlines the three levels, the corresponding factors – as well as its interrelationships – which in our view define the main ingredients of how Silicon Valley became the global engine of innovative startups. A region that sets the tone.

The Silicon Valley Innovation and Startup Model

CULTURE

Angel & VC Funding

Universities & Research Centers

CULTURE

CULTURE

Product: Big Idea

Marketing: Pivot & perserverance

Organization: Team & Talent

Government

CULTURE

Network Support System

CULTURE

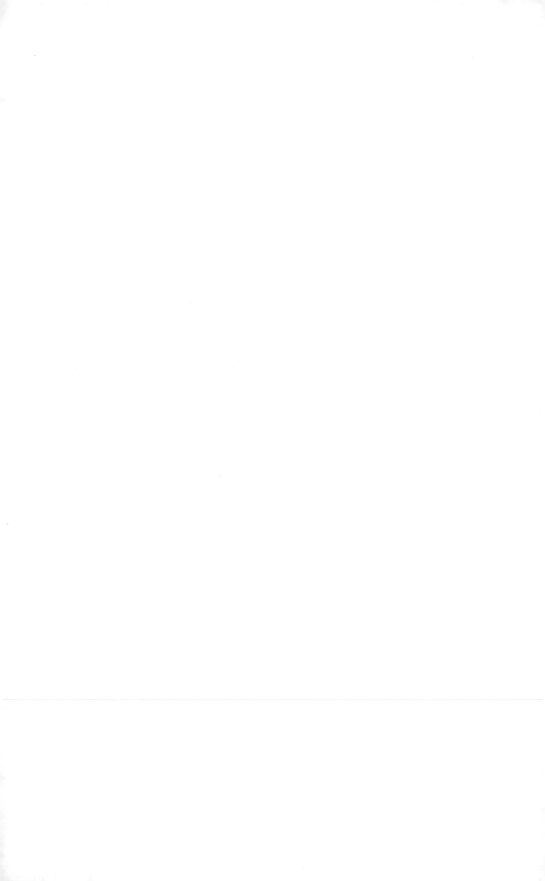

3. Product: Innovation Silicon Valley Style

In this chapter, we will outline some of the main characteristics of the way innovation works in Silicon Valley, particularly in the context of startups. Features such as Think Big, disruptive innovation, innovation approaches, and innovation differences between hightech ventures will be described and explained. The development from idea to product, from upstream to downstream innovation, is the core of the analysis and illustrates the micro-level of our 'Silicon Valley Innovation & Startup Model'. The second part of the chapter reports on the model elements that were decisive pull and push factors for Dutch entrepreneurs to start their new venture in Silicon Valley.

Think big

"Small is beautiful" is definitely not part of the Silicon Valley frame of mind. Quite the opposite: scalability is seen as the key to successful innovation and entrepreneurship. Think Big is the leading motto which mirrors an ambitious business climate that aims high and sets ambitious goals. It indicates that startups should not be satisfied with limited product impact and poor market share, but should shoot for the moon. The corresponding idea is to trigger entrepreneurial heuristics that go beyond the here and now and address real issues. Think Big shows the drive to grow one's business and to get rid of hurdles that block growth. It implies leadership, mission, direction, focus, and above all an innovative and visionary product portfolio. But it is more than entrepreneurial psychology alone. Investment logic is at least as important. As we will outline in chapter 6, VCs go for substantial returns on their startup investments. In order to reduce uncertainty, a fast growth perspective can win them over. The better the growth perspective, the easier it will be for new ventures to raise VC funding. Setting low goals, so the belief goes, will result in mediocre outcomes. It will bring about underperformance. That is not the world of smart VCs, neither, of course, of ambitious startups. VCs are interested in making money, and that can be done by one of two exit strategies. Either an IPO (an initial public offering, i.e. a stock market launch), or sell the company.

VCs not only want fast growth but they also expect fast returns on their investments which inevitably results in short (18-24 months) runways for startups. The implication is that startups who qualify for the Think Big paradigm also have to develop and prove their product idea in a relatively short time. A product beta version, a proof of concept, is a good appetizer.

Fast startup growth means the launching of a scalable product that will reach sizeable volumes of customers. Silicon Valley has a solid position in this respect as it provides access to a large US home market and functions as a gateway to significant international markets.[1] Hightech companies such as Google, Apple, WhatsApp, or LinkedIn owe their mega-success to their matchless global impact and ditto consumer market penetration. They are key-players on their markets and some of them even set the rules and dominate the competition. They share a vision of how their software and hardware can turn existing consumer markets upside down. The current mobile apps revolution and the thousands of startups dreaming that their app will revolutionize technology and consumer markets, clearly echo the Think Big growth axiom. But even with a comprehensive vision most startups will fail. Thinking Big is no guarantee for success. WhatsApp (which still describes itself as an early stage technology startup) with, by April 2015, over 800 million active users is the premier case of an outstandingly successful mobile app startup. Nanotechnology, big data, and cloud computing are further examples of Thinking Big in the hightech sector. Both ambitious startups that aim at making a difference in their markets and VCs seeking serious returns on their startup investments are permanently looking for the Next New Thing or in Silicon Valley slang: the New New Thing. The idea, as Michael Lewis, biographer of Netscape founder Jim Clark, writes is that it: "is a push away from general acceptance and, when it gets that push, will change the world."[2] The New Google, the New WhatsApp, or the new market changing application or product, is what startup entrepreneurs and VCs are after.

Think Big is part of Silicon's Valley entrepreneurial spirit. Nevertheless, some observers and experts have raised the issue whether the Valley is still excelling in this innovation paradigm.[3] Isn't there a shift observable from focusing on finding solutions to Big Problems to developing fashionable me-too products? As Facebook's CEO Mark Zuckerberg stated: "A lot of companies I see are working on small problems (...). Companies getting started now are trying to copy stuff others are doing and just aren't going to be successful."[4] Peter Fenton, managing partner at VC fund Benchmark Capital, sees it differently. "In my experience, what's common among the companies that have broken out to be sensationally big was No. 1: a narrowly focused starting point. It wasn't an abstract, grandiose idea. It was a hyper-focused, laser-like precision on an experience those companies are trying to create, but then it grows and compounds."[5] Twitter, Fenton argues, is a good example of such a company. "It started with 140 characters and (...) only became a big idea by chance." Peter Thiel, successful serial entrepreneur and venture capitalist is probably Silicon Valley's greatest propagandist of the Think Big axiom. His venture capital Founders Fund specifically targets startups that have a grand vision on societal and technological developments and center on problems that matter. "We invest in smart people solving difficult problems."[6] Thiel is quite critical about mainstream VC startup funding. "VC has ceased to be the funder of the future, and instead become the funder of features, widgets, irrelevances."[7] In spite of these diverging views, the fact remains that the most successful Silicon Valley hightech companies have one thing in common: their products have a tremendously big impact which profoundly affect our lives. Moreover, the existing tech giants are not passively watching the hightech arena. In fact they play a very proactive role in which they strategically acquire successful startups that stand out in developing Think Big products. Facebook acquired WhatsApp, Yahoo bought Tumblr, Oracle obtained Taleo, Google purchased Waze, and Apple acquired Beats, to give just a few examples. This acquisition strategy is a determined attempt to bring in inventive Think Big new ventures that strengthen the companies' own innovation potential. Both in terms of new products and new talent. These ventures function as satellites that expand the renewal capability of the Valley's hightech giants. It keeps them sharp, alert, and focused.

Think disruptive

Our brief history in the previous chapter of the different innovation periods in Silicon Valley showed that these periods corresponded with structural technological paradigm shifts. These shifts were marked by discordant and sometimes even clashing technological innovations (vacuum tube, the integrated circuit, the personal computer, the Internet). The innovations had an unparalleled market impact. The standard term for such paradig-matic changes is "disruptive innovation". It signifies changes that radically challenge and surpass existing technologies and shake markets. The term disruptive innovation was coined by Clayton Christensen, professor of Business Administration at Harvard Business School, and describes "a process by which a product or service takes root initially at the bottom of a market and then relentlessly moves up market, eventually displacing established competitors."[8] Examples of disruptive innovations, according to Christensen, are personal computers, cellular phones, discount retailers. More recent illustrations are 3D printing, the Internet of things, drones, mobile self-monitoring medical devices, and soon to come: autonomous vehicles. Telling examples of companies that made their business out of disruptive innovation and transformed markets include Uber (taxi market), Airbnb (hotel market), Skype (phone market), Amazon (book market), eBay (shopping market), and Apple's iTunes (CD market). These innovations came to outperform seemingly superior products or services, and in doing so redefined existing markets and attracted new customer segments. Some of these disruptive innovations are technologically highly advanced, but most are not. In Christensen's words: "Generally, disruptive innovations were technologically straightforward, consisting of off-the-shelf components put together in a product architecture that was often simpler than prior approaches. They offered less of what customers in established markets wanted and so could rarely be initially employed there. They offered a different package of attributes valued only in emerging markets remote from, and unimportant to, the mainstream."[9] Disruptive innovation is contrasted by Christensen with sustained innovation that merely incrementally improves current products. The innovation dilemma facing market players is whether to take the route of sustained innovation by doing their standard business a bit better or to go for creating new markets by adopting new but uncertain innovations. An example of a company that made the wrong trade-off is Kodak (which once had a 90% market share) that held on too long to photographic film in an era that was increasingly dominated by digital photography. Another example is DEC, once a leading vendor of computer systems, that did not make the shift from minicomputers to the PC which quickly eroded the company's core business.

The essence of disruptive innovation is its ability to create new markets, to reach new consumer segments, to change market relations. The personal computer revolution was disruptive because PCs became available to the masses, whereas the previous highly expensive mainframe computers were only sold in very specific markets. Successful disruptive innovation leads to a market shake up that separates new competitors from the established players. Disruptive has to do more with business models and market impact than with the technological nature of the innovation. Christensen argues that disruptive innovations share a number of characteristics such as simplicity, convenience, accessibility, and affordability.[10] These characteristics start to draw new customers, usually at the lower end of the market, which rapidly undermines the market position of technology giants. As phrased by Christensen's consultancy company Innosight: "By creating new markets or reshaping existing markets by delivering relatively simple, convenient, low-cost innovations to a set of customers ignored by other industry leaders, these pioneers significantly supplemented growth in their core businesses with disruptive growth."[11] Emergent business strategies are needed that combine market feedback with flexible response. Strategies that enable growth in uncertain markets.

Silicon Valley has embraced the idea of disruptive innovation to a degree that it almost became a gospel. To disrupt or become disrupted seems to be the near-messianic message. Disruption itself has become big business: there are disruption consultancy agencies that help companies and startups to disrupt, and disruptive innovation awards. TechCrunch organizes a yearly disruption conference, and there are many events celebrating disruptive innovation among which the Disruptive Innovation Festival.[12]

The disruptive innovation paradigm contains much wisdom, but is not undisputed.[13] The continuing immense market success of, for instance, Apple's iPhone, now (2015) in its sixth generation, is difficult to understand from the basic premises of the paradigm. It ran in no time through all the stages of the technology adoption life cycle and comfortably manages to attract a huge number of customers without any serious disruption attacks. The greatest criticaster of the disruptive innovation, probably, is Harvard history professor Jill Lepore, who wrote a lengthy disapproving article in The New Yorker on disruptive innovation theory.[14] Lepore argues that disruption theory is a biased chronicle of the past and has limited predictive value. "It is a theory of change founded on panic, anxiety, and shaky evidence."[15] It is at best, in her opinion, a theory about why businesses fail, it does not explain change.[16] It is not a law of nature. These objections may have some validity, but what cannot be rejected is that hightech companies must confront the innovation dilemma: persist in incremental innovation or go for disruptive change? There will always be entrepreneurs who will rethink a currently existing business. By rethinking a disruptive idea, these entrepreneurs may come up with an idea which may turn out to be a feasible and efficient way of doing an existing business in a better way. If such an entrepreneur succeeds, a new disruption occurs. It may not be planned all the way, but it is the result of strategic rethinking. An innovation dilemma is a recurrent theme in many strategic discussions in Silicon Valley's corporate boardrooms but is also a lifeline for disruptive startups.

Think innovation

Silicon Valley lives off innovation which is the quintessence of its existence. The commercialization of innovations is the backbone of the Valley.

Bringing new and innovative products to the marketplace is the nucleus of its entrepreneurial spirit and leadership.

Entrepreneurship is the vehicle by which innovations become (or do not become) reality, depending on the adoption rate of its customer target group. Startups play a distinctive role in the innovation process as it is their core business to come up with new ideas, new products, and new services. Just as in society at large, where social renewal and social change are being stirred up by the youngest generation, startups are the new generation of business innovators that often have a pioneering change function in innovation trajectories. Successful startups are the ones that effectively challenge established companies and go for rejuvenation and revitalization of business development by centering on designing new solutions to pressing problems. Silicon Valley and innovative entrepreneurship are two sides of the same coin.

One of the greatest dilemmas startups (and established companies) have to cope with, is finding the right balance between upstream and downstream innovation. Upstream innovation refers to the routing from idea to product. Downstream innovation is about bringing the new product to the marketplace. Particularly in hightech startups, there exists a sometimes natural tendency to keep on fine-tuning until product optimization is nearly perfect. But the downside is that these startups may quickly approach the end of their runway. The Valley of Death – running out of resources after the first round of financing – is a real danger. Often these startups have technical founders and their prime fascination is to almost permanently refine and polish their main innovation. This may lead to quite lengthy and costly R&D phases. But startups do not make money out of faultless product innovation but out of timely and successful go-to-market. In the end, the real confrontation is how well the new product is doing in the market. That is when the product has to prove itself as it depends on customer adoption. A technologically highly sophisticated product looking for a market is not a wise innovation policy. Neglecting the downstream phase is disastrous for startups. Valorization is key. Successful value creation and market entry is what startups are all about. That is the alpha and omega of a startup's commercial raison d'être. Or as Ruben Daniëls, one of the participating hightech entrepreneurs in our study, appropriately says: "a startup is a vessel to find a business model around the technology you are developing."

The rules of the innovation game are very different in the upstream phase of a startup innovation compared with its downstream stage. Market entry requires different competences and skills than product development. Marketing becomes even more important in downstream strategy. Startups, therefore, have to deal with the question of how to accommodate upstream and downstream innovation.[17] Its leadership needs a solid synthesis between product development and marketing talent. Determining the right time-to-market is one of the most difficult issues for any startup.

New hightech ventures in Silicon Valley seem to be quite aware of the need to balance upstream and downstream innovation. The prevailing incentive structure favors Thinking Big but also strongly emphasizes the commercialization of innovative products. The dominant VC funding regime simply demands a strong and direct connection between product development and market launch. VCs are willing to fund further R&D on promising new hightech products but will also insist on timely market entry. And as we will see in the next chapter, the Silicon Valley rigorous pivot culture considerably shortens product development cycles. Moreover, many incubators and accelerators in the Valley are available to help startups in this crucial phase to decide when and how to launch its innovative product and to clarify the underlying decision-making criteria. Innovation Silicon Valley style is based on the idea that upstream and downstream innovation should be combined, product development and go-to-market must be best friends.

There is a voluminous and rich literature on innovation. This is not the place to discuss its various theories, concepts, and methodologies. Such an endeavor is beyond the scope of this book. We will, however, review some persistent myths surrounding business innovation strategies and discuss solutions to recurring innovation issues. The ongoing debate on innovation, its merits and pitfalls, shows a number of stereotypical biases that need proper debunking. These misconceptions, some of which are quite persistent, prevent a correct view of innovation perspectives. Moreover, they obstruct a well-founded choice of innovation strategies by established companies and startups. Guy Bauwen, a Belgian innovation expert, points out eight of the most common innovation myths.[18] We mention the two that we think are especially relevant to Silicon Valley. The first myth is that incremental innovation efforts will make a competitive difference. What companies need, on the contrary, is more radical and non-risk averse innovation. This refers to the discussion earlier in this chapter: is Silicon Valley moving towards an area increasingly focused on incremental innovation, or does it stay ahead with radical and disruptive ones? A second myth is that we need more creativity at the front end of innovation. This is not true, but remains a pitfall for technically oriented entrepreneurs. The important question is whether or not new ideas lead to a profitable business. The demand site of innovation must become much more prominent in innovation activities, as we will also discuss in the next chapter. Addressing these two innovation myths accurately may prevent Silicon Valley startups and established ventures for innovation failures. As we have outlined in this chapter, disruptive innovation is very much at the heart of Silicon Valley. Creating profitable business, however, remains an important aspect about which much is still to be learned and experienced.

Think different: Need seekers, market readers or technology drivers

The danger of writing in quite general terms about Silicon Valley (or the Bay Area) as the unrivalled global hotspot of innovative hightech companies, is that one loses sight of the inter-firm differences in approaching innovation. Further fine-tuning is necessary to get hold of these differences in order to get a fuller and richer picture of how companies respond to innovation stimuli and how their innovation policy aligns with the broader corporate strategy. Are there particular segments in terms of innovation aspirations and achievement needs that have to be distinguished among the many Silicon Valley hightech ventures that make their living out of innovation? Is there an effect of corporate leadership and corporate culture? The answer, as we will see in this section, is a qualified "yes". Depending on their product and market strategies, so our hypothesis runs, both existing ventures and startups are likely to differentiate their innovation role: taking the lead vs. following the trends. Product and market characteristics will define companies' innovation strategy, varying from taking a cutting-edge to a more incremental approach. Not all hightech firms are innovation pacesetters, policies differ according to mission, product segment, and customer target group. Our interviews with Dutch startup founders reported in the second part of this chapter will also illustrate this point.

A recent joint study by Booz & Company and the Bay Area Council Economic Institute provides some highly interesting data on this issue.[19] The research is based on the annual Global Innovation Study conducted by PWC (formerly Booz) among 1,000 public companies around the world. An additional 2011 module among 600 global innovation leaders focused on the impact of corporate leadership and culture on innovation policy. The Bay Area Council Institute conducted a similar study among its member companies which enables a comparison of the global innovation distinctiveness of the region. The Global Innovation 1000 study observed three main profiles in classifying a company's innovation strategy based on the role that end-customers play in nominating future product needs. The first profile is called "Need Seekers" and is a first-mover innovation strategy. These ventures invite their customers to help define new products based on their unique understanding and personal user experience. "These companies often address unarticulated needs and then work to be the first to market with the resulting new products and services."[20] The second profile is named "Market Readers". These companies closely follow their customers and the competition. In terms of innovation they are supreme trackers, not leaders. "They focus largely on creating value through incremental innovations to their products and being 'fast followers' in the marketplace."[21] The third profile is labeled "Technology Drivers", these firms depend on their own technical expertise to develop and market products, which may be incremental or breakthrough innovations, and take their time to do so. "Theirs is the least proactive of the three approaches in directly contacting customers. They often seek the unarticulated needs of the customers through leading-edge new technology."[22] The study by Booz & Company reports that Need Seekers show the best fit between the alignment of company innovation, business strategy, and corporate culture, and demonstrate the strongest financial performance. Need Seekers do best but as the researchers rightfully add, all three profiles have their winners: Google is a Technology Driver, Samsung is a Market Reader, and Apple is the prime example of a Need Seeker frontrunner. A further analysis of the findings indicates that compared to the companies participating in the global survey, Bay Area firms show a stronger alignment between innovation and business strategy and a much stronger cultural endorsement of such an innovation policy. These firms, according to the results, clearly perform better with regards to profitability and enterprise value.[23] It turns out that 46% of the Bay Area firms are Need Seekers, 18% are Market Readers, and 36% are Technology Drivers (Global Innovation 1000 overall percentages for all participating companies are 28%, 34%, and 38%, respectively).[24] The relative overrepresentation of Need Seekers in the Bay Area is revealing as they "excel not just at technology but also at gaining insights into the needs and desires, both articulated and unarticulated, of their present and future customers."[25] These companies combine passionate and early innovation, customer consultation and identification, with timely openness to new markets. Furthermore, outcomes show that Bay Area ventures do a better job with respect to in-company communication of their innovation strategy throughout the organization (development teams, marketing, and sales) also regarding its integration with the broader company business strategy. Moreover, these ventures have a much higher share of innovation team leaders reporting directly to their CEO compared to the average company. Their innovation and product development receive higher marks for consistency and rigor. This study convincingly indicates that Bay Area companies are especially effective in a holistic approach to innovation by balancing their business strategy, innovation policy, communication style, and organizational culture. It seems that at the crossroads of this quadrangle lies the competitive advantage of innovative hightech companies, both of existing ventures and startups.

Entrepreneurs: Coming to Silicon Valley

In this section, we will discuss the push and pull factors which our sample of Dutch startup entrepreneurs took into account in deciding to move to Silicon Valley and to launch their new venture in this acclaimed region of innovation and entrepreneurship. As we will see, their stories differ considerably, as they depend on career paths and migration motives. Some entrepreneurs started quite a while ago, others recently crossed the ocean. Some entrepreneurs initiated their startup as a spinoff from an existing Dutch Silicon Valley based company (e.g. Philips), whereas others began their new business from scratch. Some startup founders are serial entrepreneurs, for others it is their first company. Some entrepreneurs are young, some are more seasoned. Some want to grow as fast as possible and eventually go for an IPO, others share more autonomous goals. Some startup entrepreneurs are already successful, other founders anticipate better times. But they all share a passion for entrepreneurship, for innovation, and they all want to realize their business ambitions and dreams. All entrepreneurs were attracted by the mesmerizing appeal of the Valley's ecosystem and the inspiring culture that goes with it. At the same time they all suffered misfortunes, experienced setbacks, had to cope with financial trouble, and needed to refocus their business. But they felt and feel that their future is in Silicon Valley. That is where things happen. In the words of Curtis Mo, Partner at DLA Piper, Silicon Valley is "the Hollywood of technology". Below are their stories, we will aptly start with the entrepreneur who has recently received a very significant investment from Hollywood, in particular from Walt Disney.

Push & pull factors

Serial startup founder Arthur van Hoff came to Silicon Valley via Scotland where he was working as a computer scientist for the renowned Turing

Institute in Glasgow, specializing in artificial intelligence. In the early 1990s Arthur was recruited by Sun Microsystems in Silicon Valley where he and his team did pioneering work on developing the Java programming language, leading to the first release of Netscape. Arthur knew Silicon Valley quite well. "I had been here a number of times already so I knew about the environment. Silicon Valley was nectar for computer scientists like me, that's the reason I moved." (Arthur van Hoff, Jaunt). A few years later he launched his startup Marimba where he further developed Java products as the company's CTO. "I always have a really hard time working for people in general, I like to do it my way. If you want to be really successful you need to start your own project, and that's kind of what we felt like as the four founders of the Java team. We just started our project, the company got funded really well which was easy at the time simply because we had a great reputation. But we had no idea what we were going to do, zero, no product idea, no nothing. We just started and made something up and go with it." A few years later Marimba was sold for $239 million to BMC Software. Several startups (Strangeberry, Zing Systems, Ellerdale, Flipboard) would follow. Presently Arthur van Hoff is CTO (and founder) of Jaunt, a Palo Alto startup developing a comprehensive toolset for creating cinematic virtual reality.

Geologist and economist Pieter Bas Leezenberg started his business career in Silicon Valley after his PhD position at Stanford University. "For me it didn't begin with the entrepreneurial or the startup scene here in Silicon Valley, but I started with the world class research I was doing at Stanford. I just sort of got dragged into the startup world only later in life, as it became obvious to me that I didn't want to be involved in academic institutes but rather in a corporate environment. And the second thing was that I didn't want to go back to Holland, so here we are." (Pieter Bas Leezenberg, SkyGeo). Pieter Bas worked for IBM and Maxtor before launching his startup SkyGeo that specializes in monitoring and analyzing satellite data to make dams, levees, and communities safer. A perfect Dutch niche market: water management.

Adrie Reinders started his first US businesses already in the early 1980s in Austin, Texas, and in Boston, Massachusetts. "I always liked doing business in the US, as it is much more entrepreneurial than in Holland. Moreover, the US is a huge home market. The market there is very good for entrepreneurs." (Adrie Reinders, EFactor). Adrie noticed that there were no tech-based networks for entrepreneurs (similar to LinkedIn or Facebook) to share innovation experiences, match potential partners, and exchange new business ideas. It resulted in founding EFactor which turned into a major global entrepreneur social network, headquartered in San Francisco.

David Mayer, health entrepreneur, also had a strong click with America. "My vision from early on was to build a wellness company in the US, make it successful here, and then once that is accomplished, expand it to the Netherlands. So ten years from now I will have the luxury to work in both places." (David Mayer, RENDLE). David has co-founded RENDLE and is its Chief Product Officer. RENDLE provides healthy lifestyle products and services. Their business focuses on employers, and RENDLE's goal is to reduce medical expenditures and increase productivity and company morale. David enjoys working in the US: "I worked in the Netherlands in the wellness field as a health coach, but the industry is much more developed in the US." And David adds: "it was completely clear I wanted to stay since innovation was taking place here".

Entrepreneur Dirk de Kok came to the US during college, visiting for a year. Dirk already had startup experience in the Netherlands through his co-founded venture HelloInbox, an iPhone application that collected different digital messages in one universal inbox. Silicon Valley was not really on his mind "but then I had the opportunity to visit Silicon Valley and meet all these technology entrepreneurs here. I was amazed by the whole openness, the size of the ecosystem, how concentrated it is, and the success of the people. My startup was not going that well, so I sold the company, and started my new business Mobtest here. Right now it was a bigger decision than I envisioned. But still I had my house, my family back home in the Netherlands. I can go back if I want to." (Dirk de Kok, Mobtest). Dirk's startup Mobtest focuses on user testing or mobile apps.

Maarten Sierhuis, co-founder of Ejenta, came to Silicon Valley as a student too. After his studies he started to work at NASA where he conducted research on modeling and simulating human behavior. Maarten and his team created their own programming language and automated the flight machine controller for the International Space Station. He realized he topped the bar and wanted to start a business of his own by applying his software running machine control to "real problems on earth". As Maarten says: "I wanted to make something, the only thing I had not done in my career yet was to do something as an entrepreneur. And you are in the Valley, hearing so many stories on startups and entrepreneurs." During the Christmas vacation a proposal was written for DARPA, the US Defense Advanced Research Projects Agency, and the company was created. After six months they received an email from DARPA saying: "congratulations, you have funding." (Maarten Sierhuis, Ejenta).

Rip Pruisken, CEO and co-founder of Rip van Wafels, studied at Brown University and started making the wafels in his college dorm room. Together with college friend and co-founder Marco De Leon they moved the business to San Francisco in 2012. "We saw the natural alignment with the value proposition of our product and the Bay Area; The sophisticated coffee culture, the sporting culture, the complementary snacking for employees at tech companies and the healthy outdoors lifestyle." (Rip Pruisken, Rip van Wafels).

Faruk Ateş, founder of Presentate, came to Silicon Valley through his then employer Apple. Working as a developer and programmer in the Netherlands, Faruk was recruited by Apple to work on its on-line store and remote video interfuse. After two years he left the company and had to decide on his future as his visa was tied to working for Apple. "I didn't really feel like going back to the Netherlands, like moving my life back. I was quite happy here, built a new life here with lots of friends. I saw the most interesting activity in the tech and web industry happening here. It is such a good place to start new ideas, so I wanted to stick around. I did some freelancing for another startup and then decided to start my own business. I did not want to work for a big company, I decided to pursue my own dream." (Faruk Ateş, Presentate). His startup develops interactive presentation software "where we try to fix the whole Death by PowerPoint Syndrome", aiming at making presenters more confident and audience-oriented in telling their story.

Some of the Dutch startup entrepreneurs were originally employed at Philips Semiconductors – now NXP Semiconductors – in Silicon Valley and founded their own business after the company was sold to a consortium of private equity firms.[26] Jan Grotenbreg is one of them. Before moving to the US, he worked for Philips in the Netherlands, Taiwan, Germany, and China. As a business developer, Jan was impressed by the entrepreneurial activity going on in the Valley. "Everybody is enterprising. The biggest opportunity was much bigger here." Jan's consulting company SiliconValleyLink assists European and particularly Dutch firms that want to expand their business in this part of the world but don't yet have the resources and networks to build up. "That's my target market, that's my skill. I was always at the front of the market everywhere in the world." Jan left us with this great Hotel California type of quote at the end of his interview: "It is very easy to come to this Valley, but it is very hard to leave."[27] To which he adds: "There is always a moment where you feel that there is something that you have to do as an entrepreneur, and that is how I ended up here." (Jan Grotenbreg, SiliconValleyLink).

Pieter Noordam also worked for Philips Semiconductors and for some earlier Philips ventures in Silicon Valley as well. In the mid-2000s, Philips, according to Pieter, "was really scaled down in the Valley because of the down cycle of the chips industry" and he decided to start his own business: RFIsoft. His company does data analytics and workflow management, especially with respect to energy monitoring. Networking for Pieter was both a big challenge and a strong feature of the Valley's ecosystem. "You have your Philips networks, local and overseas. But every big company is a universe in itself. The disadvantage of working for a big multinational is that you stay within the four walls of the company, you are not encouraged to get out." (Pieter Noordam, RFIsoft). Pieter admires the Valley's mindset and ecosystem, but also points at the relaxed lifestyle and the fact that his business allows him to self-direct his professional and private life. "I am a happy camper. My drive is to have fun with new work coming out of what is basically my hobby. Do I make as much as I did at Philips? Most likely not, but I like it to be a good life. I am very self-motivated."

Jurriaan Kamp, is co-founder of the media company and global magazine *The Intelligent Optimist.* As its name indicates the magazine primarily centers on intelligent solutions to worldwide problems such as food scarcity, renewable energy, global warming, pollution, stress or obesities. Jurriaan strongly believes in the power of optimism and feels that the greater San Francisco area is the premier area to work and breathe the energy of centering on solutions rather than to lose oneself in problems. "If we want to be part of the future, California is closest to where it is al happening. And if it is not happening here, it is bordering on where it is happening and that is not in Europe." (Jurriaan Kamp, *The Intelligent Optimist*). The focus on thinking in terms of solutions, so Jurriaan argues, strongly benefits from the innovative and entrepreneurial climate in the region. The willingness to take risks, the emphasis on bringing innovations to the marketplace, and the catching entrepreneurial environment, fits the mission of Jurriaan and his media company well.

Marieke van der Poel is also in the creative business. She is Chief Creative Officer of her company Proef Trend Forecasting in San Francisco. Marieke wanted to work for bigger and more interesting clients, and the West Coast seemed an obvious choice with companies such as Gap, Boeing, and Levi's. She spoke at a lot of events like Magic, the big Las Vegas fashion show, and did television and radio interviews. The magnetic force worked. "I really came out of opportunity and I always have been someone who likes to lead and run my own way (...). I came to a new country and there were a lot of cool, smart people. I loved that. I think that is the best way to selling anything. But I still find America a bit enigmatic." (Marieke van der Poel, Proef Trend Forecasting).

Serial startup founder Neil Blaak has a different story to tell. "I think I am a little bit different than most Dutch entrepreneurs here because I was born in the US, then grew up in the Netherlands, came back to the US for college, and then settled in Silicon Valley." (Neil Blaak, ZappoTV). Neil has a clear vision how to benefit from his multicultural background: "My goal was to be able to use my background of multiple cultures, multiple languages and to help a Dutch company getting settled in the US and close some business deals, because that is my expertise." His former advertising company was sold to a European news publisher and Neil managed to get the rights to sell the TV technology to third parties. That is how his startup ZappoTV was created: a deliberate choice for Silicon Valley because of its culture, entrepreneurship, market opportunities, and business climate.

Vincent van der Poll is a young and highly energetic CEO and co-founder of GROM, a B2B startup that makes 3D printed cases. Even at his young age, Vincent already had a number of startups in the Netherlands. He finds the Valley culture dazzling. "Everybody here in Silicon Valley loves entrepreneurs, the energy, trying to break down walls, doing new things, the crazier the better, the bigger the better." (Vincent van der Poll, GROM). But his move to America was actually based on very pragmatic considerations: his wife got a job offer in San Francisco. "It took me half a second to say yes, because of the sort of dreams and the fairytales you hear from the Valley."

Ronald Mannak had a very atypical reason to move to the US. His startup in the Netherlands failed, as we will explain in Chapter 9, and in order to avoid bankruptcy due to the Dutch personal liability legislation, he basically fled to America. Was Silicon Valley a purposeful choice? "To be honest, I didn't know exactly what Silicon Valley was. I mean I had heard the term. The first time I went there was for a developers' conference and I noticed like wow there are startups all over the place. And I saw the great infrastructure and ecosystem supporting startups. That triggered me. Before that I never had the ambition to come here." (Ronald Mannak, JumpCam). Ronald is, at the time of the interview, JumpCam's lead iOS engineer, a startup that enables people to create joint videos.

Harm TenHoff is a healthcare innovation consultant. He helps Dutch and European medical companies to grow in Silicon Valley. Harm has moved a couple of times as an entrepreneur between Silicon Valley and the Netherlands in the last two decades. He first came to America (in 1993) to work for Boston Scientific, was then transferred to Silicon Valley, and worked for a couple of medical startups. After the dot-com bubble, Harm moved back to the Netherlands and returned to Silicon Valley a few years later to launch his startup BayLink, a medical device incubator and accelerator and health consultancy firm. He describes his coming to Boston and later to Silicon Valley as "a combination of youthful opportunism and adventure." Besides the entrepreneurial climate, the access to a higher ambition level, talent and expertise, the global market, and US funding, pull factors for Harm also include his appreciation for societal pluriformity and freedom. "Silicon Valley offers no panacea in this respect but celebrates pluriformity in a much more consistent and constructive way." (Harm TenHoff, BayLink).

Thijs Boekhoff is a health consultant as well. Thijs recently started his business in the Bay Area and attempts to implement some of the good elements of Dutch health policies in the region. Thijs is CEO and founder of Ingen-Housz, a new medical startup in San Francisco. Focusing on the elderly and chronically ill, Thijs introduces best Dutch medical practices in the American context. Why did he come to the Bay Area? Basically, he says, it was the excitement of starting something completely new after having created a successful consultancy firm (Squarewise) in the Netherlands. "I think for me it was really the time to change and coming to this entrepreneurial area was a great opportunity. I looked at the business perspective and San Francisco was ideal. I am sort of a maverick really. Life here fits us well, but we keep our Dutch identity."

The last three Dutch startup entrepreneurs in Silicon Valley all founded hightech ventures: Valentin Smirnoff (now at the Wells Fargo Incubator), Salar al Khafaji (Silk), and Ruben Daniëls (Cloud9 IDE).

Valentin Smirnoff, former co-founder of Tinypay (an e-commerce platform), was already intrigued as a young boy by Silicon Valley. "At an early age I was fascinated by the early internet companies that came from Silicon Valley. Ever since I was a child, I always had that dream to someday come here and start my own business." But his interest in America was also broader. "Somehow I was always fascinated by things that were going on in the US, the culture, the music, the movies, and the video games." (Valentin Smirnoff, Wells Fargo). Businesswise it also made sense to move to Silicon Valley since half of his customers and users were from the US. The transition, moreover, facilitated the cooperation between his startup Tinypay and PayPal, the worldwide online payments system.

Salar al Khafaji, co-founder and CEO of Silk, a startup building a platform for structured data on the web, has high ambitions with his startup. "We want to be a really big company; scaling is key." Dutch investors did not share this mission ("they think like bankers") but Salar and his cofounder managed to get funding from a VC fund based in London. From there Silk moved to Silicon Valley. Why? "We realized that the first round of money we raised would not be sufficient. We needed more funding and that would most likely come from Silicon Valley. Companies like Silk, I think, almost have like no other place to raise money. Even in the US, you have to be in Silicon Valley." (Salar al Khafaji, Silk). But there is more besides funding. "The understanding of the people, the energy, the optimism, the sharing." The move turned out to be successful, Salar raised $3.5 million for his startup.

Cloud9 IDE, a cloud-based development environment, was founded by its CEO Ruben Daniëls. Why did he move (part of his) startup to Silicon Valley? "I had to be here, definitely. I wanted to be bigger. That feeling became even stronger after the move. We feel very comfortable here. People understand what we are doing while we felt sort of misunderstood in Amsterdam and in Europe. The energy here and the cross-pollination between all those different companies and institutions really stuck. That is what drew us. That is why we want to be here." Ruben managed to get VC funding in the Valley for his startup of about $5 million. The funding is important for his growth ambitions, a mission that is at the heart of the Silicon Valley hightech business culture. "We need to aim high. That is what people do here. And I think it is the only way." (Ruben Daniëls, Cloud9 IDE).

The migration stories and the underlying push and pull factors show considerable diversity. The stories are centered around different career paths, different company trajectories, different entrepreneurs' motivations, and different life stages. But, as we saw, there is at the same time considerable consensus about the distinct attractiveness of Silicon Valley to start a new venture in terms of entrepreneurial mentality, talent, knowledge, and funding. The analysis also showed that our sample of Dutch startups is quite heterogeneous regarding type of venture and type of product. Some startups are good examples of hightech startups (e.g. Silk, Cloud9 IDE, Login VSI, Presentate), others center at innovative technological manufacturing (Jaunt, JumpCam, GROM, Ejenta, Groasis); some startups are active in the creative industry (ZappoTV, The Intelligent Optimist, Proef Trend Forecasting) others do consultancy work in the health sector (RENDLE, BayLink, Ingen-Housz) or do more general consultancy (SiliconValleyLink). Other startups concentrate their business on platform building (EFactor, Eventbrite) or on testing and monitoring (Mobtest, RFIsoft, SkyGeo). And some make great wafels (Rip van Wafels).

4. Market: Pivot and Perseverance

To bring an innovation successfully to the marketplace is a tedious job. It indicates whether a startup (or an existing venture) applied the right survival techniques and made an effective transition from idea to market adoption. Bestselling books on innovation focus, for instance, on improving internal management processes[1] or on sharpening market strategy.[2] The innovation failure rate – where failure is defined as not realizing the pre-launch anticipated benefits – is usually estimated at 80-90%.[3] It is therefore not surprising that many a company's innovation manager relies on incremental innovations, such as introducing a new milkshake flavor or improving a bank's online webcare services, rather than risking his career with some highly unpredictable disruptive innovation. It takes guts, perseverance, and a deep understanding of the market to come up with successful disruptive innovative products or services. The focus of this chapter will be on the market and its consumers. In the end, they are the ones that must be willing to pay for whatever innovation enters the market. Innovation success depends on customer adoption, on the diffusion of the new product or service among consumers. A convincing customer strategy should be a top priority among startups. Having a technologically perfect product is simply not enough to enter the market, developing a persuasive marketing strategy is essential. Upstream (product creation) and downstream innovation (going-to-market), as we explained, should go hand in hand. Startups typically fail because they overlook the vital importance of combining smart upstream and effective downstream innovation.[4]

An innovation, of course, starts with an idea. In Silicon Valley, this idea is preferably disruptive, by shaking the status quo as we discussed in more detail in the previous chapter. Is it difficult to come up with disruptive ideas? Apparently not, since there are many disruptive ideas launched by startups. There are so many ideas, you do not even have to worry yours will be stolen. We quote Eric Ries from his already classic book *The Lean Startup*: "Part of the special challenge of being a startup is the near impossibility of having your idea, company, or product being noticed by anyone, let alone a competitor. (...) [T]ake one of your ideas (...) find the name of the relevant product manager at an established company (...) and try to get that company to steal your idea. Call them up, write them a memo, and send them a press release (...). The truth is that most managers are already overwhelmed with good ideas. Their challenge lies in prioritization and execution."[5] In other words, Ries claims that although there are many innovative ideas, the struggle is to get the idea noticed, to get your pioneering product to the market. The "Book of Ries" may qualify as the the most popular book in the Valley. Every investor, every entrepreneur, every startup founder, seems to have it on their bookshelf. Sometimes it is even the only book. Apparently, Ries has written something that matters, that touches upon the essence of startups. His book is a very accessible and practical guide on how to make a startup successful, with lots of tips and tricks for the starting entrepreneur. But the book also excels in analytical thinking and methodological scrutiny. We will therefore highlight some of his observations and methods of working. One simply cannot write about Silicon Valley without reference to *The Lean Startup*. The leading principle that Ries advances is that "learning is the essential unit for startups".[6] To systemize this learning process he introduces the Build-Measure-Learn feedback loop, which is at the core of the Lean Startup model. It comes down to first building a minimum viable product (MVP), defined as "a version of the product that enables a full turn of the Build-Measure-Learn loop with a minimum amount of effort and the least amount of development time".[7] Once this MVP is ready, a startup is going to assess where they are in terms of customer appreciation: customers' reactions, use of the product, willingness to pay, etc. On the basis of this feedback, a startup should learn what needs to be improved, and what product changes are necessary. It is crucial to do iterations in order to finally come up with a definitive product that is a success in the market. This way of working, according to Ries, is about getting the business model to work: "if we're not moving the drivers of our business model, we're not making progress. That becomes a sure sign that it's time to pivot."[8] The term "pivot" found a ready reception because of Ries' highly successful book and has become a leading concept in Silicon Valley's flashy startup vocabulary. It refers to the iterations of the envisaged product-market combination that a startup has to go through. When something is flawed (strategy or product), when envisaged buyers are not interested, a startup needs to redefine its core activity. This change may be anywhere in the business model, but in the next iteration it should be correct. Therefore, MVPs must not be full products, since the chance of having developed such a product that is not answering a consumer need is far too big. It could even be disastrous and mark the fall of a new venture. For startup entrepreneurs with a strong internal drive, such an MVP is often the most difficult decision to take. Not in building the MVP, but in *not* building the full product and pivot at the right moment. "Ask most entrepreneurs who have decided to pivot and they will tell you that they wish they had made the decision sooner."[9] "The decision to pivot is so difficult that many companies fail to make it."[10] Pivoting is necessary, but very hard to practice. Ries teaches startup entrepreneurs wise lessons; his book is a must-read for new ventures faced with the question whether or not to pivot. Pivoting, so much is clear, is not an innocent concept but a serious business activity.

Unfortunately, data on startup pivot strategies are scarce. There are hardly any large-scale empirical studies available on why, when, and how new ventures decide to correct their initial business course on the basis of market signals and customer feedback. We know little of startups' decisions to pivot as prompted by first learning experiences in order to achieve either lift-off or fail. Most studies are based on single case studies which complicates generalization and comparison. There is, fortunately, an interesting exception: The Stanford Innovation Study. This study, which will be further outlined in Chapters 5 and 8, was conducted among a huge sample of Stanford alumni (almost 28,000 respondents) and faculty and research staff (over 2,100 respondents). The alumni sample included some 8,000 entrepreneurs and 4,300 alumni who founded an incorporated business. A quarter of Stanford faculty started their own business. Part of this extensive innovation study was to explore the magnitude of companies founded by Stanford entrepreneurs that pivoted their original business model and product strategy. What were the main trends? Overall, about 60 percent indicated that they had changed their business; among younger businesses (founded in the last three years), the percentage of startup founders that modified their initial business ideas and plans is even higher: 70 percent. Over a quarter of the entrepreneurs pointed out that they had re-targeted their customer segment considerably, by over 50 percent in their estimation.[11] One-fifth mentioned that their business' technology had changed by half or more from the technology they started with as a new venture. And over one-quarter of the business founders said that their revenue model had been redefined, by again more than 50 percent. Sales channels also differed markedly from what entrepreneurs planned at launch. About one-third of the founders reported that they had shifted their sales plans by 25 percent or more. And almost 30 percent of entrepreneurs remarked that they had significantly modified their initial plan for key corporate partners and suppliers. One-fifth of the Stanford entrepreneurs even stated that their value proposition to their customers and users had changed substantially (a shift of 50 percent or more) from their original ideas. And, probably related, more than one-quarter revealed that they had considerably modified their initial marketing plans. Pivoting, so the conclusion holds, is quite standard among startups and some of the modifications and adjustments are far-reaching. The findings of the Stanford Innovation Study, according to the researchers, "indicate a picture of the early entrepreneurial firm that is often very flexible and nimble".[12] Startup founders need to skillfully navigate their new venture by carefully listening to market responses and be willing to pivot their core business strategy. Startups must agilely maneuver between the Scylla and Charybdis of perils and pitfalls that are typical for new ventures in the early stage of their business cycle.

Already in 1962, Everett Rogers proposed the innovation adoption model in his well-known book *Diffusion of Innovations*, which became one of the most cited books in the social sciences and a cherished handbook for communication experts and marketeers.[13] It describes the different stages in which consumers are assumed to adopt an innovation. Rogers' model shows a Bell curve with innovators being the top 2.5% in a particular market to adopt an innovation first, followed by 13.5% early adopters. From that point, an innovation should hit the market when the next 34%, called the early majority, adopts the new product. Late Majority (34%) and laggards (16%) follow after that. This model has been shown to work, at least as a useful framework to think about who is going to buy an innovation. It is clear that one person might be an innovator when it comes to new food products whereas this same person is a laggard concerning new cars, and belongs to the early majority in adopting new mobile devices. In other words, the diffusion model will work for each product, but different people may assume different roles for different product categories. During the past 50 years, numerous diffusion of innovation models have been forwarded by social scientists and marketeers, many of which are directly or indirectly variations on the Rogers' model. One example is the Technology Adoption Life Cycle by Geoffrey Moore,[14] which he explicitly links to technological innovations created in Silicon Valley. Since the model was developed in the US, the question is whether it works in every country; whether, in other words, it shows a pattern of cross-national stability. The answer is positive, but the percentages do differ. For example, the joint groups of innovators and early adopters is 16% in the US, but 24% in the UK, and 9% in Spain.[15] There is a strong positive correlation between innovation adoption and two cultural dimensions (individualism and acceptance of uncertainty) that we will further explain in Chapter 7. This means that an innovation will more quickly hit break-even in countries such as the UK, Ireland, the Netherlands, and Scandinavia than in other countries. Silicon Valley's dynamic startup culture, that we will describe in-depth in Chapter 7, is so unique particularly because taking risks is part of its entrepreneurial psychology. This collective mindset is related to having so many people around that are thrilled by innovation and by starting new ventures, and hence share a risk seeking attitude towards the world. They will also act as innovators or early adopters when it comes to new products, they have a tendency to be Need Seekers, as outlined in the previous chapter.

The reason for innovations not being successful is *not* that there are no customers. There are just *too few* customers. This is the lure for many hightech startups: the founding entrepreneurs are in close connection with other owners and employees of hightech startups. They understand each other, they speak the same language, and they share similar experiences. They may test their alpha or beta products with other techies and conclude that they have a killer app. At that moment, in terms of innovation diffusion, only the innovators and possibly early adopters have embraced the new product. To be successful one definitely needs a larger part of the market. It is exactly this issue that is addressed by Geoffrey Moore in his insightful and widely read book *Crossing the Chasm*.[16] Moore argues that innovators and early adopters are of a different make than other people, especially when it comes to technological innovation. They are technology enthusiasts (the innovators) and visionaries (early adopters). We shall use the term visionaries in the following to indicate both groups jointly. The early majority are called the pragmatists. Visionaries do not care whether the product is completely finished. They are perfectly happy with an MVP. Pragmatists prefer a proven concept that is working flawlessly and is recommended by existing users. And this contrast in customer attitudes, beliefs, and expectations denotes the chasm, a gaping *gorge* between the visionaries and the pragmatists: "the point of greatest peril in the development of a high-tech market lies in making the transition from an early market dominated by a few visionary customers to a mainstream market dominated by a large block of customers who are predominantly pragmatists in orientation."[17] A product may be liked or loved by the visionaries, whereas the pragmatists just don't get it, don't see it. Startups that are unable to cross the chasm between an early market and a mainstream market are doomed to fail. The do-or-die trick, according to Moore, is to sell disruptive products to mainstream customers by accelerating adoption rates among all consumer segments.

Moore identifies four characteristics that define the chasm between visionaries and pragmatists.[18] First of all, it is the ability of visionaries to see possibilities in underdeveloped products. Pragmatists would rather see an industry reference list. Secondly, visionaries like to imagine the future, where pragmatists are more oriented to the here and now. Thirdly, pragmatists have vested interests, they have built their career on other people, other ways of working etc. Visionaries do not really care about that, they build systems from the ground up. Finally, pragmatists tend to be committed to the company and their profession, whereas visionaries "don't plan to stick around long".[19] It is exactly this last observation that is the nightmare of employers in Silicon Valley. Employees are always looking around for the next move, lasting loyalty to the employer is virtually non-existent (see Chapter 5).

Silicon Valley likely has a large share of visionaries. People who want to disrupt the market and who are enthusiastic and passionate about technology and its possibilities. It is definitely one of the reasons why Silicon Valley is so successful and a role model for many startup entrepreneurs. On the other hand, this is exactly the pitfall: when a startup is testing its product among 100 or 1000 users, and they are all (friends of friends of) friends living in Silicon Valley, there will be a structural bias towards visionaries in the sample. If they embrace your product, or suggest improvements, this does not mean that pragmatists are agreeing, or that the mainstream market will be reached. The critical danger is that the startup will stay on the wrong side of the chasm.

Key Success Factors

There are marketing agencies in Silicon Valley, obviously. However, the size of these agencies is not what you would expect, given the high number of companies. The biggest is Liquid, with a gross income of $20M (2013) and 45 fte's.[20] They may count companies such as Google, Cisco, and HP among their clients. The second largest is CatapultWorks, recently joined with and adopting the name of R2integrated. Their gross income amounts to $13.3M in 2013, with clients such as Citrix and ServiceNow. Scott Gardner, president and CEO of Liquid, explains that "the in-house marketing teams of companies such as Apple, Google and Facebook are the biggest marketing teams in the Valley". Bigger than the external agencies. They typically come to a company such as Liquid for the more strategic questions, such as positioning and brand identity. Tom Beck, president and CEO of R2integrated, adds to that: "The upcoming of big internal marketing teams at Apple and their lot, has resulted in higher level assignments for us. The operational work is handled more and more at the clients' side."

Self-conscious consultants typically have their own set of 3, 5, 10 or any number of steps, factors, and prerequisites of successful innovation trajectories, all said to be backed up by scientific research. We have picked a few of our own that we deem relevant for Silicon Valley and which are in line with the beliefs and experiences expressed by our group of startup entrepreneurs.

1. Customer involvement. Align market and technology. Listen to the customer, involve the customer, for instance by applying Ries' feedback loop. The technology push, for sure, may be bigger when a technologically challenging product is being developed and continuously fine-tuned, but this comes at the risk of forgetting about the market, of not taking customer needs into account. It is always about balance. Without customer involvement, pivoting will be difficult and even pointless. Of course, one could argue in accordance with Steve Jobs that "People don't know what they want until you show it to them. That's why I never rely on market research."[21] Steve Jobs, however, seems to be the exception rather than the rule. And from a different perspective one may hold that Jobs was a marketing genius as reflected by the innovative early Apple ads and the customary massive events on launching new Apple products.

2. Team. We will underline this point throughout the book: a strong team is the most important asset of a startup (see Chapter 5). Disruptive innovations are almost always multidisciplinary, and that means that the coder should be able to talk to the financial controller, and both in turn should be able to understand the marketeer. But understanding and talking obviously is not enough; it goes much further and deeper: team members should integrate the other disciplines in the work that they themselves are doing on product development or market entry. Co-operation and multidisciplinarity are key factors in a startup's innovation trajectory. That is precisely why techniques such as Scrum[22] are so prevalent in especially software development. Companies such as Spotify, Apple (iPhone probably being the most cited example), Instagram, Dropbox, and Salesforce have effectively used Scrum to manage the innovation process and help team members working together.

3. Passion and perseverance. The startup drive to realize its goals should be all-encompassing by leading and energizing team members and employees. Investors explicitly search for passionate startup entrepreneurs (see Chapter 6). Perseverance is above all relevant directly before, during, and after a pivot. Pivoting is often associated with failure, but failure is also seen – particularly in Silicon Valley – as a precondition for learning. Furthermore, employees will be motivated and stimulated by dedicated entrepreneurs who set startup goals that exceed the worldly realm of turnover and profit.

4. Focus on the right business. Many startup innovation ideas need money from investors in order to be realized, but these investors ultimately

want an exit strategy (acquisition or IPO, see Chapter 6). Angels and VCs go for a tempting return on their investment. This means that startup founders must always have a keen eye on the business model: who is going to pay, why, and for what. It is this last question that is easy to pose but often difficult to answer. The "who" is your target group, and much internal discussion arises when this decisive issue is addressed within a startup company. The "why" is about the customer's pain, or what is the problem that needs to be resolved? The "what" is about your solution, what is it exactly that is going to relieve the pain that the customer experiences? Only too often does a startup go astray because one of the above questions is not answered correctly or only partially. These three questions (who, why, what) are the basic subjects for every investor upon deciding whether or not to invest in a startup.

We believe these four conditions are essential in realizing a successful go-to-market strategy. It is the transition from upstream to downstream innovation that racks most startup founders' brains.

Marketing redefined

How to get a product sold? It is the age-old marketing question. It is the ultimate problem that every startup has to face. Silicon Valley is finding new ways and is partly driving a new way of marketing. How do people come to know about and use Google, Facebook, WhatsApp, Instagram? Most likely from someone else. They definitely did not see a TV ad in these companies' early days. Somewhere the rumor got started. It is called word-of-mouth, and we will come back to that.

So how do you go about as a brand? We see a few trends in marketing that we want to share. The list of four points presented here is based on our interviews with entrepreneurs and on cases from bigger Silicon Valley companies (all former startups), of which we will introduce a few. The first two points are related to upstream innovation, the latter two are related to downstream innovation. This emphasizes the continued importance of marketing throughout the whole process of innovation.

1. Having a superior product is a must. This is true for new and existing ventures. Before the internet and the transparency it brought, a brand was able to convince customers with smooth ads claiming that their product was better than anyone else's, but these days have gone. People will talk about products and services in forums, on review sites,

on blogs etc. If a product is mediocre, or worse than its competitors', customers will simply say so. This is not different than before, but the speed of diffusion and magnitude of a positive or negative message is much greater. There is a tendency, especially in newly created markets, towards a "winner-takes-all" dynamic. Examples are Uber, Airbnb, WhatsApp, and Facebook. For example, there used to be many local 'Facebook-type' social networking sites, such as Hyves in the Netherlands, but many have been swallowed up or ousted by Facebook. This tendency is not limited to new companies, similar dynamics can be seen in department stores (Walmart and H&M) where superior is defined as discount enabled by superior logistics) or smartphones such as iPhone's first-class design and user-friendliness (who remembers Nokia?). As we discussed above, making an exceptional product means pivoting when needed.

2. Build on customer insights. Uber sells taxi service without owning a single taxi, Airbnb offers travel accommodation without owning a single hotel. What they do superbly, is to give customers what they want: a fixed price for the cab ride, a more personal way of staying somewhere at a good price. Finding the right customer preferences may be quite a problem. Pivoting is often part of this search for the customer decision metrics and product choice. If done correctly, it may pay off greatly. Therefore this point is intertwined with the first point. Product and market are very, very tightly connected. Disruption may work best in industries that are irritating customers. Banks may be an example (crowd funding is an answer), or car dealers (Tesla can do without them). On top of that, startups must ensure that their first customer is the right customer. They will act as ambassadors of the company's product.

3. Content is king. "Content is actually the best thing to happen to the marketing profession in decades."[23] The smooth payoff of the TV ad has been substituted by content that is actually meaningful. The surge of storytelling comes from this as well: shouting doesn't work anymore, but telling a compelling story of how a brand started, how or why a customer uses a product etc. works. The story may also tell something that is not directly related to the brand or product. Content management is very much linked to customer insights, since there is a need to know what kind of information customers are seeking and how they process the acquired information. It also helps in getting the company's story across.

4. PR and word-of-mouth. Since the rise of social media, word-of-mouth seems to be more and more the key to success. People talk about a

startup if it developed an excellent product with a great story. Just look at the hypes that are happening every day on Twitter, Facebook, and Instagram. Whether it is a Coke and Mentos experience[24] or an Ice Bucket Challenge[25], it is the way that consumers are drawn into a story that gets them to engage in the story and share it.[26] A proven way of working to create word-of-mouth is by starting to offer a product, or part of it, for free. Users of WhatsApp can use the product for free, and indeed many apps start and remain for free, such as Evernote, Spotify, LinkedIn, DropBox, Flickr, and PayPal.[27] Chris Anderson describes giving products away for free as one of the nine rules of the long tail.[28] Phil Libin (CEO at Evernote) states: "The easiest way to get one million people paying is get one billion people using."[29]

The third point (content is king) is a form of outbound marketing. Outbound marketing is often described as an old-fashioned type of marketing, since it is about sending the message out through e.g. TV, internet banners or cold calls. It is, in other words, about attracting the (potential) customer's attention. Content marketing is also a form of outbound marketing and is definitely not considered old school. It is rapidly increasing in popularity.[30] The fourth point (PR and word-of-mouth) contains examples of inbound marketing, i.e. earning the attention of customers rather than working hard to get them to pay attention. Blogging and vlogging are examples. Typical forms of inbound marketing occur on social media, where customers engage in the company message or talk about it (word-of-mouth). Free publicity through magazines, newspapers, and websites may also be seen as inbound marketing.

Of course, this list is not complete and can be augmented by numerous other issues, but based on our interviews we believe these are the most important ones: start with an excellent product that offers a solution for a significant customer base, topped with relevant content and a good story, and help customers to talk about it to other customers. Now let us examine whether this fits with some of Silicon Valley's successful company stories.

Palantir makes "products for human-driven analysis of real-world data". Customers are able to "answer complex questions without requiring (...) to master querying languages [or] statistical modeling".[31] It proves to be a very interesting business, as Palantir has recently (June 24, 2015) been valued at $20B.[32] Being in the business of making data accessible, Bloomberg and similar agencies seem to be perfect first customers. Palantir managed to get to talk to them and pitch their product. Of course, this is only possible if the product is outstanding. And from there, business basically took off. These first customers started telling the Palantir story. Did they only talk about the product itself? Probably not. The company's name has a mysterious ring about it. Palantir is one of Three Rings in Tolkien's Lord of the Rings, a mystical account of a fantasy world.[33] With Palantir one sees things afar which are not visible to the naked eye. This story relates directly to Palantir's core business, and is therefore a very strong and compelling narrative. The interesting thing of storytelling is that it drags people into a story. Whether an investor or not, people like stories because it touches our emotions. As Fog et al. (2010) state: "A strong brand is a combination of facts and emotions. We rationalize and legitimize with our brains, but we buy with our hearts, be it shampoo or insurance. The product has to be up to scratch in order for us to rationalize our choice, but it is the heart and not the head doing the persuading."[34] Palantir applied all points on both of our lists on how to manage a successful innovation and how to launch a narrative marketing strategy.

Zendesk is a company that helps supporting customers better. Zendesk offers Software as a Service (SaaS) – the software is hosted on a central unit, customers subscribe through a license. Customers, by having SaaS, are free of the nagging procedure of updating software on all company computers, because the updates will be done centrally on an outside server. Zendesk went a long way to understand their customers. They examined the customer journey: all interactions that a customer may have with a particular company. Then they created content around that journey. Interestingly, they found out that the typical enterprise customer has 10-30 interactions with a company before buying its software.[35] During these interactions, Zendesk made the difference by helping customers through solving tactical issues, interconnecting between different channels, etc. The marketing communications department is called PR, aimed at getting the brand narrative across their customers and potential customers. All points of our innovation and marketing list are put to work at Zendesk.

We already mentioned the iPhone while describing these innovation and marketing prerequisites. Apple uses a technique of exclusivity: there is a grand show, the Apple Event, where their CEO introduces the Big New Things to be expected shortly. This creates the second buzz. The first buzz was already created in the weeks before the event, where people who are 'in the know' predict features of the new iPhone or new products to come. After the first and the second buzz, the third buzz is created by consumers actually having bought the product. Consumer and expert reviews appear everywhere: in blogs, magazines, and on YouTube. iPhones are designed on the basis of consumer insights. A very special one is the insight that consumers who buy a beautifully designed electronic device, experience this as a gift (from others or from themselves). Therefore, Apple products are always beautifully packed. There are numerous videos on YouTube where the unpacking of an Apple product is filmed.[36] Also the Apple iPhone uses all points of both of our lists.

Having said that, there is an additional strong point in Apple's marketing strategy that deserves mentioning. Distribution is a big issue. Apple's new iPhone is usually quickly out of stock. Not because they are bad at planning in Cupertino, but because they intentionally plan to run out of stock. This creates scarcity, rumor around the product and the brand, people blogging about it, animosity between iPhone haves and iPhone have-nots. This all works to get people to want the product, even if they didn't care when they first heard about it. It is a technique of inducing exclusivity, of in-group marketing. Apple and other hightech firms use other, often less sympathetic, ways to use distribution as a marketing tool. They sometimes force customers to use something. This may be about products that most people do not really care about such as an Intel processor. But a PC comes with Internet Explorer, an iPhone app can only be bought in an iTunes-store. And there is no, or no easy, way around such rigid sales conditional.

We will come back to both lists when introducing the marketing beliefs of the startup entrepreneurs that we interviewed, which combined with the topic of pivoting, are addressed in the following and final section of this chapter.

Entrepreneurs on pivot & perseverance

Pivoting the startup

Typically, Tom Beck, president and CEO at R2integrated, explains, a novel startup does not come to R2integrated: "They don't give a damn about marketing." They are pushed either by investors or other market forces, such as an upcoming IPO into the direction of a marketing agency, because the stakes are much higher then. Sometimes, at that point, some damage has already been done to the brand. Hence, Tom Beck says, "we tend to work with clients who have funding from $20M to $4B, that's our sweet spot." Scott Gardner, president and CEO at Liquid, confirms this, saying "we work with companies that have funding from, say, $50M." At that point, marketing and branding becomes very important and, moreover, the companies have more money to spend on marketing. Both Liquid and R2integrated have experimented with deferred payments and taking equity in ventures. However, they have both stopped doing so. Scott: "All our work needs to be paid, we do not take financial risks with companies anymore." It is only too logical: marketing agencies have a too small client portfolio, compared to investors or big law firms, to level out winners and losers.

We asked our sample of startup founders whether they had changed their original business plan, and if so in which direction. Was pivoting based on clear market feedback, and how did founders respond to customer reactions to their product? Below are some of the pivot experiences of our startup entrepreneurs.

David Mayer, CEO of health care startup RENDLE, explicitly pivoted the core business of his new venture. The change was from cure to prevention, and from the individual to the employer. "Pivoting processes take time. Our initial idea was an online platform that aimed at enhancing people's health, and monitoring the changes. But the actual health problems in the US caused by lifestyle, smoking, overweight, eating habits did make me realize we should focus on prevention more than on mere cure measures" (David Mayer, RENDLE). The second pivot was to center on the enterprise since health insurance in the US is provided through one's employer. "So now we focus on corporate health and wellness solutions." The overall idea is that these pivots improve employees' health and their productivity, and decreases the company's health care costs. "Simple kindergarten math" as David adds.

Maarten Sierhuis, founder of Ejenta, is also in the health care business. Their product is on wearable sensors measuring health through a cloud-based service with intelligent agents interpreting the data, and personal assistants helping customers with health problems. Ejenta is in the process of defining its core market. "As a startup we pivot, we need to specify our business model. We have a scenario we are working on but we are still struggling whether we should have a consumer product or an enterprise product (...) We are at a pivotal moment to figure this out" (Maarten Sierhuis, Ejenta).

Choosing between a B2C or a B2B market model is a classic issue facing many startups. GROM is one of them. This smartphone case printing startup needed to determine its prime market. They started out with smart phone users as their main target group but realized that this is a colossal market for which you need designers, marketeers, logistics people, etc. "We decided to switch from focusing on consumers to retailers. It took us basically one and a half year to come to that decision. We did not believe in it at first, we were stubborn. But I am happy we did it, although our pivot had many consequences. Our sales stopped for three or four months because of the switch from consumers to businesses" (Vincent van de Poll, GROM). Vincent's startup now serves companies that sell his smart phone cases to their customers, including the largest retailers in the world. Co-founders, Rip and Marco of Rip van Wafels, also pivoted their startup, particularly after moving the company to San Francisco. "Our go-to-market strategy changed from focusing on colleges to focusing on a regional geographic approach. We made quite a lot of product modifications over the years. We've made the product healthier, tastier and have been working hard on improving the product experience. We really want to make a product that enables busy Americans to savor the time they spend snacking. We want to make savoring a Rip van Wafels a staple snacking ritual in the US" (Rip Pruisken, Rip van Wafels). Ruben Daniëls radically changed the business course of his startup Cloud9 IDE from a consultancy firm in the Netherlands to a hightech software company in Silicon Valley. This was a truly major pivot that not only impacted the core activities of his business but also had implications for the employees Ruben needed for his transformed company. There was not a perfect match between the people he needed and the people he had currently employed. "We were a consultancy firm of fifteen people when we got funding here in Silicon Valley. To make such a pivot means some people did not fit." Ruben's startup product is a cloud-based integrated development environment (Cloud9 IDE) that was pivoted several times. "We launched the product, we went to open source, we made a lot of noise, and it worked. We created alterations with different ideas throughout the pivot, and it worked, it sort of spread, people talked about us and wanted to talk with us" (Ruben Daniëls, Cloud9 IDE). Ronald Mannak tells us about the creative way his company JumpCam pivoted their video app. The old app they were working on needed some fundamental improvements, which as such is nothing new but, in this case, it had to be done in a very short time. "Almost every startup must pivot, that can be pretty dramatic because in the end you are building a product nobody has made before. You don't know if it is going to be successful or not. You can do all kinds of research, do market interviews, but many things can go wrong" (Ronald Mannak, JumpCam). The smart pivot idea was that they provided test apps to college students – they started at the University of Kansas and the University of Pennsylvania – and organized college parties at which they ask students for their feedback which then was used to further improve the app. Universities are both a test audience but also a sales target group. Working with and through universities greatly enhanced the number of app sign ups. "We are now set up for rolling out twenty-five universities later this year. We are trying to apply what we learned from the first two universities and develop a blueprint of how to roll out our app. Maybe the next market will be a country, not just a university."

Bianca Oudshoff (Dutch Ministry of Economic Affairs), who worked at the Dutch consulate in San Francisco for several years, compares Dutch and American entrepreneurs when it comes to pivoting: "In Holland, we are very much inclined to completely develop a product. We want it to be perfect and beautiful, and then we go to the market. In the Valley, they start at the other side: first prove that there is someone who is going to buy your product. Then you start developing that product further together with that customer. That way of thinking and acting is very difficult for Dutch people. Especially for Dutch technicians."

The question *when* to involve the market and the customer is a difficult one. Our respondents do not seem to completely agree. Harm TenHoff (BayLink) is very outspoken: "It's all about marketing," he claims, "It is a very big necessity in a very early stage to have marketing understand what the market wants or what we can make the market want. Therefore a company has to fully understand not only what that market is today." Harm stresses having a solid sense of market understanding right at the beginning of a new venture. Other entrepreneurs have a slightly different view. Faruk Ateş (Presentate): "We haven't looked at the public yet since we are still comparatively early stage really." Somewhat later in the interview Faruk states: "There are some things that I would do differently (…) I would probably focus a little bit more on getting something out there that we could launch publically so people could start using it earlier on. Even if it meant that we will have to rebuild the stuff and even if it meant that we would slow down in future development for a long time. Just having people to use our product is incredibly valuable." Here, Faruk alludes to bringing out an MVP earlier. As we discussed, this appears to be one of the most difficult business decisions for startup entrepreneurs. With regard to marketing, Ruben Daniëls (Cloud9 IDE) notices: "I think in the early stages of the company you only want have to have a product team most of the time. I mean there are some products where you want to sell the beta." To him, though, the product team is "purely focused on finding out what product, what market, and all those different variables." To Ruben, these functions are completely intertwined, and that is exactly what pivoting and market-oriented product development is about. Arthur van Hoff (Jaunt) says it more explicitly: "there is nobody who hires marketing people here." Arthur also means to indicate that though as a startup founder you have to look at the market, you always do that in combination with the product developer, with the engineer, with the designer. Faruk Ateş (Presentate) also seeks market feedback without having someone in his company who is specialized in marketing: "We've casually spread the word via Twitter and Facebook; people signed for the alpha and then we conducted a poll with questions like 'Do you have an urgent need and are you okay with using an alpha product?' We've also had a number of people we didn't know and then invited into our office and talk." The Mountain View Chamber of Commerce helps their local companies also in this respect. Oscar Garcia (CoC, Mountain View): "According to the city there are about 100 startups in Mountain View and sometimes we get requests from startups that will say (...) we need half a dozen businesses that are willing to test our product (...) What the Chamber does is facilitate introductions to other organizations where the startups can test and promote their product."

Launch and sales

Getting money from investors is partly team effort, partly the idea, but there is also some marketing needed for that. Serial entrepreneur Arthur van Hoff (Jaunt) tells us how that works: "When you raise financing for companies you kind of learn what works, what doesn't work (...) From a marketing perspective selling your ideas is the hardest thing, nothing to go on it's just you (...) that's why I always tell people you got to have an emotional hook." Arthur specifically mentions storytelling as an interesting way to establish an emotional connection: "there was this guy pitching an idea for a watch, a smart watch. The guy didn't pitch by saying I developed this smart watch and it's got such and such features. No, he told a little story: 'I grew up in Egypt; my father was a nomad, my grandfather was a nomad. My grandfather was traveling through the desert during the First World War and he saved a British soldier. The soldier gave him this watch, this beautiful gold watch on a chain in return, and that watch got passed down from my grandfather to my father, to me. I hold that watch really dearly, that's been my inspiration and I've been inspired to create this smart watch.' (...) His whole story was about creating this emotional connection. Arthur van Hoff's account is similar to what has been described about Palantir in the previous section. Storytelling is a great way to start your PR, to get interest from investors, from the media or entertain people at a party. It is also a great way to inspire startup teams. Cees Jan Koomen (VC and entrepreneur) also tells us a story about a watch (this must be a coincidence) that he used when working at Philips: "We also used metaphors, one metaphor I used for the RF [Radio Frequency, PE/AM] business. You probably still remember the cartoon Flash Gordon from a long time ago. Flash Gordon was one of the first science fiction heroes, I think, he was kind of an investigator, a crime investigator. Or something like that. But he was a hero, and he had some new gadgets. So one of the gadgets was a kind of a watch but it also had an image in it, and you could flip it. We took that as a metaphor for our development program, we called it the risk communicator project. So we kind of drove our innovation out of that vision. And that helped to develop the RF business at Philip Semiconductor tremendously. In such a way that still today they are a leader in the market." Scott Gardner, president and CEO of Liquid, supports Arthur's remarks: "Storytelling is really important." Tom Beck, president and CEO of R2integrated, adds: "Storytelling starts with the care-abouts: what are the big pains. On the basis of that, the concepting of the story starts."

Cees-Jan Koomen is very clear about the go-to-market phase: "Commercialization is always a challenge. If you have people who have already commercial experiences in the market (...) that makes a big difference." Ruben Daniëls (Cloud9 IDE) specifically mentions Moore's chasm: "making the jump over the chasm to the mainstream is very difficult". So, how do you go about doing this? How do you get from one side of the chasm to the other? Pieter Noordam (RFIsoft) needs just one word: "Referral." Interestingly, that is exactly what the early majority, at the other side of the chasm, is looking for: proven concepts, proven technologies, word-of-mouth. No visionary stuff. Pieter Noordam further explains: "Let's say a guy who I worked for at a company goes to another company and they (...) are having lunch or coffee and talk about what I did for them. (...) That is actually how I keep busy." Especially in B2B, the first customer is very important. This customer should start the word-of-mouth. Thijs Boekhoff (Ingen-Housz): "My first customer was also the toughest one, so I spent a lot of time on him." Pieter Noordam (RFIsoft): "Actually the first customer gets a lot of attention, right. It has to be perfect and even if it's a small thing, even if it takes you five hours to do it, without any questions, you just do it."

Word-of-mouth can be further stimulated by giving away your product as a freemium, or by letting people beta-test it. Faruk Ateş (Presentate): "We have a free version, it's basically a premium business model where we have premium accounts and a free version for everyone to use. Any time people use it and put the presentation in public, you know, they share with other people and we have tons of new signups." Rip Pruisken (Rip van Wafels) expands: "The reason why we moved to the Bay Area is because a lot of tech companies give food away for free to their employees. It was a great way to introduce the product, to get the product trialed at very low cost." To get the talking going, it may be wise to have a community manager, especially assigned for creating just that. Ronald Mannak (JumpCam) elaborates: "Our community manager was in touch with the community making sure everybody was happy, deleting content that wasn't appropriate, all that kind of stuff."

Companies are looking more and more towards content marketing. Social media is an excellent way of sharing content directly with customers. Tom Beck, president and CEO of R2integrated: "content marketing often starts with a buyers' journey. What are the touchpoints, what is the right content for each phase?" However, the idea that social media costs nothing, is often found to be mistaken. "Social media delivers for free. No bleeping way," Tom summarizes.

Is the "old stuff", such as events and corporate marketing not relevant anymore? We would not make that claim. Some of our respondents mention that area of the business as (still) important. But it is definitely less prominent than a decade ago. Eric-Jan van Leeuwen (Login VSI): "Basically my marketing director is responsible for corporate branding and corporate mission, and then on the local level we also have marketing people who are responsible for organizing events and local marketing activities." And of course, big companies such as Apple, who got famous with the iconic 1984 MacIntosh commercial[37] and their Mac vs. PC ads,[38] still use commercials to advertise their products. But other big companies like Google and Facebook hardly, if ever, use TV as an advertising tool. Neal Blaak (ZappoTV): "In the beginning we've done a bit of marketing. We've done five or ten blog posts, where we just participated in conversations and just said 'hey did you check out ZappoTV? You can do this on the TV' and that was it. And that's three years ago, that were our first 5,000 users."

Getting PR is the way most entrepreneurs would like to go. It is free and the source is unsuspected. Ruben Daniëls: "What we did was that prior to raising money we started doing a lot of PR and so (...) Mozilla announced that we were working with them (...). Later, there was also a big TechCrunch article." And this was for investors, to raise money? "Yeah definitely, you want to paint them a picture or give them a perspective that you are on to something."

Thus, marketing and PR are not only crucial to attract customers, but also to convince investors. There are basic differences in this respect between the US and Europe. We will delve into that in Chapter 7. But we will mention some marketing issues here. Most importantly, the European market is much more fragmented. Arthur van Hoff (Jaunt) puts it very clearly: "Here you have a hundred million families that all have credit cards and use dollars; who all speak English, and that's not the case in Europe." However convenient that is, it does not mean that the US is an easy market. Eric Gabrys (Bay Area trade and investment commissioner at Brussels Invest & Export) explains: "Sometimes people want to rush into the US: 'We have a great product in Europe, we are so successful. I don't understand that we wouldn't be able to sell it in the US…' And then guess what, they get feedback and they don't understand the feedback of customers just because they skipped the step of validating their products for the US market. So that's a very critical success factor we're going to talk about with our startups (…). Think about customer support, think about the timing of response. Sometimes I have companies I had to wait for three days to get an answer. I told them if you do that to an American, you are out."

Tom Beck nicely sums up how clients in the Valley sometimes differ from 'normal' clients: "A new client said to us: I want you to fail! Please try new ideas, I want to see new things." It is this spirit of the Valley that has led and will lead to new ideas coming out of the Valley, also in marketing. Scott Gardner expects a lot of changes due to data analytics: "I think that in the future, we will be working even more with data analytics. It will help us decide what to do real-time, but also what to do for the long term."

5. Team and Talent

Startup founding teams: From pals to professionalization

The life of a startup founder is no picnic. It can be extremely stressful, demanding, and hard. To create a successful startup is a Herculean undertaking that takes guts, passion, and perseverance. Becoming a startup entrepreneur often implies a rigorous break with one's past, the need to acquire new business skills, and the challenge of facing a highly uncertain future. It often involves a total reorganization of one's private life. Startup founders must cope with painful mistakes, wrong judgments, and lacking expertise. Most new venture entrepreneurs cannot fall back on previous experiences, so they cannot rely on availability heuristics. They know that most startups fail, and financial worries dominate their daily concerns. Startup founders must secure company funding, develop the basic startup idea and turn it into an innovative and competitive product, come up with a solid product/market fit, effectively profile its customer segment, define a convincing marketing strategy, and take timely pivoting decisions. Furthermore, founders need to invest in the professionalization of their new business venture: recruit and coach employees, structure the organization, budget its activities, control the cash flow, and create an energetic and positive business culture. They have to survive in an ultra-competitive market with numerous rivaling businesses that all aim high and all want to have their share of the pie. Startups, in short, are vulnerable ventures that face a multitude of barriers and dilemmas. It takes a lot of mental strength to maneuver new ventures through this early business stage. Research has shown that the first two to three years of a firm's life cycle are the most risky and precarious episode and determine the startup's survival chances.[1] On top of all these tough hurdles, our non-US sample of startup pioneers had to deal with extra constraints as they moved to Silicon Valley from abroad and had to adjust to a new environment, to a new culture, and to new rules. Moreover, they had to build new networks and a new customer portfolio. And did so mostly from scratch.

Startup entrepreneurs need to operate strategically at different levels and at different playing fields. Startup management is like simultaneous chess. Beginning a new business on your own, without co-founders, is usually not a good idea as it generates many difficulties. Akin to swimming into deep water, as it were. All the issues mentioned above require calculated decision-making and risk-taking, carefully weighing various positive and negative outcomes, and the tenacity to keep on going. Running a startup in its early stage can be very chaotic and demands quick responses to a variety of managerial complexities. Teams of startup founders, so the consensus seems to be in Silicon Valley and elsewhere, are better suited to handle these problems and challenges than solo founders. As Paul Graham, co-founder of Y Combinator – a successful seed capital firm headquartered in Mountain View – maintains: "all startups are the same, you need two people to spread the load".[2] When Y Combinator was launched it had a clear formal rule: no funding of startups with only one founder.[3] The Silicon Valley startup community knows that VC's strongly favor founding teams over single founders and most startups looking for funding are consequently headed by a team of two or more entrepreneurs. Jon Katzenbach and Douglas Smith, authors of *The wisdom of teams: Creating the high-performance organization*, come up with a useful definition of what makes a good team: "a small number of people with complementary skills who are committed to a common purpose, set of performance goals, and approach for which they hold themselves mutually accountable".[4] They also point at the wider psychological significance of the team's mission: "credible team purposes have an element related to winning, being first, revolutionizing, or being on the cutting edge."[5] They share energy and reach for synergy. Research indicates that startups founded by teams on average perform better and are more successful than firms started by single founders. This is particularly true for hightech startups. In his review study of entrepreneurial teams, Thomas Lechler concludes that "overall the main argument for the advantages of teams is based on the positive effects of a combination of people with different personalities, characteristics, knowledge, skills, and abilities".[6] The main focus of entrepreneurial teams is on creativity and innovation, on the ability of new ventures to develop and market innovative ideas and on its practical applicability. Startup teams need to be goal-driven, achievement-oriented, collaborative, and they should make use of the experience, expertise, and competence of team members.[7]

Younger startup teams typically consist of founders who know each other from college. Many of the hightech new ventures in Silicon Valley were – and are – started by college friends who studied computer science, engineering, or other technical disciplines. They often developed their startup initiative during their college years, in many cases supported by the entrepreneurial spirit and climate of their university. As we will see further on in this chapter and in more detail in chapter 8, the Bay Area universities take these startup activities by its students very seriously and offer specific courses and facilities to foster their entrepreneurial activities. Having a team of hightech startup founders from the same technical discipline has clear advantages. It is good for the technological refining and perfection of the startup's innovation idea, but it is not so good for the launching of the new venture in all of its other critical business dimensions: funding, budget control, accounting, marketing, recruiting, organization, and day-to-day operational management. In order for startups to be successful, complementary skill sets of its founders are decisive. Effective new venture founding teams consist of members with unique startup competences and talents that add to integral and balanced management who are able to address the many challenges startups have to respond to. As Bernd Schoner, vice president of business development for ThingMagic, concludes: "Having the right team determines the path and outcome of a new venture more than any decision in the lifecycle of a company."[8] As a rule of thumb, startup teams need to at least cover the following competences: visionary skills, capable execution skills, administrative and financial skills, and talent recruitment skills. In combination these fundamental competences represent the startup's resources, its entrepreneurial capital so to speak. Team composition, therefore, greatly matters. The more popular literature provides many examples of catchy names for key roles of startup team members. According to Bernd Schoner, a new venture team needs at least the following six "personalities" to be successful: the prima donna genius (the innovation expert and most high-risk team member), the superstar (multi-tasking charismatic nerd), the leader (informal decision-maker other team members are willing to follow), the industry veteran (experienced market insider), the sales animal (accomplished seller of the startup's main product), and, finally, the financial suit (the startup's financial wizard).[9] The literature also highlights best practices for interdependent high-performing teams. Leadership is of overriding importance. Team performance expert and social psychologist Richard Hackman distinguishes five conditions leadership must establish in order for teams to function effectively: create a real team, with a compelling direction, an enabling structure, a supportive organizational context, and expert coaching.[10] Based on this classification, psychologists Kevin Stagl, Eduardo Salas, and Shawn Burke formulated ten basic rules for high-performance teams: define and create interdependencies (team members' roles), establish goals (shared goals and team commitment), specify decision-making rules (conflict reduction), provide clear feedback (team performance and improvement), ensure stable team membership (co-operative joint learning), stimulate challenging the status quo (openness to innovation and change), attract new talent and expertise (identifying and recruiting talent), establish a team-based reward system (combining individual and collective performance incentives), create a learning environment (team development and skills advancement), and focus on the common mission (sharing the higher purpose).[11] A super team excels in self-efficacy, the need for achievement, mutual trust and accountability, and confidence. It knows how to deal with interpersonal difficulties and nourishes intra-team communication and interaction. Particularly in times of crisis, a super team shows its strength and ability to lead. Team dynamics, obviously, are elementary in the early and growth startup stages and, in the post-honeymoon period. Rules are still informal, there is no crystallized structure or routine for decision-making and conflict resolution, and team members' roles are weakly defined. The ability of startup founding teams to cope with its internal group dynamics is essential for the new firm's survival and further development. Research has indicated that new business venture performance is related to team cohesion, mission sharing, team conflict regulation, team learning, and the team's social capital and networks.[12] The role of the founding team CEO is central, he or she according to successful serial Silicon Valley startup entrepreneur Steve Blank, is "the first among equals in the founding team. Ironically they are almost never the most intelligent or technically astute person on the team. What sets them apart from the rest of the team is that they can project a fearless reality distortion field that they use to recruit, fund raise, pivot and position the company. They are the ultimate true believers in the company and have the vision, passion, and skill to communicate why this seemingly crazy idea will work and change the world."[13] The founding CEO is on a mission, a calling almost, and thrives on operating in a context of chaos and uncertainty. The CEO's main task is to empower the business, its management team and employees, to lead the company through a process of uncertainty and ambiguity. Steven Blank again: "While the rest of the team is focused on their specific jobs, the founding CEO is trying to solve a complicated equation where almost all the variables are unknown – unknown customers, unknown features that will make those customers buy, unknown pricing, unknown demand creation activities that will get them into your sales channel, etc."[14]

Effective startup founding teams dispose of collective resources that go above and beyond the team members' individual resources. And this is exactly why founding teams are more able than single startup founders to guide a startup through its developmental transitions, "since individual entrepreneurs may lack critical resources to grow their businesses".[15] Founding team members need to bring in competences and talents that strengthens and broadens team performance. Complementary dissimilar competences and skills, as we indicated, make for strong startup teams. It creates synergy. The simple team math here is that the whole is greater than the sum of its parts.

Talent: Excelling in hard & soft skills

Talented software programmers, engineers, and computer scientists are in great demand in Silicon Valley, both by existing and by new hightech ventures. They are the core human resources of the hightech sector and indispensable for developing distinctive innovative products that disrupt technological paradigms and change consumer markets. Talented employees are of paramount importance in the basic innovation process of idea generation, idea elaboration, and of turning ideas into inventive and marketable products or services. Talent makes the difference in how well companies and startups are doing and therefore is the main ingredient of a company's human capital. The talent capacity of a startup determines its survival likelihood, innovation potential, growth perspective, and performance outcomes. How do we define talented employees? Human resource management expert Clem Molloy gives a good operational definition: "If they have solved difficult problems, made critical decisions effectively, envisioned and led change, inspired creativity and innovation and generally contributed to the performance and long-term viability of the organization, then there would be little doubt that they have talent."[16] Hightech talent in the Silicon Valley context is not just about having excellent hard skills, i.e. knowing how to program, how to write code, and how to develop user-friendly software, and doing so at the highest level. Talent Valley-style must also dispose of outstanding soft skills, i.e. being creative and open-minded, able to work in diverse team settings, have an entrepreneurial mindset, be good at networking, have a flexible but dedicated attitude, intrinsically motivated and opportunity-focused, willing to deliver and learn, customer-oriented, and focused on one's personal development.[17] An exceptional combination of these hard and soft skills is what defines talent. A skill set that is characteristic of the 21st century economy and workforce.[18] Job demands and job skills are fast changing and talented employees know how to adjust and update their core competences through lifelong learning. As NOVA Workforce Development, a Silicon Valley employment and training agency, concludes on ICT employees: "Technical skills are obviously important, but attitudes and characteristics such as flexibility, curiosity, and initiative foster important bridging activities. These activities include

networking, self-awareness, organizational reading, relationship management, and mentorship, and demonstrate to employers that they have a team
member who will continue to seek to add value to the firm."[19] Google's talent
description underlines this conclusion. According to Laszlo Bock, senior vice
president for people operations, Google (who receives 2 million applications
a year) looks for four key qualities in recruiting candidates: general cognitive
ability, leadership, "Googleyness", and role-related knowledge.[20] Note the
descending order from "general smarts" to specific job skills. A clear fit
between venture and potential employees ("Googlers") is what all ventures
look for. As Facebook CEO Mark Zuckerberg pointedly formulated: "I will
only hire someone to work directly for me if I would work for that person."[21]

In a sector that is so dependent on human capital, on knowledge workers,
Silicon Valley hightech companies need to heavily invest in binding and
bonding its talent, in retaining its gifted employees. These companies
are involved in a permanent struggle for attracting the best talents available on the market. As it depends on a steady stream of talent, recruiting
bright and brilliant people is a top priority for the hightech sector. People
that are not just smart but who fit and carry the culture and mission of
the business. The competition for talent in Silicon Valley is a very serious
business which in a booming economy may even result in a "war for talent".
Smaller companies may outsource their personnel hiring to professional
recruitment agencies in the Valley. The big hightech companies have developed full-swing human resource policies to keep their employees happy
and to be an attractive employer for new talent, by offering competitive
salaries, flexible working hours, stock options, creative work spaces, free
transport, time for innovative projects, free meals, professional fitness
centers, etc. Companies know that talented people seek challenging work
that gets the best out of them. They know that they have to create an
inspiring organization culture and positive corporate identity that add to
the company's reputation. Employer brand, next to employee benefits, is
a major element in the perception of prospective employees of the firm's
reputation, which in turn affects their decision to join the firm.[22] Here is
how Google communicates its employee benefits: "Our benefits are part
of who we are, and they're designed to take care of the whole you and
keep you healthy, whether physically, emotionally, financially or socially
(…). We want to make your life better and easier. We want our benefits
to work for you. We care about you AND your family."[23] Big words from
a big company that wants to create and communicate a social, healthy
business culture that connects employee interests and corporate concerns.
Google's employee benefits and perks include on-site medical services

and health care, travel insurance, maternity leave, taking courses, legal aid, one day per week to work on a side project of one's choosing, free home to work transport, and free meals.[24] Apple offers similar benefit employee packages, framed within the context of its talent mission state- ment. "We're perfectionists. Idealists. Inventors. Forever tinkering with products and processes, always on the lookout for better. Whether you work at one of our global offices, offsite, or even at home, a job at Apple will be demanding. But it also rewards bright, original thinking and hard work. And none of us here would have it any other way."[25] Apple recently updated its employee benefits policy to attract new talent.[26] Its new and updated perks include longer parental leave, education reimbursement for classes taken by employees, expanded donation-matching program (matching employees for their time spent on philanthropic causes up to $25 per hour with a total cap of $10,000), subsidized student loan refinancing, and full acceleration of stock in the event of an employee's death.[27] Apple markets its corporate career opportunities as a niche where intrinsic work values flourish but in a demanding environment. Talent is cherished but also challenged. "With so many ways to contribute here, chances are good you'll find a way to do what you love. We need the best of the best to create hardware and software, and we expect nothing less from the people who market, support, and manage our products, our process, and our people."[28]

There is a certain paradox that results from the binding and bonding policies of the hightech giants. It reinforces an investor mentality among employees that may prompt rational choice over company loyalty. They weigh the pros and cons of working for top tier firms, and compare the employee benefits. The psychological contract between employee and their company in Silicon Valley is therefore quite fluid. It makes that employees, especially talented employees with a high market value, are permanently looking for the better job offer. And the competition does not hesitate to do so in a labor market where talent is scarce. For startups, however, it is almost impossible to compete with the big hightech firms in recruiting top talent. They cannot offer the same niceties and perks but primarily depend on the drive of potential employees to excel in a hectic startup environment, and the excitement and satisfaction it gives, to share its value-driven mission and culture, see its market prospects, enjoy working in a small company, that is passionate about the product it develops and to which they have a unique personal contribution. And there is a segment of tech workers that for these reasons deliberately chose to work for a startup as they thrive on the frantic impulses that a new venture radiates. To them, the big hightech companies equal bureaucracy and red tape.

Recruiting highly talented employees is one thing, keeping them is another. The Silicon Valley labor market is a high-velocity market where job hopping is a normal phenomenon.[29] Changing jobs every year or every two years is quite usual. Bruce Fallick, Charles Fleischman, and James Rebitzer analyzed job mobility data and found that job hopping rates in Silicon Valley's computer industry are much higher than in out-of-state computer clusters.[30] Between-company mobility among ICT workers is considerable. This leads, according to standard economic theory, to substantial human capital externalities creating spillover effects. The high frequency transitions of skilled employees between competing hightech firms is characteristic for the Valley's open innovation culture. But this is only part of the mobility story. A major institutional explanation is that California state law prohibits the enforcement by employers of non-compete agreements, i.e. a binding clause for employees not to work for competing firms upon the termination of or resignation from their present job.[31] This rather exceptional legal veto facilitates the free flow of talents between rivalry companies. High inter-company mobility of skilled software programmers, engineers, and computer scientists in Silicon Valley is therefore rooted in both an open innovation and pro-mobility culture but also in a supporting legal system.

According to various stakeholders and labor market experts, a talent shortage in Silicon Valley in the near future is likely. The Public Policy Institute of California (PPIC) forecasts that by 2025 the total shortfall in California will be about one million graduates with at least a bachelor degree.[32] Several factors make this a plausible prediction. Demand for higher skilled tech workers is growing in this post-recession era but the labor market supply is unable to fill these vacancies: the (large) baby boom generation is retiring, the workforce is ageing, ethnic groups with lower educational levels – such as Latinos – constitute a large share of the population, the Bay Area educational system is of exceptional caliber but still does not produce enough highly qualified graduates at the masters level to meet demand, funding for public higher education has decreased significantly and student tuition and fees have increased, and, finally, foreign competition for ICT talent is rising.[33] Immigration helps but is still restricted by quota's. PPIC concludes that "to close the gap, the state should set new statewide goals for higher education that are consistent with the demands of the 21st century. New investments in higher education will be necessary to meet those goals."[34]

Extra policy efforts are needed to minimize the predicted misbalance between labor market supply and demand in the ICT sector. The Valley's business elite, as found in a recent survey study, "overwhelmingly voiced the need for more qualified scientists and engineers to fuel the engines of innovation in Silicon Valley. The demand for workers with advanced degrees in these fields far outpaces the current output, and much of the discussion centers on an early and inclusive commitment to science, technology, engineering, and math (STEM)."[35]

Despite all these challenges Silicon Valley entrepreneurs, according to research, believe that one of the strongest points of the Valley ecosystem is its access to high-level talent. "There is simply no other place in the world with such a concentration of engineers, scientists, entrepreneurs, and other highly skilled professionals."[36]

The extreme importance of talent for existing and new hightech companies is not without its downside. Labor costs in Silicon Valley are very high. Salaries for senior software engineers, apart from stock options and other equity and bonuses, as shown in a study by Riviera and Partners, are roughly averaging around $150,000; for juniors this average is roughly $100,000.[37] Actual salaries depend on company stage and the engineers' role in the firm. The 2014 CEO Business Climate Survey, conducted by the Silicon Valley Leadership Group (SVLG) survey, ranks the cost of employee recruitment and retention as the number two business challenge in the region (employee housing costs is number one).[38] The top strength of doing business in Silicon Valley according to the participating CEO's is access to skilled labor and next the entrepreneurial mindset in the area.

Talent, in summary, is a self-evident dimension of our 'Silicon Valley Innovation & Startup Model'. The rich talent pool is a major competitive advantage of the Valley. But as our findings indicate: the talent pool needs serious maintenance in order for the area's existing and new ventures to prosper in the future.

By way of example: Stanford University as talent pool

As we saw in chapter two and will further elaborate in chapter eight, Stanford University was and is a main supplier of talent to Silicon Valley's hightech companies and startups. This section will present some data on how Stanford's graduates pursue their career as either entrepreneurs or employees. But particularly on their role as startup founders. Findings are based on the Stanford Innovation Survey (2011) by Charles Eesley and William Miller among almost 28,000 Stanford University alumni and over 2,100 faculty and research staff.[39] The empirical data collected in this large-scale and encompassing survey provide a unique opportunity to picture the career paths of Stanford's talents and their role in the Valley's startup economy. As we will further outline in chapter eight, almost 40,000 companies can trace their roots to Stanford University. It is a clear indicator of the substantial role of Stanford in educating entrepreneurs and in supporting the university's paradigm to take technological innovations and inventions to the marketplace. And it is a clear indicator of the role of talent in a knowledge economy. The findings of the Stanford Innovation Study show that almost one-third of all participating Stanford alumni and one-quarter of Stanford faculty had founded a company. Over 1,000 startups were founded by students while still at Stanford or within a year of their graduation. Over the years, Stanford entrepreneurs start their new ventures sooner and at earlier ages. During each decade since the 1950s more and more of Stanford's alumni pursue a career as entrepreneur. The number of female entrepreneurs rose from 5% in the 1950s to almost 30% in the first decade of the 21st century. Results show furthermore that the number of Stanford serial entrepreneurs is increasing over the decades, illustrating as the researchers convincingly argue, that entrepreneurship has become an effective "career path like any other".[40] Becoming an entrepreneur is as normal as becoming an employee among Stanford alumni.

More than half of Stanford's graduates who became entrepreneurs in the past decade acknowledges that the university's entrepreneurial environment and mindset were a prime reason for studying at their alma mater. Did Stanford graduates find companies that excel in innovation? Were they able to capitalize their talents? Eesley and Miller calculate that 25% of Stanford-affiliated firms are majorly innovative, another 25% are moderately innovative, and 50% of the companies are minorly innovative. The majorly and moderately innovative Stanford firms account for almost 70% of the combined revenues and almost 60% of total employment.[41] There are some clear shifts in the type of Stanford startups over the last six decades. The 1950s had its focus on electronics, communications, and publishing. The 1990s saw booming software and internet-based companies, and the 2000s inspired many Stanford alumni to start a business in energy and clean-tech.

Stanford entrepreneurial talents have invested substantially in Silicon Valley and the Bay Area. The study points out that since 1990 over one-third of Stanford alumni remained within 60 miles of the university after their graduation, and slightly over 20% within 20 miles. 36% of their companies are located within 60 miles of Stanford, and 23% within 20 miles. These data demonstrate the magnetic role of Silicon Valley in employing its home-educated talents and the eagerness of Stanford's talents to work in the Valley's hightech industry. In this sense, proximity reflects the internal strength and macro-stability of our 'Silicon Valley Innovation & Startup Model'. The dense and close spatial and social networks between Stanford University and its alumni workforce of entrepreneurs and employees are part of the way Silicon Valley succeeds in matching demand for and supply of highly skilled talent. As Eesley and Miller conclude: "Stanford's approach is to encourage proximity and the back-and-forth exchange that occurs between the campus community and fledging and established businesses."[42] The Valley, in short, is quite effective in retaining the high quality Stanford-trained workforce. And, vice versa, Stanford University is quite successful in guiding its talent pool to founding startups in the area and to the regional labor market.

Having said all of the above, one could easily think that startup founders are young, "a 20-something man who spent his childhood playing on computers in his basement and who later dropped out of college to become a billionaire entrepreneur".[43] Toby Stuart and Weiyi Ng from Berkeley University's Haas School of Business found the average age of a startup founder is 38, with 16 years of experience. He (mostly, only 12% is a she) has a Master's degree and 38% is over 40. Stuart and Ng further found out that the likelihood to become an entrepreneur increases when someone has worked for a venture-backed company in the past.[44] In our sample of Dutch entrepreneurs we found people who worked e.g. for Apple (Faruk Ateş, Ronald Mannak) or Sun Microsystems (Arthur van Hoff).

Ian Sobieski (Band of Angels) understands where this idea of 'young people doing the startups' comes from: "The problem with the media is that they love a simple story and it loves the story of people doing things on the web. So I think they get a disproportionate share of the media attention, because the design automation company or the semiconductor company is not very interesting. We had a company last month that sloshes the fluid that comes out of a semiconductor machinery that improves yield by 3 percent. And no one is going to write a Tech Crunch article about that or put them on a cover." (...) "It just makes better media. But I don't think it is representing the full market." During our visit to the Band of Angels (see the next chapter) we also encountered some people who were definitely belonging to the "older" 38%.

Entrepreneurs on team & talent

Team composition and talent hiring are among the top concerns of our sample of Silicon Valley startup entrepreneurs. Having the right human capital defines the difference between success and failure of a new venture. All of our startup founders struggled with this issue of finding the right people, both in management and product development. They all experienced the severe competition in Silicon Valley for recruiting hightech talents who not only know how to program but also bring the new product or service up to market needs and requirements. And they all experienced the absolute necessity of having a strong team of co-founders or executives that are able to lead the startup to the next phase. In this section, we will outline the main views of our startup initiators on effective team creation and on talent binding and bonding. Two human resource conditions that are absolutely essential for new businesses to grow and flourish. After all, startups are people's businesses.

Great teams will win

What are the qualities startup founders are looking for in building their management team? How important are complementary competences? Arthur van Hoff, founder and CTO of Jaunt, has a strong opinion on this topic: "Personally, I look for people I want to work with. You need people that can stand chaos, because a startup is extremely chaotic especially early on. Team composition is very hard to hire for, I'd rather hire people that are flexible and willing to do any task." Ruben Daniëls also points at the typical starting phase of new ventures: "I think in the early stage of the company you only want to have a product team most of the time. Especially if you want to sell off the beta version than you want to have a team purely focused on finding out what the new product can do, what its market is, etc." (Ruben Daniëls, Cloud9 IDE). Dirk de Kok (Mobtest) is a team player too. "I need to have a team around me. You need co-founders in your team to have management capability with respect to all the facets of running the company and you need discussions on the direction of the new venture. Co-founders who take the same risk as you, invest a lot of time, effort, and money and have that completely different mindset."

A balanced skills portfolio is underlined by several respondents. Valentin Smirnoff in looking at his team: "Our specific skills are very different from each other, very complementary. My co-founder is a developer, I am more of a designer. I like to create graphics, he is very technical. But we are both passionate about what we do and the way we see the world is very similar." (Valentin Smirnoff, Wells Fargo). Rip Pruisken, co-founder and CEO of Rip van Wafels) is a believer too in the necessity of complementary competences of startup teams. "Absolutely. As co-founders, Marco and my skills are very complementary. I focus on sales, motivation and investor relations and my co-founder focuses on operations, finance, and logistics. Those are the core things that we really need to execute on and we both add more value than the other. We both decide on the overall company strategy and vision together. We have very much of a meritocratic culture at our company. We leave our egos aside and are devoted to championing and implementing the best ideas and strategy possible to achieve our company goals." (Rip Pruisken, Rip van Wafels). Neal Blaak also underlines the importance of complementary skills sets for startup founders. "My co-founder is very much into the technology of ZappoTV and operationally involved with people. I am more of an ideation visionary guy, to me it is the experience, and it's the app: you turn it on, and cool content comes to you (…). We are great sparring partners, we listen to each other. I need him and he needs me." Knowing your limitations as a startup founder is imperative. As David Mayer (RENDLE) reveals: "From day one you have to understand what you can do yourself and where your limitations are. You need to find people around you who are strong where you are limited (…). Every person we work with is senior with a strong track record. They are willing to put in capital and equity, forgoing higher salaries." Vincent van de Poll also emphasizes the role of supplementary skills. "My co-founder is a very theoretical guy and wrote a very extensive business plan on 3D printing. The only thing that was missing was a business partner on the sales and financial side and also an actual product. My role in the company is to make quite complicated things into very simple solutions." (Vincent van de Poll, GROM). Joint decisions are vital in a young startup team. Vincent and his co-founder have a clear agreement. "All the decisions are made together. Only when we really wouldn't be able to agree we have written down who decides on what, although this has never happened in three years. For instance, if we would come in a situation that we disagree on production, my partner will decide. If it is sales, I will decide. We don't compromise on anything, and that is, I think, our strength. We are both very emotional guys, but we always base our decisions on arguments and facts." Such a role division between a technical and a commercial team member, can often be observed in startup teams. "There usually is a combination of the more technical guy and the more commercial guy. But they need to understand both sides, particularly the CEO. This might change when formal money comes in. When the VCs get there, the structure might change and sometimes they bring in a CEO who has already done a couple of exits, so he knows how to organize things." (Harm TenHoff, BayLink). But some startup entrepreneurs believe that in the hightech startup business, technical team members should have the lead. As Ronald Mannak concludes: "When you look at the most successful companies in Silicon Valley, I mean Oracle, Apple or Google, they were all founded by teams of technical people and not by sales people. Even Steve Jobs was a nerd in business terms." Arthur van Hoff agrees and sees a big difference with startup teams in the Netherlands. "There they usually are business people, here they are engineers. Steve Jobs, Steve Wozniak, Bill Gates, Larry Page, Sergey Brin, they are all engineers. And they are all general engineers. But they are very creative people (...). We need creative people, people that can make something."

Ejenta is a startup founded by Maarten Sierhuis and his partner Rachna Dhamija. Being a team in a double sense may generate extra complexities. But Maarten feels that Ejenta is in the right flow, they "really balance each other out. I am the technical person and Rachna is the business person. We are complementary in a very nice way, it almost becomes effortless." (Maarten Sierhuis, Ejenta). Team chemistry is what good startup teams distinguishes from weak teams. "When I met my co-founder the first time, we were making very geeky jokes about certain database technologies. We meshed well together, we got along. We could really do a holistic approach, combining back-end programming, product design, and usability. It is a great collaboration." (Faruk Ateş, Presentate). Faruk does not hide a weaker point of his team: "We both lack the sales perspective, which is sort of a recurring shortcoming which causes some friction. A weaker side of the team. We are trying to fix that once we launch our alpha. We will have a product and it means we need to go and sell it, get more users and do marketing." Eric-Jan van Leeuwen too experienced the need for a stronger marketing representation in his team. "With me being here in the Valley, the only thing I needed was very clear: to work with a marketing director. Who could work on corporate branding, on launching new products, a tight marketing plan, and marketing actions on the US and Canada level." (Eric-Jan van Leeuwen, Login VSI). A broader team member perspective also counts. As Ronald Mannak says: "Our CEO has traveled a lot, worked in London, and is familiar with European culture. People who have been living abroad have a different view. They see America through different eyes, which makes it easier to work with them." (Ronald Mannak, JumpCam). Ronald, by the way, is thinking of building a new startup. Having a strong team is important to him: "I could start on my own, but it is more fun and better to do it in a small team. I started my companies with friends. You know each other. But you need to keep on learning. You don't use the same team twice, because you kind of burn each other out in startups. It's pretty intense; very, very intense even." Teams of friends may even break up due to these struggling times. As Valentin Smirnoff shares: "I started a company with a friend that did not work out. Things were said and I got very emotional at one point. That was not a very good experience. Maybe the friendship was not based on the right foundation or it was not right to start a company together. There were a lot of things not said and we were not completely honest with each other." Investing in team formation, in team building, is decisive in early startup development. Salar al Khafaji learned his lesson. "Finding the right people is extremely important. In fact, I should have spent more time on team dynamics, building networks, and all that. I think it is ok now, but that is the one thing I could have done better in the first six months." (Salar al Khafaji, Silk). Salar, like Ruben Daniëls, has his engineering team in the Netherlands. He also learned that VCs in Silicon Valley like to have the CEO or the startup team in the area. "Most of them do not like outsourcing. They feel if you outsource, the IP you're building is probably just a commodity." Salar's company Silk is modeled after many successful Israeli businesses that have their executive team in Silicon Valley and their development team in Tel Aviv.

As we concluded earlier in this chapter, team dynamics are critical for startups but so is creating the right organizational culture. Teams have a prime responsibility in working towards a challenging and entrepreneurial culture. Ruben Daniëls has an interesting view on this topic. Sharing and consensus are important values to him in building a startup. "Nobody can have a successful startup by himself. If you got into a startup and you don't see it as your company then you are doing it wrong. You always do this together with other people and so you need to share. You need to learn how to share. Now sharing too much is of course detrimental because you also need to maintain some level of power." Ruben believes that "creating culture is not something you can dictate. You need consensus. Which is quite different from making compromises, it just means that people need to agree or accept." Rip Pruisken and Marco De Leon also put a lot of time in creating the right culture for their business. "Culture is the X factor to give the company a unique personality, it is the set of traits that we all embody at our company. We've defined our culture by a set of values that we live by. Our company values serve as a benchmark to assess new hires and assess the performance of each of our team members including ourselves." Startup teams, finally, are not static but may change over time, particularly when VC money is coming in. Cees Jan Koomen, VC and entrepreneur, reviews the situation as follows. "A startup founder CEO assembles the team, is the wizard himself too, the prime among equals sort of thing. He has to be creative, has to understand what people need, and make them (and himself) do exciting work. Later the team layout may change. A CEO in the next phases of a startup needs different qualities than a CEO in the initial startup stage." When investors become involved in a startup this may modify the team setup and may lead to management replacements. Also students realize the importance of teams. As one of the interviewed students, Waad Jaradat, says: "if I start up my own company, I will definitely go for a team of people to work together".

Team composition and team functioning, thus, are crucial for startups to grow and be successful. Having a team rather than be a solo startup CEO is important in itself. VCs, as we will see in the next chapter, are very hesitant to invest in new ventures that are not run by a management team. They feel that the formula of single leadership is too vulnerable. They ardently support Cees Jan Koomen's basic startup message that "strong teams will win".

Talent is gold

Silicon Valley startups and existing ventures are involved in a never ending competition in attracting hightech talent. Highly skilled employees that are able and genuinely motivated to develop that one killer app or unique world class product that will radically change our digital existence. An innovation that will drastically affect the way we think, live, work, and play. An innovation that will definitely establish the startup's brand name and route to success. But real talent, even in a technological hotspot such as Silicon Valley, is scarce which has a strong impact on labor demand and supply relations. What do our startup entrepreneurs look for in recruiting new employees? What are the main qualities they search for in hiring software programmers and engineers? What do they offer potential employees to work for them? Can they compete with the large hightech companies in the Valley?

The importance of finding the right talent is illustrated by how Arthur van Hoff organized the launching of his startup Jaunt: the first person he hired after appointing an office manager was a recruiter. Hiring is a time-consuming business: "Maybe you talk to 200 people, interview 20 of them, and hire one. That is a huge job for one position. Plus it is very competitive so even if you're making offers, they might not accept. They get offers from other companies too. You can do a lot yourself but I have done too many startups so we have a fulltime recruiter. It is a very expensive solution. He makes a lot of money plus gets paid extra for everybody he hires." For Ruben Daniëls, recruiting is a collective startup activity. "It is a team process. I did the first conversation and a group of us interviewed different candidates.

Everyone has a veto." Getting access to talent also depends on the name and reputation of the startup founders. Maarten Sierhuis of Ejenta is very explicit on this topic: "One benefit we have is that Rachna [his partner and CEO, PE/AM] comes from Berkeley, she has a name; I come from NASA, and I have a name. We do the hiring ourselves. It is not at all that difficult to find people, what is difficult, is to find the right people." Salar al Khafaji, CEO of Silk, has a similar experience but from a different geographic perspective. As we mentioned before, most of his engineering team is based in Amsterdam. A few of his people are stationed in Silk's San Francisco office. "Without being arrogant, I think we are one of the few high-profile startups in the Netherlands. People that we hoped we could hire actually want to come to work for us. We just hired two engineers from Sweden who are amazing. That is one of the advantages of being in the EU."

Hiring employees is a big step for every startup. For new ventures with growth ambitions it is a necessary move but not one without consequences. As Maarten Sierhuis confides: "Rachna always said to me that 'having your own company is fun but wait until you have employees, then the pressure is on'. Especially when you have employees with families, because then failure of your company means that other people will be hurt too. So the pressure is starting. We really need more outside funding to cope with that." To hire or not to hire is a big decision for startups. As Harm TenHoff comments: "Especially the first persons that you hire within a company you're building up are the most critical ones." Valentin Smirnoff clearly remembers. "In the beginning we were really trying to take it slow because we heard a lot of stories about startups going through their money very quickly. We were trying to be more cautious but we needed developers. We got office space at RocketSpace [a well-known incubator in San Francisco, see chapter 10, PE/AM], where many recruiters dropped by. We needed somebody to start very quickly, so we hired our first developer through a recruiter there. We had to pay a stiff fee, they are not cheap. Maybe we were trying too quickly or trying to take a short cut. But that is how we started." Hiring too rapidly is a major problem and difficult challenge for startups. This is how Ruben Daniëls looks back. "A clear mistake that we made was that we hired too quickly and didn't fire. We were already a consultancy firm of fifteen people before we made a pivot. This meant that some people no longer fit because of new job requirements. We did not let people go and just kept on growing. We still kept them around and grew way too big for our runway." The intended size of the company matters in startups' recruitment policy. As Arthur van Hoff states: "In the beginning you can hire your friends but that very quickly becomes an exhausted pool. When you are with ten to fifteen people you start hiring great employees and you still can be very selective. But by the time you have hired one hundred people you have hired one of every kind: the good, the bad, and the ugly. That is just reality and we try to keep up the good track record but it is very difficult." Ronald Mannak is not the kind of entrepreneur who dreams of leading a big company. "It is fun to have your own startup and go through the whole process. I learned a lot from that. But working with a large group doesn't seem very attractive to me. It is not where I get a lot of joy. It is not my goal."

The typical question is what qualities startup entrepreneurs are looking for in hiring new employees. This is especially true in the very early startup phase when there is neither a clear organizational structure nor a professional division of tasks. Pieter Bas Leezenberg knows what he wants: "I look for passionate people with a good track record. Not necessarily in the corporate world because I believe that things that make you successful in a corporate career can be quite different from a startup. How much chaos can you stand, are you willing to sweep the floor, and put paper in the printer?" (Pieter Bas Leezenberg, SkyGeo). Entrepreneurship is another distinguishing quality. "One of the things we actively filter out is that people need to be entrepreneurial. People who we don't feel need to be managed. I don't think you want that in a small team. You get easily impressed with people who worked for the big name hightech companies here. A lot of them are no good fits for small teams because they are used to a lot of management overhead. I look for employees that are flexible and can cope with chaos." (Ruben Daniëls). Rip Pruisken highlights the importance of culture and personality. "You need to find people that fit the culture of your business. We are looking for people who embody our set of company values and have the right complementary skill sets needed to grow our business. We also look for bold out-of-the-box thinkers and doers that see their job not only as a source of income but also an opportunity to be a part of something game changing. We believe in human potential and value immense effort, the ability to grow, push and redefine one's limitations over experience. We have a long term viewpoint on hiring as we'd rather hire someone to stay and grow at our company for the years to come rather to fulfill only the short term needs of the business. To ensure this we ask our new hires whether they'd be willing to be with us for at least 2 years."

Freelancing and flexibility are common work arrangements. Marieke van der Poel did it her way: "I have a very interesting setup. I only have two people left who work for me fulltime and the rest are all people that are in the field and we hire them as freelancers. That can be up to twenty people on a specific project that we manage." Freelancing and flexibility are also important in Jan Grotenbreg's line of work. "What is nice about here, is that you can find people who can work part-time. There are people who don't have more time available and there are young people who want some extra hours."

The Silicon Valley labor market is not all that bright and healthy as our entrepreneurs convincingly point out. Two reasons dominate: low retention rates and high salaries. Salar al Khafaji confirms that "loyalty is a problem in the Bay Area. Even people in successful companies keep switching jobs every two years. I know startup founders here that have twenty employees and assume that they need to hire four people extra in order to maintain their team size. That is how bad it is right now. A lot of engineers [in the Bay Area] think like investors, they want a portfolio of options. So they keep changing jobs hoping to build a portfolio of potentially successful companies through their stock options." Eric-Jan van Leeuwen has similar experiences. "There are very interesting candidates but it is hard to find the right one at the right price. I spoke to nearly 30 marketing candidates with very interesting and long résumés. But the problem is the culture here; people will come and people will go very easily. And if you don't have a very tight option plan in place, then especially here in the Valley, people are not very enthusiastic to work for you."

The biggest personnel issue that keeps startup founders awake at night, however, is the high salaries in Silicon Valley, way beyond what is common in Europe. "It kills your dreams" says David Mayer. "The average kid with a computer science degree is 22 and has a starting salary of six figures. Then you have about 25% employer costs on top of that. And the problem with junior engineers is that they don't have any experience so they need to work closely with your senior engineers. It takes time to find the right people. The shortage for software engineers is growing every year, even though more engineers are coming to the Bay Area." To which Dirk de Kok of Mobtest adds: "There is so much competition here, big companies may easily pay $150,000-200,000. Why would somebody risk working for a startup that maybe has a one percent chance of succeeding?" Arthur van Hoff recognizes the calculating mentality of potential employees. "The first question they ask in an interview is what the cap table is, what the percentage is, how many shares you are giving, and what the investment schedule is." Ruben Daniëls also points at the high salaries. "It is very difficult to get experienced people here, they are making $200,000 or $300,000 a year. They've got their house, they are pampered by their companies, and they have stuff taken care of. Working for a startup means you have to do everything yourself, all sorts of things that are not even in your job description, but it gives you back a lot of excitement. You definitely have to go out of your comfort zone, you are learning all the time as you are growing as a person." Eric-Jan van Leeuwen put a lot of time in recruiting for his new venture. "Finding the proper personnel is actually the issue, not the number of potential candidates. If you think you got the right one, then you end up negotiating a contract and then they basically want to earn even twice the money I make here as the one who is responsible for the company. That's quite hard." The other side of high salaries for hightech employees are simple dismissal procedures. As Neal Blaak explains: "In the US it is much easier than in Europe to fire people. It's two weeks or if you're lucky you have a month notice, and if you're really lucky you get paid a few months. You can hire and fire people at will."

Team and talent, in short, define the success likelihood of startups. Particularly in a highly competitive and meritocratic environment as Silicon Valley. But finding the right team members and the right employees is the issue. In a culture that prompts entrepreneurship employees also internalize an entrepreneurial mindset. It determines how they look at the world and how they look at the job market. In a situation of relative scarcity of talent this means that employees can force up their demands. And that is exactly what they do. It has become part of the Silicon Valley culture. Many big hightech companies outcompete one another in comforting their employees. Startups face the problem of how to address this severe contest. They can't compete with Apple or Google for employees. Their best bet seems to be a combination of fostering pioneering innovation, cherishing intrinsic work values, the chaotic charm of startup life, and financial participation. A combination that historically has been a core element of the 'Silicon Valley Innovation & Startup Model'.

And what about the talents themselves? The San Jose State University students that participated in our study really experience that they are in great demand. "I was just in the country, and got approached while at Target and was offered a job." (Philipp Schubert, student from Germany). "There are lots of job opportunities here." (Waad Jaradat, student from Palestine). "To me the high ambitions here in the Valley are very positive and inspiring." (Alexandre Gallardo). But the bar is high too. As Dutch student Quirijn Kleppe concludes: "You should dream big enough." To which Philipp quickly adds: "but you don't have to be afraid to fail." A nice summary of the Valley's self-understanding.

6. Funding

Angel investors & venture capitalists

Sand Hill Road in Menlo Park is the Wall Street of Silicon Valley, home to many well-known venture capital firms. Several of which have a legendary status as they funded some of the most successful hightech companies in the Valley. Companies which all began as innovative startups eagerly looking for money to grow their business, and which are now global industries with a global brand name and reputation. Sequoia Capital, founded in 1972 and one of the most influential VC firms in the Valley, funded Apple, Atari, Cisco, Oracle, Google, Yahoo, YouTube, LinkedIn, PayPal, WhatsApp, Airbnb, Instagram, to mention just a few of the bigger names. Sequoia's funds raised amount to $3.1 billion, the firm did 47 IPOs and 99 acquisitions.[1] Its recent success, WhatsApp, was sold to Facebook in 2014 for $19 billion which made it the then largest acquisition of a venture-backed company in history.[2] TechCrunch calculated that if Sequoia owned 20 percent of WhatsApp it saw a return of about $3 billion (50 times) on its $60 million investment in the company.[3] Kleiner, Perkins, Caufield & Byers, another major VC with $2.8 billion of funds raised, 33 IPOs and 66 acquisitions.[4] It was involved in funding AOL, Citrix, Compaq, Lotus, Intuit, Symantec, Genentech, Zynga, Amazon, and Twitter, to name just a few.[5] Other top Silicon Valley VC funds include Andreessen & Horowitz, Benchmark Ventures, Khosla Ventures, New Enterprise Associates, Accel, and Greylock. The four main US institutional investors in VC funds are public pension funds, private pension funds, university endowments, and foundations.[6] Commercial banks do not play a pivotal role in funding startups. The reason according to former banker John Dean is, that "the prevailing culture of banks, particularly large ones, is risk-aversive; it isn't quite suited to the freewheeling, risk-embracing ethos of Silicon Valley".[7] Banks, in the words of Stanford economist Thomas Hellmann, go for a financial portfolio that diversifies controllable risks. "By contrast, a venture capital firm will hold a very high-risk but high-return portfolio."[8] The investment logic of banks and VC's differ markedly.

Venture capital is big in Silicon Valley, both literally and figuratively. It is an integral and indispensable part of our 'Silicon Valley Innovation & Startup Model'. As Hellmann states: "the financing of startups by venture capitalists is a central ingredient in the economic success of Silicon Valley."[9] No invention without capital. Or in the more imaginative language of Silicon Valley expert Tapan Munroe: "ideas are the soul of innovation. Money is the life blood."[10] Some figures may illustrate the significance of venture capital for the growth of hightech startups in Silicon Valley, a position that is unique both inside and outside the United States. Most recent figures show that 51% of all venture capital dollars in the USA are invested in Silicon Valley companies.[11] No other region in the world captures such a high share of domestic and foreign VC investment or has such a high concentration of venture capitalists. Since 2009, VC firms invested $31.5 billion in Silicon Valley ventures.[12] Roughly equal to Bolivia's annual GDP. In 2014, total US equity investments into venture-backed companies amounted to $48.2 billion, of which $19.8 billion was invested in software companies, and $8.6 billion in life sciences (biotechnology plus medical devices).[13] Silicon Valley, according to PriceWaterhouseCooper, attracted as much as 48% ($24.3 billion) in 2014 of total US venture capital dollars, more than all other US regions combined. The 2014 VC results were highly affected by a few quite large investment deals: Uber ($2.4 billion), Cloudera ($900 million), AirBnB ($475 million), Palantir ($444 million), and Dropbox ($350 million).[14] Corporate Venture Capital (CVC) is quickly becoming a prominent funding source, both nationwide in the US and in Silicon Valley. CVC US investments amounted to $5.4 billion in 2014, an 11% share of total VC investments. Leading Silicon Valley companies such as Google, Apple, PayPal, Cisco, Intel have their own CVC funds to invest in cutting-edge new ventures. Google Ventures capital commitment is $300 million annually and in 2014 it launched a $100 million fund to invest in European startups.[15] Corporate venture funds keep hightech companies in touch with the major technology market trends and may – so it is not always a first priority – allow them to do strategic startup acquisitions, either in terms of access to its technology or to their talent ("acqui-hire").[16]

What about the types of startups VCs are interested in? Software represents 55% of total VC investment in the Valley; biotechnology ranks second with 11%.[17] Clean technology is important too, reaching an all-time high in 2014 of almost $3.3 billion. The combined cleantech VC investments of Silicon Valley and San Francisco are good for 53% of total US and 80% of California's investments in this sector.[18] About 40% of the Valley's VC cleantech investments is into energy efficiency, 15% in solar energy. Biofuels & biochemicals, fuel cells & hydrogen, smart grid, and transportation acquired increased VC investments between 2012 and 2013.[19] These cleantech venture capital developments clearly reflect the Valley's startup preoccupation with environmental concerns. These concerns, apparently, do not only dominate the public agenda and the private choices of many citizens in Silicon Valley, but also the innovation priorities of its startup community. VCs and startups seem to share a vision that there is a profitable market for environmental innovations. A good example is Kleiner, Perkins, Caufield & Byers (KPCB) which in 2008 launched its $500 million Green Growth Fund aiming to help accelerate mass market adoption of climate change solutions. It separately introduced a $700 million fund that invests in greentech, information technology, and life sciences. The first fund supports companies that have already entered its growth phase; the second fund helps early stage entrepreneurs. "We urgently need to advance our greentech industry at a speed and scale commensurate with the challenges we face," said KPCB Partner John Doerr. "We believe green technologies are both the key to solving our energy crisis and a tremendous business opportunity."[20] Substantial funds are required as biotechnology and cleantech startups are capital intensive, more difficult to scale, and take longer to realize returns on investment.

VC money is big in Silicon Valley, but that does not mean that startups have a smooth job in raising sufficient and sustainable funding. There are thousands of startups competing for VC money. Demand overshadows supply. In fact, most startups do not succeed in getting adequate funding, and most startups fail. Only the very best will survive. Having a startup in Silicon Valley is expensive. Their financial runway is usually short as the cash burn rate is high. VCs, moreover, are less interested in funding the initial stages of startups. They go for maximum return on their investment which is more feasible when startups mature and proved their market potential. VCs like to see a "hockey stick" growth curve: the revenue curve takes an initial linear (slow) growth curve but then suddenly turns into a much faster continuous exponential growth rate. But this will only be possible for the few startups that are able to quickly scale up to large markets. And that is why VC funds are always looking for the Next Big Thing. Scaling is the buzz word: that is how VCs can realize substantial returns on their investments. One big winner, as they say, can cover a lot of losers.

Investment in new ventures range from friends & family, to seed stage, early stage, expansion stage, and later stages. In VC terminology: Series Seed, Series A, Series B, Series C, Series D+). Most startups begin with raising money for their new venture among their friends and family, people they trust and who trust them. Their friends and relatives know how much effort, creativity, perseverance, and belief the founders have put into their startup. As friends and family they are in the right position to judge the personal ability of the founder to push their startup (usually not more than an idea or product concept) to the next stage. But the money raised will normally be limited and good for covering the costs of the very initial phase of the startup. VC authority and author Marc Philips, partner in Arafura Ventures, a Palo Alto venture capital fund, provides an experience-based overview of the capital ranges in the various startup investment series.[21] Seed capital, Philips writes, roughly ranges between $250,000 and $2,000,000 and should provide the financial runway for about one year. This is the stage angel investors are interested in; the next investment stages are dominated by VC funds. Series A investments, again according to Philips, are generally between $7 million to $15 million for advancing the business model and finding the true product/market fit. Identifying and picking winners early is a major challenge for VC funds. Fast growing and highly profitable "unicorns" (companies reaching a billion-dollar valuation) are typically detected by VCs in later funding stages that require massive financing.[22] They are, apparently, not very good in predicting innovation success in early stages.[23] Series B ranges from $7 million to tens of millions and is about scaling the business model and the user base. All estimates depend, of course, on the capital intensity and the valuation of the startup. Series C, D, and E are later-stage investment rounds of venture capital that often enter the picture before an exit, either via a trade sale or an IPO. With each successful round of funding, the startup lengthens its financial runway. At the same time, the VC fund is after maximizing its return on investment. Fast growth is essential in these later stages. "It's all about scale for VCs, and by that I mean how fast and steep the hockey stick of growth can be."[24] A VC investor will usually require a startup share of not more than 20-25% in the first funding round in order to ensure that its founders have a financial stimulus to make their new company successful and to make it attractive for other investors to step in. This balances the interests of founders and investors. But with more funding rounds, the balance will change. Philips points to the greater say that VCs demand in later investment stages. The stakes are simply higher, and so are the investments risks. "You're swimming with sharks now."[25] The greater VC control often implies a change of the startup's management team. From being the founder to the CEO of a startup is a natural transition, but remaining the CEO of a highly venture-funded more mature company is a different ballgame. It requires different entrepreneurial qualities, facing more complex market and organizational challenges, handling more difficult commercial responsibilities, and keeping their VCs happy at the monthly boardroom meetings. VCs will not hesitate to "kill" a startup if they feel the business model is not guaranteeing their return on investment.

Angel investors, as mentioned, are particularly active in the first startup seed rounds. Angels, typically, are somewhat older and largely male high-net worth investors with considerable entrepreneurial and business experience.[26] They offer a combination of cash, know-how, time, mentorship, and personal networks that are specifically relevant to startup founders and beginning entrepreneurs. In this sense they are "guardian angels" seeking financial return but who also get personal gratification from helping startups, from "giving back." It gives energy, keeps them connected, and the excitement of seeing startups grow. A new category of angels also emerged: younger cashed-out entrepreneurs who go for investing in socially valuable transformational technologies such as biotechnology, cleantech, and medical innovations.

Nationwide the US median angel round sizes remained rather stable over the last three years (2011-2013): approximately $600,000 annually. California is good for almost 20% of the national angel investments and deals.[27] The Center of Venture Research of the University of New Hampshire estimates total US angel investment at $24.8 billion in 2013, totaling almost 300,000 angels.[28] Software accounts for almost a quarter of the investments, media for 16%, healthcare for 14%, and biotechnology for 11%. Zooming in at Silicon Valley the data show that in 2012, Seed and Series A – where angels have a prime investment role – funding combined accounts for 21% of the funding share; D+ Series takes 21%.[29] Additional data indicate that the angel investment portfolio in the Valley has increased its Series A+ funding, from $460 million in 2011 to $726 million in 2012, and to slightly over $1 billion in the first three quarters of 2013.[30]

How successful are VCs actually in bringing startups to the next phase and in realizing a high return on their investments? That is a complicated issue, if only because one faces a typical observation bias: only prosperous startups will survive and failing new ventures simply disappear. Consequently, VC positive investment stories are mostly based on a selective sample of flourishing startups, stories that are often magnified by high publicity examples of huge IPO returns (WhatsApp, PayPal, Facebook, LinkedIn, Google). As *Forbes* contributor Bruce Booth concludes: "Much of the public dialogue about venture capital returns is based more on myth than fact (…). A big part of the problem is that anecdotal stories about great returns drive much of the thinking."[31] VC investments, as we stated, are risky and returns on investment are uncertain. Venture investors make their money from occasional big winners.

We already mentioned that VCs have problems in picking winners in early funding stages. Losing money on startup investments is a daily VC reality. And losses there are. But they are part of a bigger picture.[32] A detailed study by Adams Street Partners, a global private equity firm, analyzing 5600 exits covering the 1979-2011 period, demonstrated that the best VC deals create less relative value than they did in the past due to a lower frequency of outsized winners.[33] Furthermore, it is found that winners do not take up more VC capital than the average deal. This again illustrates that VCs have difficulties in picking winners.[34] The data also reveal that VCs are not doing a better job in the last ten years in avoiding losers. The "fail fast" mantra seems a pretty constant phenomenon. As Josh Lerner, Harvard professor of Investment Banking, concludes: "Despite all the care and expertise of venture capitalists, disappointment is the rule rather than the exception (...). There is usually no clear-cut evidence that an investment will yield attractive returns."[35] It is tempting, according to Kenney and Von Burg, to see Silicon Valley's economic successes as the result "of the brilliance or foresight of venture capitalists (...). The reality is more capricious. Venture capitalists have lost huge sums on perfectly reasonable investments in technologies such as pen-based computing, superminicomputers, and artificial intelligence. But the system is self-correcting. After a number of failures, the venture capitalists see no return, the firms fail, and that technological space no longer receives funding."[36]

Pitching for money

The Band of Angels is the oldest and one of the best-known angel investor groups in Silicon Valley, and the first angel group in the US, founded in 1994.[37] Their focus is on early stage seed funding of new ventures. We were invited to attend one of their pitching rounds for startup entrepreneurs. An invitation we gladly accepted and which gave us some firsthand insights in how this funding process works. The Band is a group of seasoned former and current entrepreneurs investing their (private) money and time in promising hightech startups. Its accumulated personal startup experience is impressive. Most of them are serial entrepreneurs. Not only their money, but also their know-how and networks are great assets. The Band of Angels has seeded over 277 startups, including 55 profitable merger and acquisition (M&A) exits and 10 Nasdaq IPOs. Its investments total over $230 million.[38] Band members themselves have been founders of highly successful companies such as Symantec, Logitech, and National Semiconductor, and have been senior executives at the likes of Sun Microsystems, Hewlett Packard, and Intuit. The membership procedure is stringent: to become a qualified investor you must be worth at least $5 million, a minimum standard; and potential members have to be nominated by other members. Furthermore, angels have to have made their own (not inherited) money with a high technology activity. As Ian Sobieski, the Band's managing director and gifted investor himself, tells us: "Band members that made their money in doing companies in a similar life cycle as the companies that pitch for funding. All of the companies that get funded get a Band member to help them, a mentor so to speak. That makes us really apart from any other sources of angel capital. We have an extremely good group of people, self-motivated and sophisticated. (...). And incidentally, most companies that receive money from the Band tell us it is the mentor's advice more than the money that they valued most."

In the seeding round that we attended, six startups pitched for funding. A truly remarkable experience. Shark Tank, but then in real life. The participating startups made it through the pre-selection phase and all the paperwork that goes with it. This is the first meeting that they are face-to-face with their potential investors. The intention is clear: they need funding to help their startup to the next stage, and the fourteen angel investors present are looking for a good deal. The tension is there, but the pitchers need to act cool and make a dedicated and self-confident impression. What do angels look like? As Europeans we came to the meeting in our Sunday suit, only to find out that angels can wear shorts, faded T-shirts, and barefoot sandals. No suits, no ties. Interestingly, the exception was the only female angel investor present who was dressed most elegantly. But the overall rule is a highly informal dress code and corresponding setting. And mind you: we are talking about investors of substance. But it reflects the casual Silicon Valley culture and lifestyle.

As soon as the two pitchers of the first startups entered, the atmosphere immediately changed from easygoing to businesslike. No round of introductions, no "hello, my name is..." But: "here is a chair, sit down, and tell us your story. And briefly please." In this Eldorado of technology, pitchers (at least in this stage) are demanded to present their young company without digital aids. No slick PowerPoint but an old-fashioned oral explanation of the startup's core business, its market, and how the new venture is going to make money. Five minutes max, followed by twenty minutes of sharp and to-the-point angels' questions focused on the core idea, the business model, the startup team. Sure, there was laughter and jokes being made, but business dominates. It is all about investing, all about hard dollars, and about many dollars. The angels had startup summaries in front of them. First criterion was: "what is the pain & what is the solution?" In other words, what is the problem that the startup is trying to solve? Next five topics: technology, competition, defensibility, business model, and go-to-market strategy. Each topic is explained in a few sentences. To be followed by milestones, some financial data, and some information on the startup founders. All on one A-4 sheet. No extensive business plans. Simple but efficient. And what about the startup pitchers themselves, were they all young people? Well maybe one or two, but most pitchers were over thirty. And no suits by the way.

What is the next step in the funding process? The six startups that pitched were chosen from the 50 applications that the Band of Angels typically receives per month. Of the six pitching teams only three will be invited for the next interview at a private dinner meeting. In this meeting the startup entrepreneurs will present (now by using a PowerPoint!) their business in more detail, followed by another round of Q & A's. As Ian Sobieski states: "everything before that is just a way of picking the most incredible companies. It is high risk making decisions in the face of uncertainty." After the dinner, investors interested will meet for several hours with the startup of their choice to dig deeper and to decide whether they want make an actual investment. All in all, a highly competitive procedure: getting funding is serious business. But the competitive nature also holds for the angel firms themselves. There are over 300 angel funds like the Band in the US nowadays, all looking for up-and-coming startups that are worth investing in. Ian Sobieski is well aware of the competition. "It is easier than ever to raise money as a startup. Through Angellist or Kickstarter and other crowdsourcing platforms, through individual angels that operate on their own, through angels groups or small venture funds. A startup entrepreneur can relatively easily raise $100,000 dollars."

Pitching is an essential phase in receiving VC or angel funding. A good pitch can make you, a bad pitch can break you. Dutch entrepreneur and VC Cees Jan Koomen, active both in Silicon Valley and in the Netherlands, and member of the Band of Angels, emphasizes it is not only the business plan that makes a good startup pitch. If only because the first plan is never successful. "It is also how they present themselves. Do they talk startup company language, do they talk about the people they hire, their team, do they talk about the market, the product and the product roadmap?"

Elizabeth Yin, startup investor at 500 Startups, explains that they basically look for teams comprised of two types of people in the team: "we're looking for teams with a hacker and a hustler", i.e. the person(s) responsible for product development and the person(s) responsible for sales. 500 Startups wants to see these two roles filled before making an investment. Bill Reichert, managing director at Garage Technology Ventures, explains that 90% of applications from startups can be filtered out relatively easily. Investors scan for what Bill calls "knock-out factors", specific elements that tell you that this is not the startup to invest in. Examples are, for instance, non-technological startups such as nail salons or restaurants. Perfectly reasonable businesses, but not appropriate for venture capital investment because they cannot achieve the scale and value that a venture capital investor needs. Other knock-out factors may be a delusional growth scenario – projecting a billion dollars in revenues in five years. On the other side, there may also be a lack of ambition – projecting $4 million in revenues in five years. Both cases, Bill says, "raise a red flag". If a startup belongs to the remaining 10%, Garage looks for a compelling value proposition, a sustainable competitive advantage, a great team, some traction and unique, defensible technology. Garage does not only wait for the applicants to come to them. It would be unwise, Bill claims, to think as some venture capital firms do "if they are not able to find me, they are not worth my money". "You have to reach out; you have to be open", Bill continues, and due to that strategy they have many companies from overseas that apply.

Vish Mishra, venture director at Clearstone, gives the following criteria. First of all, there should be a "big hairy problem", and a startup should explain how they know this is such a problem. Secondly, who is already working on that problem? "Since it is big and hairy, you will probably not be the only one to have noticed", Vish remarks. Third, how are you going to solve this problem, what is your approach? Fourth, what does it take you get there, what kind of help do you need, what do you bring in yourselves? And last but not least, what is your revenue model? Vish gives a very useful insight that is relevant for founders who are sometimes reluctant to have an investor in their company: "a VC wants you to succeed, even more than you want to succeed yourself".

What are the essential skills and abilities that make that pitchers reach the next round of the Band's funding procedure? Ian Sobieski who chaired numerous pitches should be the right person to know. But he admits there are no clear rules, there is a lot of serendipity and plain luck involved in creating a successful startup. Ian's intuition is his most important decision criterion. "For me, I think most entrepreneurs fail at being a little too explorative and searching rather than being more open on what they know and what they don't know. So the next three months you can plan with a great deal of certainty, but six months after that a lot less, and a year out, who knows? I am persuaded by someone who has the maturity to conceive of what is in their controlling grasp and what is not, and who has a more mature engagement with the potential of the company. For me that activates all that, but I don't think entrepreneurs should ever change who they are in order to raise money from folks or say the right things. The worst marriage is when you have people who are persuaded to invest and then simply discover that it is not a good match." (...). So put the PowerPoint presentation away, it is useless, just speak from the heart. I think the best pitch is one where you peak interest and cultivate it and get it to fire more and more until you get it consummated." Pitching, then, is about the right gut feeling that the starting entrepreneur will do anything to make his startup thriving, about authenticity, about transparency, and about a relationship being developed between entrepreneur and funder. Solid intuition, evidently, is of overriding importance to investors in judging the quality of a pitch and to decide on next funding steps. This view is shared by the VC's we interviewed. Vish Mishra, Venture Director at Clearstone, explicitly states: "I want transparency of founders. Tell what you know, but also what you don't know. Don't shoot for perfection [...] Just tell me your story." Vish adds: "Don't do Chinese math," referring to exports to China, where with only 0.01% market penetration, you will still have substantial business. About selecting the startups to invest in, Vish wholeheartedly admits: "It's emotion. You like the guy and then you try to rationalize your investment."

Bill Reichert, managing director at Garage Ventures Technology, first explains all the criteria that he uses to select a good startup. But then, he wittily adds, "you violate these rules, because you fall in love with a startup". He even makes it more explicit by downplaying rational thinking when you are in love: "you throw reason out of the window". It is logical that you must like the founders: "it's hard to hate the team, but love the concept". Also Marco ten Vaanholt, managing partner at BootUp Ventures, says that next to all hard criteria, "the base of each venture is trust", referring to less tangible aspects of business.

The investors are not unique in this respect. The saliency of intuitive heuristics in decision-making has been convincingly documented in decision theory and research as illustrated by the pioneering work of Amos Tversky and Daniel Kahneman.[39] Marc Philips, VC expert, who we mentioned earlier, wrote a nice and very accessible book *Inside Silicon Valley* that contains many helpful tips on how to pitch successfully.[40] David Beckett has written a book with useful tips, such as "share your eye-contact" and "finish with a bang".[41] Bill Reichert extends this point: "It's not good enough to finish with a bang; you have to start with a bang. Otherwise you may lose your audience before you get to your second slide." European startup pitchers could use those tips as well. One of the angels told us after the session that European startup fund raisers tend to linger too long on the problem description in their pitches and don't work up to the solution. "Pitching à la Descartes" in his words. A strong but rather deadly metaphor.

Entrepreneurs on startup funding

Raising money

We talked at length with our sample of Dutch startup founders on how they raised funds for their new venture(s) in Silicon Valley and the challenges they had to face. Their personal experiences with attracting angel and VC investors clearly illustrate the large differences in startup funding between the US and Europe. Not only in terms of financial arrangements, but also regarding its underlying investment logic and entrepreneurial psychology.

Some startups are still in the friends & family funding phase but need investors to upgrade and scale. "We raised a little bit of money from friends and family to basically keep us going. We've mostly been living on half of our savings as well. We need more funding now for doing marketing pushes or figure out if we can sell this with enough income to sustain ourselves." (Faruk Ateş, Presentate). Faruk's startup has to cope with a classic chicken-and-egg problem: the biggest clients need the most software features and that will take the most resources to build. But investors hesitate to give a multimillion dollar contract because the Presentate software doesn't include all the features that they need. A dilemma that confronts many hightech startups. Funding is important but so is advice, according to serial startup founder Neil Blaak, particularly from angel investors with an outstanding business reputation. "Some angels are considered smart money and others are more dumb money, it depends on what you are looking for as a startup. I like to have smart money because I want to have more than just their capital. I like for them to contribute their network, their expertise, their experience." (Neil Blaak, ZappoTV). Arthur Van Hoff adds his personal history with VCs: "it is not just money, you also become a part of the family. They are going to try to help you succeed. A lot of people have very negative views of VCs but they are on your side, they want you to be successful. They are only going to intrude when things are not going well." (Arthur Van Hoff, Jaunt).

Not all startups are after VC money, it very much depends on the business model, market fit, and growth ambitions. Marieke van der Poel, Chief Creative Officer of Proef Trend Forecasting, is not in the hightech software business but in creative marketing and strategic conceptualization. "We don't have to make anything, we have ideas and strategy. I have a couple of friends who are VCs. They simply told me not to raise external funding. VCs, they told me, want a say and a significant part of the company; you can do it yourself. I think that was the best advice I ever got." Harm TenHoff who leads a consultancy firm linking Silicon Valley and European health businesses, states: "my business model is not a growth business model. It's a service business working with others that need growth." (Harm TenHoff, BayLink).

But the hightech software and devices startups all have VC funding on their mind. They need the money to bring their startup to the next stage. "We are in the process of raising another round of financing, we want to scale up and need leverage. Plus it makes the company very defensive if you raise a ton of money that will scare off competitors." (Arthur van Hoff, Jaunt). "We don't want to be that little company that lives on government funding and does a little research here and there. We want to build a product that people want to use. We now want to go for a VC for Series A funding." (Maarten Sierhuis, Ejenta). Dirk de Kok, CEO of Mobtest, also wants to scale. "I'll probably be looking for about a million. A million sounds like a lot but the problem is this is a really expensive area. If you want to hire, say four engineers, that's four hundred thousand plus yourself that's $500,000 for just one year, and you have other expenses like your office, you need other employees, you need to buy advertising. A million is good for 12 to 18 months at the first phase of your startup. And after twelve months, I should already have the numbers to show investors that we are good for the second round." (Dirk de Kok). The burn rate of startup cash in the Valley is fast, very fast.

A number of startup founders successfully raised VC money for their businesses. Some in Europe, some in Silicon Valley, some in both. Salar al Khafaji raised $3.5 million for his company Silk, a cloud based (big) data publishing platform, in the United Kingdom and in Silicon Valley. "We realized that the money that we raised would not be sufficient for the future. We knew that we would need more money eventually and that money most likely would come from Silicon Valley. First because there is more money here obviously, but also because I think that companies like Silk almost have no other place to raise money. The more risk there is, the more you have to be in Silicon Valley, even within the US. We might need more money along the way if things continue to go. Ironically the better it goes, the more money we will raise." Ruben Daniëls also managed to get VC funding for his software company Cloud9 IDE: $5.5 million in Series A and is now moving his business into the next funding stage. "We want to raise another round with $25 million or something like that, good high evaluation and then growth recipe. So we are going to focus on revenue at that point, invest appropriately in enterprise story and product thoughts, and probably in new services to the platform that we are likely to integrate."

In the end, it is the investor who decides whether or not to put money in the startup. Ian Sobieski explains that it is a difficult decision: "I have made more than a 100 investments and I have to honestly say that the longer I do this, the less I know. I had all kinds of intellectual ideas and a lot of confidence and evidence behind them. The longer I do it the less I am confident about any set of didactic rules or sayings. I hate to say that, because no one likes to hear it, but there is a great deal of serendipity and luck involved. You have to work hard usually for your luck, it is unlikely that the bum on the street is going to have an IPO. But among the entrepreneurs who are working hard in reasonable markets with a reasonable effort, the variation in success has a lot to do with serendipity and the way things unfold." Trial and error, then, also in this multimillion dollar business.

Investment logic and exit

All startup founders looking for VC funding perfectly understand how the system works and how it differs from the European situation. Investors have a different calculus. "In the US they work along different lines. If you do ten investments, two will be a major success, two will be a failure, and the other six are just ok. In the Netherlands investors act like banks: they want to know for sure." (Adrie Reinders, EFactor). "Investors here are looking for a billion dollar idea, they're not looking for a ten million dollar company. They don't want to double their money, they want to get ten times or a hundred times returning their money. So they're all looking around at all the startups like who has got the Next Big Idea. They're not like in Holland where investors are much more conservative." (Arthur van Hoff, Jaunt). Pieter Hoff fully agrees: "In the Netherlands, the real problem for entrepreneurs are the banks. They are really not entrepreneurial, they do not understand business. The only thing they do is avoid risks." (Pieter Hoff, Groasis). Dirk de Kok follows up upon the different logic of investment. "It's extremely hard to have a Dutch investor that says, I have like twenty companies to invest in, I assume that nineteen will die, I will not get a single dime back from those failed companies but I'm going to be learning from them, so I'll have that. But the twentieth company return of investment is going to be like forty or hundred times and that will fund my next round of companies that I'll be investing in, and I'm willing to take that risk." (Dirk de Kok). And once you have the funding: "you have to play to win. You have to spend the money. There is no way to be conservative. I told the investors when we raised our first round of $6 million that we are going to spend it in the first year to see whether we are going to be successful. I don't want to spend five years finding out that we failed. And if we are successful we will raise a lot more money. You want to really go like pedal to the metal." (Arthur van Hoff).

Do startups have an exit strategy? Do they dream of selling big? They all, in one way or another, think of an exit but the time horizon differs. "My E-Factor Group Corp is on the Bulletin Board now but we are working hard on the uplift to the NASDAQ. It's a big step. That's is my exit strategy." (Adrie Reinders). Eric-Jan van Leeuwen has a longer exit perspective. With the right growth perspective and valuation "the exit strategy is that we get acquired by one of the companies that is out here in Silicon Valley. (...) It's all about being boxed or buying." (Eric-Jan van Leeuwen, Login VSI). "To me a successful business is the one that goes for the exit, either you go for an IPO or you go for an acquisition." (Neil Blaak). Ruben Daniëls has a strong growth and exit vision too. "We need to aim high. I mean that's what people do here and I think that's the only way. If you aim for a small company then don't take money but we definitely want to become a billion dollar company in valuation for sure. Then at that point we will either sell off or IPO, depending. If we manage to become the development platform basically of the world, where most people will come and use the ID and use many of the adjacent services; yeah we definitely have the possibility to become a large company." (Ruben Daniels). But the emotional tie between startup and startup founder is also determining. "For both Marco and I first and foremost we have a responsibility to our shareholders – to significantly grow the value of our company. For us we're enjoying the process of growing the business and are solely focused on growing the business." (Rip Pruisken, Rip van Wafels).

The pitch

Pitching is all-important in raising startup funds. It is often the first meeting between new venture founders and potential investors. As we noticed above, European pitchers according to Silicon Valley watchers can do a better job in convincing angels or VCs to invest in their business. And particularly in finding the right balance between detail and focus, between the problem and the solution. "When European companies come here to pitch, they start explaining, where they started, how old they are, how many children they have, and the like. I mean by the time you get to business nobody is interested anymore, so you have to turn it on." (Grotenbreg, SiliconValleyLink). The right sequence of selecting investors is important in the pitching process; don't start with the ones on top of your list. This is how Silk startup founder Salar al Khafaji made his pick. "I made a list of all the investors that I wanted to meet, people I got introductions to, and then I sorted it in the order from least important to most important. So I started with the people that I actually cared about the least and that's in fact useful because that allowed me to improve my pitch. It worked pretty well. I received good feedback. So the nice thing is that in the final couple of days when you meet the people you really hope will invest in you, you'll have the best pitch you could ever have at that point." (Salar al Khafaji). The whole idea about pitching for funding is that you don't have a final product, though you may have a demo. This impacts your pitch. As serial entrepreneur Arthur Van Hoff learned in his startup career: "the idea is that you cannot sell a product so you have to give a presentation in the form of a story and the story has to be about you, it has to be a personal story that is inspired. A good pitch is one that emotionally attaches people."

7. Culture

The impact of culture

Culture matters. It shapes and differentiates societies, organizations, groups, and individuals.[1] Culture impacts the macro-, meso-, and micro-level of nations and regions. It affects all layers of our 'Silicon Valley Innovation & Startup Model'. A little theory may illustrate the significance of culture in understanding cross-national differences. Cultural contrasts that are important in grasping how startup entrepreneurs who moved to Silicon Valley experience its dominant culture and how they incorporate its innovation values and business beliefs.

Culture produces societal institutions and is in turn imprinted by these institutions, they are interwoven in a dynamic pattern of interaction and causation. A culture may promote startup founding, and startups, in turn, may fuel a new business culture. A definition of culture that serves both theoretical and applied objectives is the definition by UNESCO: "Culture should be regarded as the set of distinctive spiritual, material, intellectual and emotional features of society or a social group, and that it encompasses, in addition to art and literature, lifestyles, ways of living together, value systems, traditions and beliefs."[2] The most compact definition, however, is given by cross-cultural guru Geert Hofstede, which nicely fits Silicon Valley's core business: "Culture is software of the mind (...) the collective programming of the mind which distinguishes the members of one group or category of people from another."[3] Hofstede positions different national cultures on the following six basic dimensions: power distance, uncertainty avoidance, individualism vs. collectivism, masculinity vs. femininity, long-term vs. short-term orientation, and indulgence vs. self-constraint. These cultural dimensions are directly or indirectly related to entrepreneurship, and values associated with starting new ventures.[4] Hofstede's data show that in comparing American and Dutch culture, Americans and Dutch are quite similar in terms of their attitudes towards power distance, uncertainty avoidance, and indulgence. Though both countries are western and therefore individualistic, Americans are more firmly so. The Dutch are more supportive of long term orientations. The biggest difference between the two countries is that Americans are quite masculine, whereas the Dutch are strongly feminine. Masculinity is characterized by the need for (material) success (live to work), competition and a strong role differentiation between men and women. A feminine culture can be recognized by modesty, a strong orientation towards quality of life (work to live) and overlapping gender roles.[5] It is in the realm of masculinity/femininity that we find the differences between the Silicon Valley and American culture and the Dutch culture. It should be emphasized here that we are talking about cultures, not individual persons. Of course, there are persons in the Netherlands who are very competitive, and there are persons in the USA who strongly prefer quality of life to success, but as a culture these macro-differences in orientation are significant.

Values and norms constitute the core of a culture, the cement of a society, "the way we do things." They regulate social behavior, provide identity, and strengthen societal integration. A general definition of values is offered by the European Values Study: "Values are deeply rooted dispositions, orientations, or motives guiding people to act or behave in a certain way. They are believed to be more complex, more basic, and more enduring than attitudes, opinions, and preferences."[6] Values – unlike norms – are latent constructs and cannot be measured directly. But they can be measured indirectly, i.e. in the way people evaluate actions or outcomes. An important feature of values is that they are assumed to be relatively stable or even durable: values do not change overnight. Values according to German sociologist Niklas Luhmann, are "enttäuschungsfest", they are counterfactual resistant.[7] Values are answers to the grand schemes of human existence such as equality, freedom, justice, religion, morality, sexuality, tolerance, and integration. Values according to anthropologist Clyde Kluckhohn are "beliefs about the desirable" and in the same vein psychologist Harry Triandis states that "culture is to society what memory is to individuals."[8] Values are deeply rooted beliefs and motivations acquired during one's formative years which explain the human condition and guide behavior. Values shape and justify human action, they legitimate what is "good" and what is "bad".

In this chapter, we will zoom in on major cultural characteristics of Silicon Valley and its dominant values and norms, e.g. with respect to business vision, openness and sharing, failure, risk-taking, work attitudes, diversity, and immigrant entrepreneurship. Fundamental beliefs that put the startup founders' business adventures and experiences in a broader cultural context and perspective. Cultural beliefs that non-US and immigrant startup founders in Silicon Valley need to address, comprehend, internalize, and practice.

Openness and sharing

Two of the first things that strikes one in researching the beliefs, values, and norms of the Silicon Valley startup community is its open communication mode and the general willingness to share innovation experiences. There is no business taboo about exchanging what your starting company is all about: the novelty, niche, and promise of the product, the underlying Big Idea, its strengths and weaknesses, its market potential, the marketing approach, the funding stage, the trouble to grow the company, etc. Even in a very embryonic stage of their new venture, startup founders are not hiding their business "secrets" in order not to wake the competition. This basic value of openness and sharing is quite characteristic of the Silicon Valley startup culture and mindset. In talking to many startup founders we were always positively surprised by the frank and engaging way they outlined the details of their new company, and their curiosity for input and feedback. Even though we were complete strangers. This communication style deviates markedly from the more closed and "secretive" mode of operation of European new venture creations which is dominated by the fear that competitors might run off with your idea. The more open and sharing Silicon Valley communication style has some clear strategic advantages: it broadens one's network, might generate interesting leads and further conducts, and solid feedback from others may strengthen the basic startup idea and product. Or, of course, it may call for adjusting weaker points. Chong Moon-Lee and his co-editors pointedly summarize the impact of this communication style as follows: "The prevailing business philosophy promotes openness, learning, sharing of information, the co-evolution of ideas, flexibility, mutual feedback, and fast responses to opportunities and challenges."[9]

The combination of openness and sharing has wider social and technological implications as well. It also implies openness to new business entrants such as immigrant entrepreneurs, openness to taking risks, and sharing by creating open innovation sources. An intriguing illustration is provided by Elon Musk, much celebrated CEO of Tesla Motors, one of the world's most innovative electric carmakers and strongly guided by sustainability values. In 2014, Musk radically decided that Tesla would share its technological patents in an open source environment. To effectively fight the carbon crisis by speeding up the production and adoption of electric cars, a revolutionary breakthrough of existing patent protection was announced. This is how Elon motivated his far-reaching innovation policy change. "Yesterday, there was a wall of Tesla patents in the lobby of our Palo Alto headquarters. That is no longer the case. They have been removed, in the spirit of the open source movement, for the advancement of electric vehicle technology (...). Tesla Motors was created to accelerate the advent of sustainable transport. If we clear a path to the creation of compelling electric vehicles, but then lay intellectual property landmines behind us to inhibit others, we are acting in a manner contrary to that goal. Tesla will not initiate patent lawsuits against anyone who, in good faith, wants to use our technology."[10] Though we have to see how the new policy will develop, it is a meaningful example of a pioneering Silicon Valley company that goes for disruptive innovation based on the fundamental values of openness and sharing.

The Valley's communicative culture of entrepreneurship, innovation, and sharing serves as inspiration for other countries that want to boost their startup economy. Some years ago, one of the first tweets from Russian President Dmitry Medvedev's new Twitter account was about his visit to Silicon Valley and his positive assessment of its remarkably open communication culture. "Silicon Valley's greatest asset is communication. People discuss their work not trifles. Russia would benefit from this kind of environment."[11]

If we would place this openness and sharing on one of Hofstede's dimensions, we would suggest it belongs to uncertainty avoidance. This dimension assumes (on the tolerance for uncertainty side) a tolerance for ambiguity, for non-hierarchical communication, autonomous non-structured working and the like. Despite Medvedev's intentions, Russia has one of the highest scores worldwide on uncertainty avoidance.[12] This would mean that such openness and sharing is hard to realize in Russia. Scandinavian countries, UK, Ireland, and the Netherlands have cultures that are typically acceptant of uncertainty.

Passion and ethos

Silicon Valley is a 24/7 economy that never stops. Its work ethos is unmatched. The Valley's preoccupation with continuous innovation, with creating new hightech products that will shake the world, with finding new and profitable markets, with staying ahead of the cut-throat competition, requires permanent focus and availability. Running a startup is simply not a nine-to-five job. It is a rat race that never ends and demands total dedication and passion. As Randall Stross, author of *The Launch Pad*, the inside story of Y Combinator, states: "in startup life, commitment comes in only one size: total".[13] The drive to excel is all around the startup scene and creates a culture of passionate and ambitious entrepreneurship. Work ethos is a big thing in Silicon Valley and it seems, at least to outside observers, that everybody is working all of the time. Bringing a startup to the next phase and getting the funds to do so, dominates the entrepreneur's life, and calls for many hours. Regular schedules are simply not on par with everyday startup challenges. Standard working schedules do no create fast moving companies. Working weekends and pulling all-nighters to meet critical deadlines are an almost innate part of the Silicon Valley culture and work ethos. Working extremely hard, taking no vacation, and being constantly available, has an air of normality. It is "all or nothing" with growing a startup and making it successful. It is all about passion, commitment, perseverance, and long hours. Author Kay Hymnowitz critically describes the Silicon Valley high-energy and high-spirited work vibe as "ecstatic capitalism's brave new work ethic".[14]

The European (and certainly Dutch) debate on a healthy work-life balance is not a central issue in Silicon Valley's startup community. It may enter private conversations with entrepreneurs but it rarely leads to a radical reconsideration of work-life choices. Starting and managing a new venture in a highly competitive environment such as Silicon Valley absorbs all of one's energy and attention span. Being passionate and driven about turning the new venture into a thriving business is what guides the startup entrepreneur and preconditions all other life choices. Or as they say – slightly contemptuously – in the Valley, building a new company is not just a "lifestyle business"; a business that aims at sustaining a certain income level (and not more) or to enjoy a certain lifestyle with no particular growth ambition.

Working for a startup is not a nine-to-five job either. Employees put in a lot of hours as they are also infected by the Silicon Valley zealous work ethos. Having a nice salary, a pleasant package of stock options, and a convenient office environment help to overcome the negative effects of long working days, but this is not the whole story. There must be other incentives for startup employees to work so extremely hard. The new company they work for must have an inspiring story to tell with which they can identify. But what story? An interesting answer to this question was given by veteran Silicon Valley company builder Maynard Webb, former COO of eBay and presently Chairman of the Board of Yahoo, in an interview to *Forbes*. Webb believes that to motivate employees over a long period of time "you need to tap into a higher purpose. You need to explain the higher purpose of what everyone does day in and day out".[15] The work itself must be motivating and stimulating; the work content must be in line with both the employees' and the company's higher goal settings. The company should clearly explain its broader mission – beyond its financial targets – and how employees contribute to realizing this mission. Employees, in Webb's view, need to become the CEO of their own destiny and that is how the company's business agenda can be aligned with the personal agenda of its employees. Higher goals bind workers to the company and make them to perform above average. Intrinsic work motivation makes the difference.

Work-life balance, as we remarked, is not a broadly discussed cultural phenomenon in Silicon Valley, at least not among startup entrepreneurs. It seems to be taken for granted. It is the price to be paid for starting a new business. The aura of free choice prevails. It is not cool, as the dominant business culture seems to suggest, to sympathize with a more relaxed work attitude; it even seems that the work-life balance issue is being perceived as something for "losers".[16] But some advocacy groups started to criticize Silicon Valley's work ethos. Recently a group of psychologists and business academics dispraised the Valley's disproportional long work hours, both from a health perspective and in view of the adverse effects on its prime business: innovation.[17] Companies that make their money by developing innovative solutions to pressing market demands, need a workforce that is mentally and physically fit. There is not a one-to-one relationship between working hours, productivity, and innovation strength. There are obvious ceiling effects. But as the work ethos is such a cornerstone of Silicon Valley's business culture, it will take a long time before a healthier work-life balance will become reality. Unless, of course, new startups will frame this as an innovation challenge and devise new hightech and disruptive solutions to finding a better symmetry between work and life. That would certainly be in accordance with the Silicon Valley mindset and could even become a cultural game changer.

This Silicon Valley work ethos is, in terms of the Hofstede dimensions, very typical of a masculine culture. It is much more "live to work" than "work to live". We should not forget that Silicon Valley attracts people who have exactly that attitude, so it probably even strengthens this trait that is already inherent to American culture.

Risk-taking and failure

The willingness to take risks is another fundamental characteristic of American business culture. This particularly holds for new venture entrepreneurs and for startup investors as we saw in the previous chapter. Risk proneness is perceived as a positive business attitude that is essential for successful entrepreneurship. "No risk, no business" (or in plain English: "no guts, no glory") so goes the underlying heuristic. The relationship between risk-taking and business success may be curvilinear: up to a certain point the correlation is positive but too much risk-taking may cause business failure. However, not enough studies have been done to draw firm conclusions.[18] Tolerance towards failure is another basic feature of American business culture. "Fail fast, fail often" is a very popular and often repeated statement about Silicon Valley's business climate. A mantra that has a positive connotation and implies that it is ok to fail as a startup founder. Unlike the European attitude towards failure, the American business culture does not stigmatize entrepreneurs who failed. They are not subject to the modern version of tar and feather, to disgrace and contempt. As most Silicon Valley hightech new ventures fail, a business climate that negatively stereotypes failure would be a serious deterrent for setting up new businesses. This is especially true for a business culture that is risk aversive and that rewards uncertainty avoidance. But the dominant culture in Silicon Valley is pro risk-taking, does not discredit failed startup founders, and radiates a general sense of business optimism and self-confidence. Failure tolerance as a cultural phenomenon – which goes back to the old Californian gold-rush mentality – is backed up by a system of institutional factors which limits personal liability for entrepreneurs and their investors, such as bankruptcy laws and limited partnerships. This is a good example of how cultural values and beliefs interact with institutional parameters. European societies are believed to be less acceptant of risk-taking and failure which is likely related to the fact that supportive legislation – such as the US limited liability laws – is largely lacking.

Failure Silicon Valley style does not equal personal failure. The business community and culture applaud a startup entrepreneur for having the spirit to start a business, to take risks, and failure is simply seen as an intrinsic part of the startup game. But failure is not admired for its own sake. As Reid Hoffman, co-founder of LinkedIn, stated: "We don't celebrate failure in Silicon Valley. We celebrate learning." A failed startup is framed as a learning experience that empowers a startup entrepreneur for his next new venture. It broadens and deepens the failed entrepreneur's personal portfolio of business experiences which is an asset in starting a new startup. Timing is absolutely essential. The mantra of "fail fast, fail often" is precisely pointing at this sense of urgency: waiting too long with closing down your startup can be catastrophic. Fail fast is the better option; it challenges entrepreneurs to find the right balance between failing and persistence, and making this crucial calculation creates a meaningful learning experience. A miscalculation might have serious consequences, startups that go on too long may turn in what VCs call "the walking dead". The culture of failure tolerance even led to the launching of the San Francisco based annual

FailCon conference ("embracing failure") at which entrepreneurs frankly talk about their misfires and mistakes.[19] It almost seems that Silicon Valley's embrace of failure is emerging as "a badge of honor", according to *New York Times* writer Claire Martin.[20]

Fail fast, fail often is a leading Silicon Valley slogan that reveals much of its entrepreneurial and startup culture. It is important, however, to not exaggerate its positive meaning and significance. Failure remains a very painful experience, even in the absence of stigmatization. Losing your new venture is no fun. Startup founders invested all their money, time, energy, creativity, and efforts in making their new company successful. We should not turn the fail fast slogan into a hype. As *Forbes* contributor Rob Asghar wrote: "Failure can't be taken lightly. Forget the cute mantras. No one should ever set out to fail. The key, really, shouldn't be to embrace failure, but to embrace resilience and the ability to bounce back."[21] Rory Carroll, the *Guardian*'s correspondent in San Francisco, points at the "psychic toll" of unrelenting startup failure. "What about those tech entrepreneurs who lose – and keep on losing? What about those who start one company after another, refine pitches, tweak products, pivot strategies, reinvent themselves ... and never succeed? What about the angst masked behind upbeat facades?"[22] Important questions that should be taken seriously by the advocates of the failing-is-ok paradigm. Failing is a key learning process for startup founders, but it is not necessarily a rite of passage to future success.

Most startups fail. What are the main reasons? Why do they fail? *CB Insights* analyzed the top 20 reasons for startup failure by analyzing data from over 100 startup failure post-mortems. The main causes, in descending order, are: no market need, running out of cash, wrong team, getting outcompeted, pricing/cost issues, poor product, lacking business model, poor marketing, release of product at wrong time, lose focus, disharmony with investors or co-founders, pivoting gone bad, lack of passion, wrong startup location, lack of follow up financing or interested investors, legal challenges, not properly using one's network and advisors, burn out, and failure to timely pivot.[23] As one can see, the variety of startup failure causes corresponds nicely to the three levels and separate institutional and cultural factors outlined in our 'Silicon Valley Innovation & Startup Model'. Micro-level: product (idea), organization (team & talent), and marketing (pivot & perseverance). Meso-level: funding, government, research and network support). Macro-level: the impact of culture.

Although Hofstede points out that risk and uncertainty are two different concepts,[24] the willingness to accept eventual failure is related to uncertainty avoidance. Hofstede's empirical data indicated that Americans are less inclined towards uncertainty avoidance than the Dutch are. At the same time, failure does not seem to match with masculinity, on which Americans score much higher than the Dutch. The idea seems to be "better to have fought and lost, then never to have fought at all", and that is more in line with masculinity. We hypothesize that the risk taking and the acceptance of failure is a combination of these two dimensions: low on uncertainty avoidance and high on masculinity. Only Anglo-Saxon countries (Ireland, UK, Australia) and China seem to have this rather unique combination of cultural traits.

Cultural diversity and innovation

Diversity is a topical issue in Silicon Valley for two main reasons. The first is how diversity – in this section to be understood as the Valley's mixed ethnic, nationality, and gender workforce composition – impacts innovation performance. The second reason is the current heated dispute on the underrepresentation of minority groups in the Valley's ecosystem. The first topic relates to cultural and demographic antecedents of innovation achievements; the second issue concerns the rule of distributive justice of corporate recruitment policies.

Silicon Valley's population and workforce is a melting pot of many different immigrant groups from a wide variety of ethnic and national origins. The general consensus seems to be that cultural diversity is good for innovation: it brings multiple perspectives to existing and new ventures developing innovative products, it reinforces intercultural competencies which are indispensable for companies operating in global markets, it raises new questions and new answers in the innovation process, and keeps in-company innovation teams sharp in having a keen eye for diversity issues related to new products in new markets. Or as *Forbes Insights* concludes in its recent study of promoting innovation through diversity: "A diverse and inclusive workforce is necessary to drive innovation, foster creativity, and guide business strategies. Multiple voices lead to new ideas, new services, and new products, and encourage out-of-the-box thinking. Today, companies no longer view diversity and inclusion efforts as separate from their other business practices, and recognize that a diverse workforce can differentiate them from their competitors by attracting top talent and capturing new clients."[25]

But cultural diversity is not an innocent concept. It functions at different levels (countries, regions, organizations, leadership, teams, and groups of individuals) which makes it a complex phenomenon that calls for multi-level and advanced macro-, meso-, and micro study designs.[26] Such studies are not abundantly available, but some interesting findings can be highlighted, especially with respect to work teams. Corporate R&D is usually organized in innovation teams. Cultural diversity is particularly important in this context. Innovation teams that are culturally mixed are believed to bring in a wider and richer range of frames and experiences to the creative innovation process: with respect to product brainstorming, product development and consumer needs, product problem-solving, sensitivity of product adoption and is cultural dimensions, cross-cultural correlates of product diffusion, and a general sense of debunking mono-culturalism. A review study of cultural diversity in work teams by Günter Stahl and his co-authors – who conducted an encompassing meta-analysis of more than 100 studies including over 10,000 teams – came up with interesting results.[27] The study is especially relevant because it attempts to reconcile the conflicting outcomes of past, predominantly qualitative, research. They point at three potentially opposing theoretical ways of how cultural diversity may influence team performance. Similarity-attraction theory assumes that people like to work together with people who share their cultural values, attitudes, norms, and way of life.[28] Social identity and social categorization theory holds that people identify with specific groups ("in-group") and categorize others in terms of "out-group".[29] Outsiders are often stereotyped by assumed group traits. Information-processing theory states that diversity brings different cultural views to teams and taps into a broader range of networks that strengthens creativity and problem-solving.[30] The conceptual dilemma now is that the first two theories tend to hypothesize negative effects of cultural diversity on team performance and innovation, whereas the third theory assumes positive effects. Stahl and his colleagues developed a dynamic taxonomy which offers an elegant explanation of these conflicting views by focusing on team "process gains and losses". Cultural diversity tends to increase creativity and innovation as process gains, but also raises group conflicts. Cultural convergence on the other hand favors group cohesion but also leads to groupthink which causes process losses. The study's findings revealed positive main effects of cultural diversity on team creativity and satisfaction, but also on team conflicts; and negative effects on social integration. For our theme of the relationship between cultural diversity and innovation, the positive relationship between diversity and creativity is a major outcome, albeit at the loss of increased conflict. But it is hard to imagine team creativity puzzles and innovation challenges without team conflicts. Besides: disruptive innovation is all about conflicting views.

And, finally, the good news of this comprehensive meta-analytic study is that cultural diversity does not impede effective team communication. Ursula Brinkmann and Oscar van Weerdenburg, intercultural consultants, developed the Intercultural Readiness Check (IRC), which analyzes how effective organizations are in intercultural team-working and interaction, and how they can improve their diversity performance. They distinguish four core competences for working across cultures: intercultural sensitivity, intercultural communication, building commitment, and managing uncertainty.[31] The authors provide a wealth of practical insights on how these competences can bring organizations to a higher level of diversity management and intercultural achievements.[32]

The key question with regards to diversity is, in short, whether a difference makes a difference? McKinsey recently published an overview study "Diversity matters", which as the title already suggests, answers this question affirmatively.[33] The cross-national comparative study among over 360 public companies varying in level of diversity (defined as having a more mixed ethnic composition and a greater share of women in the leadership of large companies) observed some marked effects. The most important outcome is that companies in the top quartile for ethnic and gender diversity are more likely to outperform the national means in terms of financial returns, respectively by 15% and 35%. "It stands to reason (...) that more diverse companies are better able to win top talent, and improve their customer orientation, employee satisfaction, and decision making, leading to a virtuous cycle of increasing returns (...). Diversity matters because we increasingly live in a global world that has become deeply interconnected. Given the increasing returns that diversity is expected to bring, it is better to invest now, as winners will pull further ahead and laggards will fall further behind."[34] A global mindset and intercultural fluency can indeed make a difference of a difference. The McKinsey researchers argue that US companies can still do a better job in this respect. Ethnic representation of company leadership does not reflect their workforce ethnic composition and the impact of gender representation is only positive if more than 20% of the leadership teams consists of women.

In the last couple of years the major Silicon Valley hightech companies have been seriously attacked by advocacy groups because of its unequal inclusion of ethnic minorities. Ethnic workforce representation shows a substantial divide between white and Asian workers on the one side, and Latino and African-Americans on the other side. It signifies a sense of parallel worlds in the Valley's hightech business landscape. Elsa Davidson in her book on ethnic social divides and social inequality in Silicon Valley summarizes the ethnic polarization as follows: "Educated whites and Chinese, Taiwanese, and Indians often occupy highly paid technical and managerial positions in the hightech sector, and Latino and Vietnamese, Filipino, Korean, and other Southeast Asian immigrants perform low-paid services and hightech production work, creating ethnic and racial hierarchies and patterns of ethnic and occupational segregation."[35] Data support this picture of unequal ethnic representation in the Valley's higher paid ranks of software programmers and engineers and all the perks and social benefits that go with it. An overview by Working Partnership USA shows that over 90% of the US-based tech workers of Google, Facebook, Twitter, Yahoo, eBay, and LinkedIn, and over 75% of Apple, are white or Asian. Only a fraction (between 3-4%) of their workforce is either Latino or African-American, with Apple doing slightly better (13%).[36] To put these findings into perspective: almost 30% of the Santa Clara workforce is either Latino or African-American. The data also reveal a gender bias: the vast majority of hightech employees and higher managers are male. Explanations of minority and gender underrepresentation in the hightech industry given by the companies and advocacy groups are quite different and vary from educational mismatches, lacking technical skills, lower STEM (science, technology, engineering, mathematics) scores, to selective recruitment policies, cultural barriers, and prejudice. Whatever the explanation is, it seems that the prevailing talent hiring practices reinforce what has been called the "Silicon Valley's mirror effect", or the tendency that hightech companies primarily recruit from their own cultural "in-group".[37]

The heated debate on the failure of the Silicon Valley corporate world to employ Latino, African-American, and female workers, forced the leading class of hightech CEOs to respond. Apple's Tim Cook put it this way: "Let me say up front: As CEO, I'm not satisfied with the numbers. We are making progress, and we're committed to being as innovative in advancing diversity as we are in developing our products."[38] Google's Nancy Lee announced that 2014's diversity initiatives (worth $115 million) were not satisfactory; the budget has been increased to $216 million.[39] Intel's CEO Bryan Krzanich stated that "While we have made progress on our goals over time, we are not content and will continue to take bold actions to grow and develop our diverse talent."[40] Intel suited the action to the word by pledging $300 million in training and recruiting minorities and female computer scientists. Its goal? To achieve full representation of minorities by 2020. Intel Capital, its VC branch, announced to invest $125 million with diverse management.[41] Although there is some overlap, Intel said, between the two sums, its total is significant. Some Valley insiders, however, are more skeptical about stringent diversity policies. Ben Horowitz, co-founder and general partner of prominent venture capital firm Andreessen Horowitz, is one of them. In his view, Silicon Valley will only recruit a more diverse workforce if they see hard evidence that it will improve their bottom line. "When you're building a startup, you're fighting for your life. You aren't going to do anything for corporate responsibility."[42]

But for the big hightech corporations diversity matters. Not only because it fosters innovation but also because it has turned into a public issue. Strong leadership and strong management support are required to advance diversity, to turn positive intentions in effective programs, and to make sure that the tech industry broadens its talent pool.

Immigrant entrepreneurship

The contribution of immigrant startups to the economy of Silicon Valley is a remarkable success story. The Valley and the greater Bay Area clearly benefitted from the presence of innovative and hightech immigrant ventures and value its impact on the region's prosperity and cultural diversity.[43] It is difficult to imagine Silicon Valley without the many startups founded by Chinese, Indian, Taiwanese or Korean entrepreneurs. A joint study by Duke University and Berkeley University found that 52% of Silicon Valley startups indicated that their key founders were immigrants (against 25% in the US).[44] Some of these founders' names were already mentioned in previous chapters, but here is a listing of leading immigrant-founded venture-backed public companies ranked by market capitalization (2013 data).[45] Google (Sergey Brin, Russia; $295 billion), Intel (Andy Grove, Hungary; $124 billion), eBay (Pierre Omidyar, France; $69 billion), Facebook (Eduardo Luiz Saverin, Brazil; $59 billion), LinkedIn (Konstantin Guericke and Jean-Luc Vaillant, respectively Germany and France; $19 billion), SanDisk (Eli Harari, Sanjay Mehrotra, and Jack Yuan, respectively Israel, India, and Taiwan; $14 billion), Tesla Motors (Elon Musk, South Africa; $12 billion), and Altera (Rodney Smith, United Kingdom; $10 billion).[46] The total market capitalization of all immigrant-founded venture-backed companies equals $900 billion; if the value of its stock exchange would represent a country it would rank 16th in the world. These companies employ about 600,000 people, most of them in the US. Looking at their countries of origin, 20% of the company founders were from India, 10% from Taiwan, and 10% from Israel; followed by the United Kingdom (8%), Germany (7%), and Canada and France (6% each). Between 2006 and 2012 almost six out of ten venture-backed publicly traded immigrant businesses were located in California; Biotechnology was the leading sector (27%), software came next (19%), followed by semiconductors (12%), and medical devices (10%).[47] Most immigrant entrepreneurs initially entered the US as employment-sponsored immigrants or as international students.

Immigration of global talent led to a highly skilled and culturally diverse workforce, a strong entrepreneurial spirit, and a competitive economy in Silicon Valley. About 40% of the Valley's population is foreign born; three times higher than the US average (13%). Half of the Valley's residents speaks a language other than English at home. Asian Silicon Valley residents have the highest levels of educational attainment in the region: 59% earned a bachelor's, graduate or professional degree (against 55% of whites and 14% of Hispanics and Latinos; US average is 29%).[48] In the last fifteen years Indian immigrants have been particularly successful, outstripping all other minorities with average family incomes over $100,000 and highly skilled professional jobs. Half of the H-1b visas for skilled professionals in the 1997-2013 period went to Indians. Some researchers even speak of "a new elite".[49] The high educational level of immigrants and the international profile of the Bay Area is mirrored in the number of foreign students of its two leading universities: Stanford University and Berkeley University.[50] One-third of all Stanford graduate students are foreign; the same holds for 40% of the graduate students of its famous School of Engineering, who come from over 70 countries.[51] One-fourth of the Stanford 2013-14 incoming PhD cohort are international students. One-third of Stanford's renowned Graduate School of Business faculty is foreign-born. Berkeley University shows a comparable pattern. Total 2014 enrollment of international students amounts to almost 6,000 students (out of 37,500); 22% of the graduate students are foreign. Already in the mid-nineties, more than half of Berkeley's graduate degrees in science and engineering were granted to students from China.[52] Almost 25% of Berkeley's international students are PhD students. About 60% of its international students come from East Asia and the Pacific, with China as the main country of origin (32%), followed by South Korea (14%), and India (9%).[53] As many of these students find jobs in the region, it provides them with an excellent start on the labor market given their competitive educational attainment.

In the 1960s and 1970s, Chinese and Indian engineers were still treated as relative outsiders on the labor market who primarily qualified for professional but not for managerial positions. Many engineers felt that they were victim of a "glass ceiling" effect. Their reaction to this sense of exclusion was twofold.[54] Firstly, they started their own companies. The pioneering example was Lester Lee, born in Szechuan, China, and holding a PhD in mechanical engineering from Stanford University, who founded his own company called Recortec. Many immigrants would follow in his footsteps. Secondly, Chinese, Indian, and other immigrant groups initiated a process of collective self-organization. They did so by turning their immigrant social and cultural networks into business associations. In this way they mobilized their social capital in order, according to Berkeley Dean AnnaLee Saxenian, "to provide resources and support structures within their own communities".[55] To which she adds that "these associations combine elements of traditional immigrant culture with distinctly high technology practices: they simultaneously create ethnic identities within the region and facilitate the professional networking and information exchange that aid success in the highly mobile Silicon Valley economy".[56] Mainland (PRC) Chinese and Taiwanese associations ("gongsi") include the Asia America Multi-Technology Association (AAMA), the Mont Jade Science and Technology Association, the Hua Yuan Science and Technology Association (HYSTA), the Chinese American Semiconductor Professional Association (CASPA), the Silicon Valley Taiwanese American Industrial Technology Association (TAITA), the North America Taiwanese Engineering & Science Association (NATEA), the Silicon Valley Chinese Engineers Association (SCEA), and, more recently, the Chinese Enterprise Association.[57] An interesting younger Chinese association is the Silicon Valley-China Wireless Technology Association, established in 2000, that aims to support startups and caters to investors and incubators.[58] They organize startup innovation pitch contests and award startups that are most disruptive, have the best business model, the best management team, the best consumer solution, and have the largest financial impact. Two main Indian professional associations are the Silicon Valley Indian Professional Association (SIPA) and The Indus Entrepreneur (TiE). Vish Mishra, Venture Director at Clearstone, but also active in TiE, states that "disruptive innovation comes from diversity". Examples of Korean associations are the Korean-American Chamber of Commerce of Silicon Valley (KACC-SV), Global K-startup Silicon Valley, the Korean-American Scientists and Engineers Association (KSEA), and the Korean-American Semiconductor Association (KASA).

These immigrant associations provide and maintain social identity, strengthen cultural ties, reinforce social integration, and secure immigrant entrepreneurs' business and professional interests. They professionalize within-group communication, networking, and contact sharing. These associations accumulate and "cash" immigrant groups' social capital in advancing their business concerns.[59] Several of them function as mentoring communities where successful first-generation entrepreneurs council second-generation startup founders in setting up their business and teaching them the ins and outs of entrepreneurship. These first-generation role models may also become angel or VC investors in new immigrant ventures. Investing in startup incubators and accelerators becomes a growth area for investors, especially Chinese investors. First examples are InnoSpring in Santa Clara, Hanhai Z-Park in San Jose, and Hanhai-Zibo Life Science Park in Burlingame, which all focus on supporting innovative cross-border startups, particularly in the technology and life science sector.[60] Their mission is to facilitate and strengthen the connections between Silicon Valley startups and their Chinese counterparts.

Immigrant business associations are important in Silicon Valley, but their members are faced with the classic issue of balancing mainstream commercial strategies (which they need to grow their business) and tailored ethnic networks. They have, in short, to combine bridging and bonding priorities. In this broader cultural context it is interesting to observe that Chinese and Indian immigrant entrepreneurs activated their social networks in their country of origin, which opened new and massive markets for their companies. This mobilization and activation strategy, linking Silicon Valley immigrant startups with the economy of immigrants' original home country, proved to be quite effective. Given their first-hand knowledge of the culture and language of these countries, these immigrant entrepreneurs can easily find the right business partners and sell their products overseas in Asia and other regions. Many Chinese and Indian startups have an immediate internationalization advantage given their transnational cultural assets and skills, and their matching value orientations.

A low score on Hofstede's uncertainty avoidance dimension associates with "immigrants tolerated". This pertains to the USA.[61] Although acquiring a visa may be a hassle, the USA still ranks as number 7 on the list of countries where it is easy doing business.[62] Silicon Valley, evidently, is a multicultural region that welcomes immigrant entrepreneurs, many of whom founded successful startups. Still, the visa procedure meets with much criticism. The majority of foreign-born startup founders believes that to enter and remain in America to start a business is too difficult. But at the same time almost 90% states that in spite of these difficulties they would still choose the United States as the country to found their startup.[63]

When we combine the above cultural identifications of Silicon Valley, we tend to conclude the following in terms of Hofstede dimensions: to have a sizzling startup culture, the Hofstede dimensions Uncertainty avoidance and Masculinity vs Femininity seem to be prevalent. Silicon Valley, and indeed all of the USA, is characterized by low uncertainty avoidance and high masculinity. These two dimensions have been associated with in-novativeness before.[64] Countries that may relatively easily develop a startup culture based upon this rather rare combination of low uncertainty avoid-ance and high masculinity are UK, Ireland and China. Southern and Eastern European countries are relatively high on uncertainty avoidance (while they are generally high on masculinity). Western and Northern European countries are low on masculinity (and generally low on uncertainty avoid-ance). Of course, by grouping together specific types of people who have the right cultural background, a region or a city can be molded into the 'culturally right' direction. However, this takes time, effort, and attention.

Entrepreneurs on culture

On risks and failure

Our sample of startup founders and entrepreneurs clearly acknowledges the cross-cultural differences in risk perception and failure attitudes between American and European societies. In fact, they all underline the importance of how these differences affect startup founding and entrepreneurship. Of how these differences impact their own businesses. The willingness to take risks and failure tolerance positively influence, in their minds, the readiness to start new ventures and the ambition to grow. It touches upon the very essence of the American entrepreneurial psychology. Eric-Jan van Leeuwen frames it as follows: "I think in the Netherlands we are quite conservative in taking decisions. We are calculating over and over again, if we should take a risk. Here in the US, it's quite different. It is more like a trial by experience, we're going to experiment and if we fail, we're going to do another experiment or we adjust and if we succeed, then we are going to make it a product and we are going to sell it to the market." (Eric-Jan van Leeuwen, Login VSI). Vincent van de Poll adds: "I think entrepreneurship in Holland is sort of de-motivating, like don't take too many risks. Dutch people like the entrepreneurs who take risks but they even like it better, so it seems, when they fail. Quite strange." (Vincent van de Poll, GROM). Risk aversion in the Netherlands is a recurring theme among our Dutch entrepreneurs working and living in Silicon Valley. As Valentin Smirnoff states: "What I really struggled with in the Netherlands with just getting businesses off the ground, is that getting funding is harder because people are more skeptical and also risk aversive in a way." (Valentin Smirnoff, Wells

Fargo). Thijs Boekhoff pragmatically relates risk taking to the assets of an entrepreneur. "If you have $100 million it's not difficult to take risks. If you lose $10 million, it doesn't really matter." (Thijs Boekhoff, Ingen-Housz).

Startup failure is the flipside of (too much) risk taking, but is not framed in the negative way as it is in Europe or in the Netherlands. As media entrepreneur Neil Blaak argues: "here in the US you are supposed to learn from your mistakes, it is a positive thing here. There is no such thing as failing." (Neil Blaak, ZappoTV). Vincent van de Poll fully agrees: "I think there is a very clear distinction between the Dutch mentality and the American mentality in this aspect. Here it is 'fail often, fail fast'. The basic fear in the Netherlands is to lose everything when your startup fails, including your ego." Failing in the American perception is related to effort. As Arthur van Hoff explains: "If you really try but your startup fails because of an economic downturn or whatever, than people will say that it was a great learning experience." (Arthur van Hoff, Jaunt). Failing and innovation go together as Ronald Mannak claims. "The biggest thing of Silicon Valley is that it is okay to fail. There is no innovation if you cannot fail; then you'll play it safe and that's what happens in Europe. People in Europe start companies but they are usually consultancy firms. There is nothing wrong with that, but it is not about innovation and innovative startups as here in Silicon Valley." (Ronald Mannak, JumpCam). Harm TenHoff adds a slightly different perspective. "Also in Silicon Valley there is no success formula per se. So part of the failures here is also because of human failure, overstretching boundaries, and taking too many risks." (Harm TenHoff, BayLink).

We also asked our sample of Silicon Valley stakeholders on their views of risk proneness and failure acceptance. Here is Ian Sobieski's view: "I really notice a difference in the tolerance for failure. Here it is celebrated and anywhere else it is not celebrated. Here you share that you have lost money, in many other countries you are done." (Ian Sobieski, Band of Angels). Stanford professor Marguerite Gong Hancock has a somewhat different standpoint. "I don't particularly like that nomenclature because I think there is a danger in celebrating failure for its own sake. It is not the failure we are celebrating, it is the risk in learning, and failure is the byproduct not the goal." Mountain View's Chamber of Commerce president Ken Rosenberg clarifies failure tolerance as follows: "Americans have a perspective that there is nothing standing in your way towards your own goal other than yourself. If you fail in a business endeavor, it may be perceived as a personal failure, so you to do whatever it takes to succeed. But here in Silicon Valley there is a separation between personal failure and business failure. If you fail in business, you (and others) don't take that personally. It does not mean that you are an incapable entrepreneur or that I cannot do business with you because you failed at one business but are now trying another."(Ken Rosenberg. Mountain View Chamber of Commerce). Sean Randolph, Bay Area Council, sees it this way. "The business culture here is very receptive to entrepreneurial activity and very accepting of failure. If you take a risk there is a strong chance that you will fail, but the business culture will credit you for taking the risk." (Sean Randolph, Bay Area Council Economic Institute). Edwin Tan, staff member of Congressman Mike Honda, finally, points at the relationship between culture, entrepreneurship, and risk taking, and highlights the positive energy it generates. "This is a culture that does value risk and encourages individuals to take the opportunity to go out on their own. Silicon Valley is a positive risk environment that people find fascinating. They find it exciting; they want to know what your business is doing, what is new, how can you innovate a product to improve a process or solve a problem. This creates a 'buzz' that further reinforces the entrepreneurial and innovative culture in Silicon Valley. There is a culture of risk taking that is embraced and not a lot of stigma for failure." (Edwin Tan, District Director Congressman Mike Honda).

Cultural codes

Cultural conventions and cultural customs matter in social life, and they equally matter in business life. Misunderstandings about prevailing cultural codes can seriously impact business relations, especially in a cross-national context. Misinterpreting cultural business codes is a critical challenge for startups settling in a foreign country. Cultural values and norms may seem self-evident, but often they are not. This is even true for American culture that many European entrepreneurs feel familiar with. And it is even true for a highly cosmopolitan area such as Silicon Valley. Non-American startup founders need to know the cultural codes that typify the Valley's way of life and mindset. The meanings underlying these cultural signs need to be decoded and internalized in order to effectively function as a new venture entrepreneur. And to be able to interact and communicate capably in a professional business setting. But first of all to be proficient in dealing with (potential) customers and establish a record of mutual understanding and respect. Language is a prime source of miscommunication. Harm TenHoff has some interesting observations about language in the American business culture and the cross-national interpretation issues it may raise. "It starts with expectation and ambition levels. Silicon Valley innovations want to conquer the world. That is implicit in all business communication. When you talk to an American your words will be put in this context. Also, some-times the Dutch take things too literally compared to the American way. You have to cut through the niceties that people put in their communications here, which can be a marketing gimmick as well as just being polite. The level of politeness is like grease, like making things move very smoothly."

Dutch entrepreneurs also need to learn to be less blunt in their interac-tions with their American counterparts, because they do not always feel the sensitivities that are involved. Eric-Jan van Leeuwen agrees: "yes, so we need to be aware that we can be over the top in directness, absolutely". But he also points at some of the advantages: "We are very direct, in how we work, we will tell people if we don't like what they do and they are not used to that. But we also expect them to tell us if they don't like what we do. Our American clients came to appreciate that attitude. But there is a huge cultural difference for sure." Vincent van de Poll prides himself in being Dutch, "I am Dutch and I'm proud of it. I wear orange all the time. But I also feel we have to 'unDutch' ourselves. Have to get out of our comfort zone more and more often, compete with the top of the top, change our vision, focus more, invest more, and change our mentality."

Business dress codes are another source of cross-national cultural distinctiveness, including a light sense of disdain. Particularly between Americans and Europeans. The definitions of looking cool and being prop-erly dressed clearly differ at both sides of the ocean. Informal dress codes are the rule in Silicon Valley, even at what seem quite formal occasions. Vincent van de Poll, the youngest entrepreneur in our sample of startup founders, generally walks around in shorts, has a keen eye for the subtleties of (the absence of) dress codes. "How you look and dress is not important. If you watch the presentations given by Silicon Valley's top CEOs they are normally dressed in a T-shirt, jeans, and sneakers. In Europe you have to wear a suit and tie. There it is very important how you present yourself, here it is really important what you present." But there appears to be a gender bias in American dress codes. Women dress much more formally at business meetings than men do. We noticed that at the various business gatherings we attended ourselves. It obviously has to do with basic male/female role contrasts. Here is Marieke van der Poel's experience: "There is a very big difference between men and women in general in America, also in business. Here women always need to look like a woman, in Holland they don't. That means that here, women are women and men are men, and they treat each other differently." This is a classic description of a woman entrepreneur com-ing from a feminine country and struggling with the different (masculine) codes. Marieke van der Poel continues: "It is a very different interaction, and you have to be aware of being a woman here. You see a lot of women – and this is a frustration to me – using their femininity to get ahead which is something you really don't see in the Netherlands that much. You have to figure out how you are going to fit yourself into that and how you are going to keep your integrity. Especially in the startup community." (Marieke van der Poel, Proef Trend Forecasting). The gender difference between America and the Netherlands has been related to distinct and overlapping gender roles, respectively.[65] Dutch society strongly emphasizes equality, also between the sexes. But celebrating equality may have a price. As Ronald Mannak argues: "In Holland you don't want to stand out too much but here in Silicon Valley it is good to stand out." Ronald feels it is valuable to be part of two cultures. "There are good things about Dutch culture and there are bad things about Dutch culture, as there are good and bad things about American culture. I am very aware it's good to be in between the two cultures." Investor Cees Jan Koomen has an outspoken view on equality in the highly competitive startup business which could not be clearer: "Forget equality. This is a war, you should not be equal."

Coming back to the issue of the importance of equal relationships and non-hierarchical organizations, Marieke van der Poel shares the following comments. "What I realized is that the Dutch, more so than Americans, are still social people, social animals. I like to work in a flat environment and I will open myself up to being vulnerable. I will say there are things I can do, and there are things I cannot do. Dutch clients will ask me to tell exactly what I will be doing when they hire me, because I am the expert. I find this does not always work with American clients because they are more individualistic and hierarchically minded, especially in the field where I work. It is a very cut-throat industry, it has always been very tiered – unlike the startup community – and so it is hard to find people that are okay with a flat structure." Vincent van de Poll, finally, points at another striking cultural difference between America and the Netherlands which is related to the fact that in the beginning his startup would not allow him to have a salary. Americans understand this, the Dutch do not. "I have to explain to Dutch people that I did not have a salary for two years. We are raising money right now, not as a loan as is customary in the Netherlands but as an investment. Dutch people find this strange."

Work attitude, drive, and commitment

A returning theme in our explanation of the 'Silicon Valley Innovation & Startup Model' is the importance of ambition, passion, perseverance, and hard work. Without these four basic entrepreneurial qualities, new ventures are generally doomed to go down. They make the difference between life and death of a startup. It requires zeal, focus, energy, and determination to bring a new company to the next phase. Startup founders who lack these primary skills will face a hard time growing their new business. In combination these qualities and skills reflect the willpower of startup entrepreneurs to succeed. The culture of Silicon Valley is based on this collective drive to make the difference, to be goal-oriented, to cope with setbacks, and to aim high. It echoes an ethos that is at the heart of the Valley's entrepreneurial spirit and startup mentality.

Our startup entrepreneurs and Silicon Valley stakeholders clearly recognize and underline the interconnectedness of passion, commitment, and the right work attitudes. Being passionate and open to the business environment about your startup idea are essential traits. In the words of Rip Pruisken: "In the US people are open to new ideas and if you are able to convey yourself clearly, with confidence and with charisma, it will take you a long way. Once you start a new business here, be very open, be courageous, take calculated risk and seize every opportunity. I mean, who would have thought that our business could have become the leading wafel brand in the US from starting in a college dorm room?" (Rip Pruisken, Rip van Wafels). Salar al Khafaji shares this belief. "Once I was here, I felt this intangible feeling of optimism and energy. Two years ago I would tell someone my business idea that we were working on, everybody here was like 'that's an amazing vision, you should meet this person I know, I'll be happy to introduce you.' Most people in the Netherlands would question the idea and respond by 'will this work, isn't this or that a problem?'" (Salar al Khafaji, Silk). Ruben Daniëls affirms this observation. "For me it was like a cultural shock but in a positive sense. I was pleasantly surprised by the energy, the opportunities, the networking, things like that." (Ruben Daniëls, Cloud9 IDE). Arthur van Hoff relates this cultural difference to the pioneering history of California and Silicon Valley. As a startup entrepreneur "you are a pioneer, that's what you got to be. You got to be able to burn all your bridges and commit, and that is a very un-Dutch thing to do." Vincent van de Poll adds: "The biggest learning for me is how American entrepreneurs think about their business. They live for their work, it is their passion, they believe in their vision, they believe in their company." Thijs Boekhoff points at the fundamental role of mavericks in the Silicon Valley startup community. "There are shipments of mavericks here. There is no real appreciation for mavericks in Holland, because that's leveled out. The maverick, the nonconformist entrepreneur that is what drives the creativity and the business here." Vincent van de Poll has an ambitious vision too. "The two reasons that I started this company is that I want to change a part of the world with it for the better, and I want to make money because at some point I will sell the company (...). We will become the global leader in hybrid manufacturing. That is the only way for me to think now and that is a very American mindset."

Having the right work ethos is elementary for a startup to flourish and to quickly respond to market demands. Maarten Sierhuis has a clear opinion on work attitude differences between Silicon Valley and the Netherlands. "If I have to say something about the differences between Holland and here, it is definitely the mentality on what it means to work. I don't think it is normal that a person from Holland takes two jobs, like I do, and does not take any vacation for five years. That simply will not happen. Here it does. The same is true for working hours. By saying it is 'Friday afternoon four o'clock so I need to go home', you will not maintain yourself here." Maarten realizes that there is price to be paid. "I have a very nice life, a beautiful house in San Francisco, the only thing is that I worked very hard for it. The last six months it has been non-stop. I came home last night at nine, worked until one, and then got up at six this morning, and had a teleconference at seven. It goes on and on. There is never a moment where we can really let down. We need to find a better work-life balance." Other startup entrepreneurs recognize this view of finding a better balance. Vladimir Smirnoff formulates it this way: "I think you can still think big, have ambitions and big dreams, but it does not always mean that you have to go on steroids to achieve that. I became a little bit more relaxed myself, but it does not mean I don't dream big. But I think there are other ways of getting there than just trying to burn through investors, customers, apps, and pivots." But commitment, definitely, remains number one. "When you are in business, you are in business. You're 100% committed, you're 100% available. If you get a call at Friday night, then you react to that." (Jan Grotenbreg, SiliconValleyLink). Drive and determination matter. "If you start a business here you really have to show perseverance and just keep on going. At the end you get somewhere and you make it. That is the American thing that everybody is talking about and I think there is some truth in that." (Pieter Noordam, RFIsoft).

All our Silicon Valley stakeholders and experts emphasize the role of passion, ambition, and commitment. And the perpetual search for new ideas that shake markets. Edwin Tan explains that "the nature of Silicon Valley is not to maintain the status quo. The nature of Silicon Valley is to change, to innovate, and to create something new. Always improve, always be competitive." Investor and entrepreneur Cees Jan Koomen has an articulate view on the subject of drive and commitment: "The people who come to Silicon

Valley, the experts or the wizards, they want to do the work that will change the world. They want to have an impact, a good learning experience, and the excitement that goes with it (...). You have to be driven and excited, dream of nothing else than making your company successful." And you need to work extremely hard as Cees Jan points out: "In Silicon Valley you see people at 1 am sleeping under their desk, they wake up at seven and continue their work. They are passionate. People join a startup not because they immediately get a lot of money – they don't. Nor because they hope to become very rich. First of all it is the excitement, it is extremely interesting, and it is something they really want to do. The feeling that they can change the world." Eric Gabrys, Bay Area trade and investment commissioner at Brussels Invest & Export, states that "Silicon Valley is first in many things like the sharing economy and a lot of people are coming here not only to start business but also to be inspired by the best practices that they can find here and apply them in Europe. Silicon Valley to European entrepreneurs and startups is a very inspiring place." Nathalie Delrue-McGuire, honorary consul of Belgium in San Francisco and co-founder of BelCham Bay Area, nicely concludes: "The combination of talent and resources has created a unique opportunity for success. However, I personally do not think that the characteristics of success vary from country to country. Most of the successful companies I have experience with, share the common attributes of innovation, timing to market and passion for customer delight and experience. These seem to be common with American and European companies that are successful, based in Belgium, here or elsewhere. The environment and ecosystem that support innovation and entrepreneurship is also crucial for success, as well as for job creation. However, it is equally important to understand the business culture in the United States. Location does not necessarily equate success. The European Entrepreneurs who relocate to San Francisco or Silicon Valley are successful when they demonstrate those attributes I mentioned, but also put strong marketing and communications concepts at work in their personal interaction to clients, venture capitalists and partners. The passion, dedication, and work ethic in Silicon Valley are unmatched anywhere in the world. The culture teaches entrepreneurs that anything is possible. That also leads to the conversation about how we can promote, create and develop more ecosystems that are similar to Silicon Valley and now San Francisco – which is becoming the Silicon Valley by the way – back in Europe. This ultimately promotes job creation and growth."

Immigrants, as we described, greatly contributed to an ethnically diverse workforce and startup community in Silicon Valley. They are skilled and motivated software programmers and engineers, and as such are very much in demand by both hightech startups and existing companies. A substantial proportion of first-generation immigrants succeeded in building flourishing businesses that had a significant economic and cultural impact. Present day Silicon Valley would be unthinkable without its highly educated immigrant workforce and immigrant startups. Immigrants from India, China, Korea, and various European countries turned the Valley into a region for global talent that really marked the area out. As employees, as entrepreneurs, and as VCs. How do entrepreneurs – many of whom are immigrant or at least foreign startup founders themselves – and regional stakeholders see this role of immigrants and their impact on the economy and culture of Silicon Valley? Eric-Jan van Leeuwen points at the well-known melting pot phenomenon. "There is not one specific US culture in the Valley. There are many cultures: Indian people, Chinese people, immigrants from Europe, etc. Actually, I am now in an office building where Alibaba is next to me, so a lot of Chinese employees are working here. They are doing interesting stuff as you can imagine. So it is a blending of many different cultures that all have their main focus on innovation and entrepreneurship." Valentin Smirnoff admires this focus. "Half of the companies here in Silicon Valley are started by immigrants. That is essentially what I like about this culture, which you cannot pinpoint down to one dominating nationality or one race. I think that does kind of even things out." Pieter Bas Leezenberg relates immigrant entrepreneurship to the way he as a startup founder had to adjust to the prevailing culture of Silicon Valley. "When I came over I was hungry for success. But I saw those guys who came from India and China: the best of the best, the brightest, hardest-nosed business drive entrepreneurs from these massive countries who are all successful here. When you come from Holland you bring something here in the back of your mind that holds you back a lot. It took me a long time to adjust to the pace and the level of ambition here in Silicon Valley." (Pieter Bas Leezenberg, SkyGeo). Bay Area experts Marguerite Gong Hancock, Edwin Tan, and Sean Randolph have some interesting views on immigrant entrepreneurs too. "The Bay Area is like a magnet for attracting immigrant entrepreneurs. Particularly the Indian and Chinese businesses have been successful because they happen to have the updraft of being in the most important emerging markets: hardware, software, semiconductors." (Marguerite Gong Hancock). Immigrants are pioneers, they are highly motivated to thrive, and immigration requires risk taking; a mindset that is truly entrepreneurial. Edwin Tan fully agrees. "It is a risk to immigrate. So immigrants come with the right mentality and have the willingness to deal with uncertainty and adapt. And if you already have a good seed and you put them in the right environment, the right soil to produce, then the opportunities are greater out here than there might be in other places for immigrants to succeed." Marguerite does not think that immigrants caused the disruptive process of innovation that typifies Silicon Valley. Other cultural characteristics, in her opinion, are more decisive: the high degree of openness, fluidity, the general sense of optimism, and self-confidence. Quite different from many of the immigrants' home countries who show "a more stationary hierarchy of social and economic roles". The Bay Area's dominant culture welcomes immigrants and its self-confidence reinforces the belief among immigrants that "I am going to be the unusual one that will change the world". Sean Randolph, finally, also singles out tolerance and openness as two defining features of the Bay Area culture that are quite favorable to immigrants. "There is a real openness and tolerance to people who come from anywhere, as long as you are smart and contribute (...). These immigrant communities are very large, often in the tens or hundreds of thousands now. A high number of these people have been successful and many have in turn become VCs themselves. Or if they started something and cashed out, instead of going off to play golf you find them in a rented office or warehouse where they have created their own incubator and are mentoring new startups they've invested in. They are serial entrepreneurs and have done this three, four or five times. Their advantage comes not just from their financial resources, but from being able to repeat the process."

8.   Universities and R&D Labs

Higher education, innovation, and new ventures

Silicon Valley's unique R&D ecosystem is another cornerstone of its innovation and startup success. As part of the greater Bay Area it is the leading region for the development of new ideas, new technologies, and new business models. The global marketplace for innovation and invention. The key institution in our 'Silicon Valley Innovation & Startup Model' is higher education. The Bay Area is home to the worldwide foremost public and private research universities, renowned federal and state research institutes, independent research facilities, and corporate R&D labs. The University of California (UC) has four campuses in the area: Berkeley, San Francisco, Davis, and Santa Cruz. Stanford University, a private institution, is located in the heart of Silicon Valley: Palo Alto. Berkeley and Stanford rank among the world's best universities.[1] California State University (CSU) has two campuses in the Bay Area: San Francisco State University and San Jose State University. And there is Santa Clara University, a small private Jesuit institution. Combined these universities enroll about 175,000 students in the Bay Area, a quarter of which are graduate students. Furthermore, there is a widely branched system of California Community Colleges which serve as important feeders of the Bay Area's universities. The Foothill-De Anza Community College District, located in the center of Silicon Valley, enrolls about 65,000 students. Such large numbers of university and college students make for a huge pool of talent that hightech companies and startups are keen to recruit from. Talent is the most important resource of corporations and new ventures that live off innovation and new technologies, and the Bay Area's educational institutions have an excellent reputation in talent training. Both at the Bachelor's and the Masters level. The thousands of PhD students doing specialized dissertation projects notably add to the state-of-the art quality of education and research, and constitute a significant part of the Bay Area highly skilled talent pool and workforce.

But the innovation ecosystem is broader than universities alone. There are many public and private, federal and state, independent and corporate research institutes and laboratories active in the area that have a solid reputation as regards innovation and R&D. They often work closely together in their respective fields of expertise. The Bay Area Council Research Institute has listed these non-university research institutes and laboratories and the result is impressive.[2] Among them are: Lawrence

Berkeley National Laboratory, Lawrence Livermore National Laboratory, Sandia National Laboratories, SLAC National Accelerator Laboratory, NASA Ames Research Center, Joint Genome Institute, SRI International, PARC, Electric Power Research Institute, QB3, CITRIS, California Institute for Regenerative Medicine, Buck Institute for Research on Ageing, Ernest Gallo Clinic and Research Center, Joint BioEnergy Institute, and of course the many (over thirty) corporate in-house R&D laboratories. These outstanding universities, research institutes, and laboratories attract the best and brightest researchers from all over the world. For those academics the Bay Area is a matchless innovation magnet, the place to pursue their career as hightech driven researchers who want to work in the most challenging and competitive environment.

This advanced and interconnected Bay Area network of knowledge institutions was built in over more than six decades, an ecosystem that has a long tradition of linking academia and industry, of launching startups that commercialize innovations and inventions. The four UC campuses alone are good for nearly 1,800 patents and 3,000 active inventions.[3] For real entrepreneurial talent, the Bay Area and its center Silicon Valley is the premier hotspot for the commercialization of research output into marketable products and services. Traditional niches are information and communications technology, greentech, cleantech, and life sciences. Universities and other centers of innovative research, as we saw in Chapter 2, always emphasized the importance of applied knowledge, of practical innovations that could be commercialized. Startup spinoffs played and play a pivotal role in prototyping new ideas and new technologies, in creating new products and services, and in bringing innovations to the market. This entrepreneurial emphasis marked the Silicon Valley academic mindset. No ivory tower science, but advanced research on innovative solutions to practical problems. As Emilio Castilla and his co-authors conclude: "the educational sector has been especially vital because the constant movement back and forth between industry and university has blurred the boundaries of both and created elaborate social networks that keep academic research focused on practical problems, and infuse industrial activity with up-to-date science".[4]

The broad array of institutions for higher education shaped the region's innovation capital which together with its networked infrastructure is the main impetus behind the perpetual dynamic of new startups. A dynamic that has created a unique and resilient value chain of new ventures. It has produced world-class hightech companies that left their innovative footprint.

In this chapter, we will look in more detail at two of the main institutions for higher learning in the Bay Area: Berkeley and Stanford University. Their impact on innovation, entrepreneurship, and new venture formation has been impressive. Both research universities have a deep history in cutting-edge technological innovation, in educating leading entrepreneurs, and in facilitating startup creation. We will therefore mainly focus on these two institutes, and briefly address the entrepreneurship activities of San Francisco State University, San Jose State University, and Santa Clara University, as well as the aforementioned research labs.

Berkeley

Founded in 1868, Berkeley, University of California, developed into a premier US public university with an outstanding record of educational excellence. It is among the leading research universities in the world. Serving over 37,000 students (27,000 undergraduates, 10,500 graduates) under the motto "Fiat lux" (Let there be light), Berkeley is a highly competitive institution for higher education. It has an acceptance ratio of 17 percent and a 17:1 student-to-faculty[5] ratio. No less than 29 Nobel prizes are held by Berkeley alumni, and current faculty holds 3 Fields Medals and 4 Pulitzer Prizes. Through its top quality educational and research programs it has contributed substantially to the advanced Bay Area ecosystem. In fact, it is one of the anchors. Its focus on innovation and entrepreneurship had a major economic impact on the region and helped the creation of new ventures with national and global significance. The ability of Berkeley "to produce graduates and attract faculty who found companies and translate knowledge into products and service has made the University an invaluable economic asset and a large-scale platform for growth an innovation".[6] It presently holds almost 1,400 active inventions and over 680 active patents. Since 1990 more than 145 companies have been founded under the umbrella of Berkeley's IP licenses.[7] Pioneering companies started by Berkeley graduates and alumni include such illustrious examples as Intel, Apple, Sybase, Oracle, Sun Microsystems, Gap, and early biotechnology companies such as Chiron Corporation, Tularik, Exelixis, and Renovis. Other successful Berkeley startups are Revolution Foods, Keyhole (which became Google Earth), Marvell Technology Group, Linear Technology Corporation, Cepheid, Enphase Energy, Net App, VMware, DigitalGlobe, Saba Software, Proactive Business Solutions, Point Source Power, Riverbed Technology, Baidu, and Tesla Motors.[8]

A 2012 study among Berkeley alumni and faculty identified over 3,700 startup founders that launched companies that are still active.[9] One out of five founders turned out to be female, a proportion that increased over the last years. Over two-thirds of founders earned a graduate degree; interestingly more than 60 percent has a law or letters & science (humanities, life sciences, computer science) degree and slightly over 20 percent an engineering or business degree. The economic impact of companies started by Berkeley founders is enormous. Based on a smaller company sample (N=2,610) it could be determined that these companies employ over half a million employees and annual revenues over $315 billion. Manufacturing (computers, electronics) dominates this picture, followed by computer systems design and related services. Totaling direct, indirect, and induced economic impact of companies founded by Berkeley alumni, graduates, and faculty, yields a figure of almost 1,250,000 jobs and $238 billion in national output (the value of goods and services produced).[10] Federal, state, and local tax revenues amount to almost 11.5 percent ($24.4 billion).

The conclusion is clear: Berkeley startup founders added considerably to the creation of new economic value in the Bay Area, California, and across the United States, in terms of employment, revenues, and economic output. How does the university succeed in being so successful in 'producing' new venture entrepreneurs? In having such an impact on the ecosystem for entrepreneurship and innovation? The answer lies in two main factors: the way Berkeley creates but in turn also profits from the Bay Area advanced ecosystem (access to venture capital, talent pool of faculty and students, pro-innovation and entrepreneurial culture, professional support networks, high concentration of other research institutes, government RD funding), and the way Berkeley organizes its internal ecosystem. How does the university encourage and strengthen innovative startups? What are the main programs and facilities that promote new ventures? We already mentioned the number of active patents and active inventions which indicates Berkeley's track record of innovativeness and applicability of its research output. This track record is reflected in the impressive number of startups that aim at commercializing and marketing of these patents and inventions. In terms of organizational streamlining the university established (in 2004) the Office of Intellectual Property and Industry Research (IPIRA) to create a "one-stop shop" for industry to partner with. The main focus is on sponsored research and commercial technology transfer. Some 170 startups have been founded to commercialize IP rights under license from Berkeley. Between 2007 and 2012 these startup companies raised over $1.3 billion and 65 startups raised an average of $13.8 million in private funding. Of these startup companies, 45% are in the life science sector, 26% in information technology, 15% in electronics and hardware, and 12% are in cleantech and energy.[11] The Lester

Center for Entrepreneurship at the Haas School of Business has a prominent position in Berkeley's internal startup ecosystem. Established in 1991 the mission of Lester School, named after sponsor Howard Lester, chairman of Williams-Sonoma, is "to redefine how we do business" and "to drive positive, disruptive change to society by building scalable enterprises".[12] The Center teaches leading edge entrepreneurial competencies, VC financing, and startup skills. Its research focus is on innovation. There is intensive interaction between the university community and the business community. Many classes are taught by experienced entrepreneurs and startup founders, VCs, and business executives.

There is a wide variety of business competitions, including the UC Berkeley Startup Competition, the VC Investment Competition, and the Intel Global Challenge. Multidisciplinarity and experimental learning are educational priorities; the business focus is on technology-enabled and socially responsible companies. The Fung Institute for Engineering Leadership of the College of Engineering, founded in 2010, offers advanced programs that transform engineers into leaders who are risk-prone and innovation driven.[13] The institute closely works together with Bay Area and Silicon Valley companies. Cleantech to Market (C2M) and Bio-Manufacturing to Market are examples of two partnerships between students, scientists, engineers, and leading business professionals to transfer innovative technologies into market-ready opportunities and startups.[14] The Bakar Fellows Program supports innovative research by early career faculty and helps them with the valorizing and commercialization of their research.[15] QB3 (the California Institute of Quantitative Biosciences) is a special UC program on life sciences and its commercial applications.[16] It offers postdoctoral students and faculty a variety of opportunities to take their research to the market, including lab space and incubator use ("The Garage"). The Foundry@CITRUS is a Berkeley incubator that helps startups at the intersection of hardware, software, and services.[17] It does so via offering workspace, prototyping, seed funding, investor pitch sessions, and on-demand mentorship. SkyDeck, a business accelerator, is a relatively new Berkeley initiative, created in 2011. Its mission is to assist startup entrepreneurs to grow their business into sustainable companies.[18] The SkyDeck facilities (10,000 sq. ft. of office space) provide startup entrepreneurs in residence access to Berkeley's resources and networks of serial entrepreneurs, investors, and academics.[19]

The Center for Entrepreneurship and Technology (CET) offers courses for engineers and scientists how to improve their innovation and entrepreneurial skills. Both for existing and new enterprises. It uses a unique pedagogy based on three interconnected layers of theory, entrepreneurial mindset, and new venture networks. A prime method is the use of a game-based learning approach to develop the entrepreneurial mindset and skills that new ventures need.[20] A final example of Berkeley's flourishing ecosystem for innovation and entrepreneurship is the Berkeley Postdoctoral Entrepreneur Program (BPEP), which aims at promoting entrepreneurship among the university's graduate and postgraduate community. The main goal is to bring innovative research outcomes to the marketplace.[21] Besides these formal research and training institutes promoting new ventures, Berkeley has a lively culture of lectures, workshops, meetings with celebrated entrepreneurs, student competitions, hackathons, etc., which reflects a dynamic environment for startup enthusiasts. One of our favorites initiatives is Bigideas@berkeley, an annual contest in which interdisciplinary student teams pitch "big ideas" and receive mentor and funding support to further develop their ideas. "The Contest challenges students to step outside of their traditional university-based academic work, take a risk, and use their education, passion, and skills to work on problems important to them."[22] Finding solutions to often pressing contemporary social problems such as clean and sustainable energy alternatives, social justice, food system innovations, global health, conflict and development, mobiles for reading, and scaling up big ideas. Bigideas@berkeley is Silicon Valley thinking in a nutshell.

Stanford University

Stanford, founded in 1885, ranks among the most prestigious US and global universities. It enrolls about 16,000 students, the majority (slightly over 9,000) of which are graduate students. Its student-to-faculty ratio is 4:1. Stanford, a private university, has as its motto: "The wind of freedom blows".[23] The university's extraordinary track record and reputation is indicated by the fact that 31 Stanford-faculty have won the Nobel Prize since the foundation of the university and 21 Nobel laureates are currently members of the Stanford community. In Chapter Two, we sketched some of the historical contributions of Stanford University to the shaping of Silicon Valley's exceptional and deep ecosystem. It is difficult to imagine the vitality of this ecosystem without the distinguished role the university played in by now over a century. The focus on outstanding applied research, integrating theory and practice, linking business and research, turning faculty innovations into business, supporting students to set up startups, cherishing liberal faculty consultancy policies, are all ingredients of Stanford's eminent academic and new ventures portfolio. Since the 1930s, over

330,000 patents have been generated by Stanford alumni and faculty. Almost 40,000 active companies are Stanford spinoffs which together produce annual revenues of $2.7 trillion and 5.4 million jobs.[24] Eesley and Miller state that "if these companies collectively formed an independent nation, its estimated economy would be the world's 10th largest".[25] According to the Stanford Innovation Survey, some 18,000 businesses headquartered in California are founded by Stanford alumni, with annual sales of about $1.27 trillion and over 3 million employees.[26] Furthermore, some 30,000 nonprofit organizations have been established by Stanford people. The same survey observed that about 1,000 companies were started by students while still enrolled at Stanford or within one year of their graduation. We already mentioned some of the most formidable companies that can directly be traced to Stanford alumni and faculty, such as Hewlett-Packard, Google, Nike, Cisco, Sun, Yahoo, Gap, VMware, PayPal, LinkedIn, and Tesla. Companies that lead their industry, changed the world, changed the way we live and work, and the way we communicate, interact, and network. Their economic, social, and cultural impact is beyond imagination. The most powerful example likely is Google – which "epitomizes the entrepreneurial culture at Stanford"[27] – an extremely successful hightech company with a global reach that dramatically disrupted and innovated the Internet. A company with sales of about $60 billion (2014), taking third place (after Apple and Hewlett-Packard) in Silicon Valley's annual company revenue rankings.[28] In 2010, 53 Stanford-affiliated Silicon Valley companies reported $34 billion in income with a total market capitalization of $650 billion.[29] Besides their financial and economic impact these companies provide internships and jobs for Stanford students. Stanford has internship agreements with e.g. Facebook, LinkedIn, and Palantir Technologies. Companies profit from Stanford and Stanford benefits from companies. It is a classic and tested win-win formula.

Looking at trends in startups founded by Stanford alumni over the last six decades, some changes can be observed. In the 1950s the main focus was on electronics, communications, and publishing; the 1990s saw a shift towards software and Internet industries; and the 2000s witnessed a change towards cleantech and energy. It is estimated that funds raised by Stanford startup founders after 1990 amount to $88 billion. The Stanford Office of Technology Licensing (OTL), created in 1970, is responsible for licensing technologies invented by the university's faculty, in particular to startup companies but also to existing ventures.[30] It claims to have disclosed about 8,300 inventions in the last forty years, generating $1.7 billion in revenues for the university. About 10-15% of OTL's licenses have an equity term. "For institutional conflict-of-interest reasons and insider trading concerns, the Stanford Management Company sells our public equities as soon as Stanford is allowed to liquidate rather than holding equity to maximize return."[31] In 2013-14, Stanford received about $110 million from 655 licensed technologies. Some of the most notable and profitable Stanford inventions include recombinant DNA, FM sound synthesis, fiber optic amplifier, functional antibodies, and improved hypertext searching.[32] The business model is quite straightforward: after deducting OTL's expenses, net royalties are divided by thirds: one-third goes to the inventor (faculty member), one-third to the inventor's department, and one-third to the inventor's school. Entrepreneurship among faculty is encouraged by individual financial incentives, but also by granting faculty members one day per week for business consultancy or longer leaves for the commercialization of innovative technologies, e.g. in creating a startup. These liberal policies go way back. In fact, as we described in Chapter Two, Frederick Terman, Stanford's visionary Dean of the Engineering School and later provost from the mid-1940s to the mid-1960s, already launched this consultancy model. Furthermore, Stanford has a President's Venture Fund for early stage startup companies which have licensed Stanford technology. In 2011 the fund invested over $28 million in about 30 businesses, with company investments ranging from $600,000 to $5 million.[33] *CB Insights* did a study of angel and VC funding to startups founded by US university alumni in the 2007-2011 period. It turned out that Stanford University ($4.3 billion) was number one, with Berkeley University ($1.3 billion) in third place.[34]

What are the main Stanford educational programs aimed at promoting innovation, entrepreneurship, and the creation of new ventures? Without pretending to be all-inclusive, the following programs, projects, and initiatives need to be mentioned. What is the underlying philosophy? According to former Stanford provost William Miller and his co-author Charles Eesley (School of Engineering) "Stanford's approach is to encourage proximity and the back-and-forth exchange that occurs between the campus community and fledgling and established businesses. The university understands it is vital to provide an environment that shows young entrepreneurs how it can be done, how the transfer of technology can take place, how an idea can become a product. This approach has proven successful across many startups and industry sectors."[35] One of the most visible and active programs on promoting and researching entrepreneurship is the Stanford Technology Ventures Program (STVP), founded in 1996 within the School of Engineering.[36] Its focus is on accelerating hightech entrepreneurship. It offers 27 introductory and advanced undergraduate and graduate courses on entrepreneurship and innovation, as well extracurricular programs, on a wide variety of subjects such as startup formation, leadership, creativity, strategy, lean startups, finance and accounting, marketing, organizational behavior, and law and patents. STVP's multidisciplinary master's and doctoral research program on entrepreneurship and innovation have a combined theoretical and applied emphasis on information and web technologies, medical devices, cleantech energy, and robotics. Research is conducted in close collaboration with the business community. Many leading entrepreneurs, venture capitalists, and successful startup founders participate in STVP. A strong point of the program is that it trains students in personal skills and competencies that are decisive in the world of business and professional nonprofit organizations. STVP also organizes the annual Mayfield Fellows Program, a nine-month combined study-internship program for a select group of Stanford undergraduate students. The program provides an intensive (theoretical and practical) entrepreneurship education for highly motivated students into the basics of innovation, creativity, and strategy and trains them in the leadership skills necessary to build new ventures. Part of the program is a paid summer internship at one of Silicon Valley's innovative early-stage startups. Stanford students Kevin Systrom and Mike Krieger, founders of Instagram, were awarded Mayfield fellowships. Another interesting STVP initiative is LaunchPad, a course offered by its Hasso Platner Institute of Design, which teaches graduate students all the different startup stages and the challenges that go with it.[37] From idea, prototyping, pricing, marketing, to selling; from design thinking to go-to-market and "the joy of success and the (passing) pain of failure along the way". Each team is being treated as a real startup and the bar is set high as it informs students: "If you do not have a passionate and overwhelming urge to start a business or launch a product or service, this class will not be a fit." STVP also hosts a very popular Entrepreneurship Corner, a website that offers free on-line access to over 3,000 videos and podcasts featuring entrepreneurship and innovation thought leaders (including Mark Zuckerberg, Larry Page, Marissa Mayer, Jack Dorsey, Melinda Gates, Reid Hoffman).[38] ECorner aims to support faculty around the world who teach courses on innovative entrepreneurship. A final triumph was that in 2011 the National Science Foundation (NSF) awarded a $10 million grant to the STVP program to launch a national center of innovation and entrepreneurship in the field of engineering. Epicenter as the nationwide initiative is called, located at the Stanford campus, aims at integrating innovative and entrepreneurial thinking in undergraduate engineering education.[39]

The Stanford Entrepreneurship Network (SEN) functions as the single point of contact on all Stanford's entrepreneurship activities (education, research, and outreach).[40] It is an umbrella organization that offers learning, exchange, and networking opportunities to Stanford students, faculty, and staff, as well as organizations that are actively engaged in studying entrepreneurship. In this sense it strengthens Stanford's internal entrepreneurship and innovation ecosystem. SEN advances a multidisciplinary mindset among the campus entrepreneurship community.

The Center for Entrepreneurial Studies (CES) of the Graduate School of Business is another leading Stanford institution on entrepreneurial and innovative thinking.[41] The mission of CES is to support outstanding research and education on entrepreneurship, to inspire and enable Stanford students and alumni to start new ventures, and to link Stanford with the greater business community. It offers a wide variety of internal and external multidisciplinary entrepreneurship courses. From MBA to executive education, from online courses to PhD programs. A most interesting CES initiative is the Stanford Venture Studio, a learning facility for all Stanford graduate students who have a passion for entrepreneurship on how to build sustainable and high-impact businesses.[42] The Venture Studio program offers one-to-one mentorship, practical skills training, and involvement of experienced entrepreneurs and VCs. Recently CES started Stanford Ignite, an international certificate program that teaches innovators to formulate, develop, and commercialize their ideas.[43] Another CES program worthwhile mentioning is SEED (Stanford institute for innovation in developing countries) that aims at fighting poverty through innovation, entrepreneurship, and the growth of businesses in the developing world.[44] BioDesign, finally, is a multidisciplinary program working at the interface of biology and medicine that focuses on the invention and implementation of health technologies.[45] Market transfer of new biomedical technologies is a major purpose of BioDesign.

These example show the commitment of Stanford to promoting innovative entrepreneurship and to creating a stimulating startup culture. Like Berkeley, the emphasis is on collaboration between the academic and the business community, by involving students, faculty, and business leaders.[46] The vibrant nature of Stanford's entrepreneurial ecosystem is also shown by the numerous Stanford workshops, seminars, events, and presentations during the year on innovative entrepreneurship. Including many high-level conferences. A fine example is the DFJ Entrepreneurial Leaders Series which for more than two decades has featured talks by business leaders and startup founders on innovation and entrepreneurship.[47] The vitality of this ecosystem is also indicated by active student organizations such as BASES, the Business Association of Stanford Entrepreneurial Students ("Empowering the next generation of Stanford entrepreneurs and beyond".)[48] BASES organizes student startup competitions, connects student entrepreneurs, and offers hackspace, a facility to speed up the growth of the hacker community at Stanford by e.g. organizing hackathons. Another good example is StartX, a student-run accelerator, founded by a former Stanford graduate.[49] StartX is not part of Stanford but the University participates through its network, expertise, and by funding some of the operational costs. Startup mentorship is provided by Silicon Valley entrepreneurs and VCs. The accelerator has supported quite a number of startups; who managed to raise an average of $2.2 million.[50] Nice detail: StartX' new headquarters on Hanover Street, Palo Alto, has a lift where startup founders can practice their elevator pitch in the most literal sense. As it is a two-floor building, the pitch has to be done in ten seconds.

San Francisco State University and San Jose State University

Both metropolitan California State public universities differ from Berkeley and Stanford in its focus on undergraduate and graduate teaching. They don't have PhD programs. San Francisco State University (SFU), founded in 1899, has almost 30,000 students. Its motto is 'Experientia Docet' (Experience teaches). SFU's College of Business ("we make innovation happen") teaches courses on entrepreneurship, has a Business Partner program, and its College of Business Enterprises is oriented towards graduate business education, executive education, consulting, and business incubation. San Jose State University (SJSU), located in the heart of Silicon Valley was founded in 1857, and is the oldest public school for higher education in California. SJSU enrolls almost 33,000 students and claims that Silicon Valley companies employ more graduates from SJSU than from any other university. Its motto is "Powering Silicon Valley". The university prides itself with the *Forbes* ranking of SJSU as one of the top 20 "Colleges that will make you rich". The Lucas College and Graduate School of Business is a particular SJSU niche institution for promoting entrepreneurship and teaching leadership skills, and closely works together with the Silicon Valley business community. Its Silicon Valley Center for Entrepreneurship interacts with businesses and investors in the Valley, organizes student business plan competitions, prepares students for creating new ventures, connects student teams with entrepreneurs to commercialize innovative ideas, and organizes the Silicon Valley Innovation Challenge.[51]

Santa Clara University

A Jesuit university, founded in 1851, serving 8,800 students under the motto 'Ad majorem Dei Gloriam' (For the greater glory of God). Many of the innovation and new venture courses and studies are organized within the Leavey School of Business of Santa Clara University (SCU).[52] Its focus is on innovative learning, blending theory and practice, business ethics, leadership skills, and finding inspiration in the Jesuit tradition and in the Silicon Valley entrepreneurial spirit. The Business School organizes the annual California Program for Entrepreneurship (CAPE), which provides training of new startup entrepreneurs to sharpen and implement their business plans, fund raising and pitching, and go-to-market strategy.[53] Mentorship is offered by veteran entrepreneurs. CAPE aims at emerging startups that will contribute to the growth and well-being of the Californian economy.

Concerns

Universities and research labs in the Bay Area are the pillars of the region's innovation and startup model. Particularly in the way they collaborate with industry, and vice versa. This state of affairs has resulted in a rich innovation ecosystem that is unique in the world. But there are worries too. Its success should not be taken for granted. For ecosystems to stay the driving force behind new ideas and new technologies, they require thorough maintenance and periodic upgrading, financial robustness and budgetary stability. And at these points universities in Silicon Valley and the greater Bay Area face serious problems, especially public universities that depend on government money. Federal R&D spending has stagnated in the US, and in California the state budget on higher education showed considerable cuts in the last decades. Higher education's share of state budget expenditures has dropped from 18% in 1977 to under 12% today; one third less. This drop in financial support for higher education particularly hurts California's public universities and colleges, having a share of 90% of student education. The Bay Area Council Economic Institute presents some further revealing and quite dramatic figures.[54] Since 1990 state financial support for student education has dropped by 60 percent and is now at the level of 1998 when the University of California had 75,000 fewer students. The situation is not much different at the California State University: state support declined from $3 billion (in 2007) to $2 billion, a drop of almost 40 percent. The budget pressures on the California Community Colleges are also felt. The Silicon Valley Foothill-De Anza Community College District has seen a budget cut of 20% since 2008 and had to significantly reduce its student enrollment. Such drastic state budget cuts leave deep marks and affect the functioning of the public ecosystem for higher learning in the region. The California public educational ecosystem, so it seems, has to reinvent itself – including its business model – to meet these extraordinary financial challenges and to secure its outstanding reputation.[55]

Entrepreneurs on universities and R&D labs

Higher education and startups

We now turn to the opinions of our sample of startup entrepreneurs on the role of public and private institutions of higher education in the Valley; and more specifically on its contribution to the founding of new ventures. To take a slightly broader view, this section will also include beliefs of Silicon Valley stakeholders. Not all of our entrepreneurs are closely working together with universities and R&D labs, though all of them underline the vital importance of the Valley's excellent knowledge infrastructure. Marguerite Gong Hancock, prominent Stanford professor of innovation and entrepreneurship, points at the long-standing emphasis at her university on applied research and practical applications. Practical learning was and is essential. The accentuation of linking knowledge and business inspired a strong tradition of launching startups. But Marguerite also stresses that students do not come to Stanford to start businesses, they come to be educated. They first of all enroll to get an outstanding education. She outlines that the primary purpose of facilitating startups "is not with financial gain. If you look at Stanford – and this is not just words and policies – its mission is to accelerate, expand, and extend the usefulness of knowledge for social good." Conflicts of interest need to be avoided. Stanford, for instance, does not allow its professors to serve on a board of a company founded by students that are currently enrolled. But the university "absolutely does believe that startups are an amazing way to help grow new businesses, to facilitate innovation and new company growth which leads to new jobs and economic development. Our curriculum teaches research-based evidence as well as cases for entrepreneurship that actually facilitate business models, creativity, and team development." Stanford has its own venture lab, physical and "mind spaces" for new startups, for student team building, and for involving Valley entrepreneurs. The university aims to integrate its various interfaculty entrepreneurship activities. Interdisciplinary collaboration, affirms Marguerite Gong Hancock, is the leading thought. "About then years ago, we created a network that actually brought all the entrepreneurship related activities and initiatives together: research, education, curriculum, office technology, licensing, and created a one stop portal. Because the one thing we definitely have learned is that transformative disruptive innovation often happens at the edge of disciplines." Part of Stanford's innovation success is its longstanding policy to allow professors to commercialize innovations and inventions. Investor Cees Jan Koomen believes this is a major asset. "Stanford has extremely liberal policies for the professors to step away and do entrepreneurial activities. It doesn't interfere with their tenure ship path or their salaries. So there is a lot of professors with startups involved or having startups on the side." (Cees Jan Koomen).

Sean Randolph, president of the Bay Area Council Economic Institute, points at the unique combination of hard and soft infrastructure in the region. "The region has what might be the world's largest aggregation of R&D capacity. There are five campuses of the University of California, Stanford, five national laboratories, and lots of collaborative research laboratories that engage multiple campuses of universities, engage national laboratories with universities, and engage private companies with universities. Some of those are very consciously designed to facilitate cross investment between corporate research and universities. So there is a deep infrastructure and capacity for R&D that attracts bright people, and many of those, because of the business opportunities just outside the door, get the idea to start a company." Having studied at Stanford or Berkeley also brings the right networks that are very helpful for starting entrepreneurs in the Valley and the larger Bay Area. It provides, says Dutch entrepreneur Jan Grotenbreg, access to people, funding, and technology. "There is a glass ceiling if you want to call it that way. I mean if you come from Stanford by the Stanford circuit or from Berkeley by the Berkeley circuit, there is a lot of successful business people that will help you with getting capital or connections." (Jan Grotenbreg, SiliconValleyLink).

Students themselves are explicitly looking for the integration of university and the startup culture. As Waad Jaradat, student Software Engineering, explains: "one of our professors [at SJSU, PE/AM] used to work for Adobe. He told us a lot about his work as a software engineer there, and that was really interesting. I learned very much from that." Also Alexandre Gallardo, studying Business, looks outside for inspiration: "the high ambitions in the Valley to me are very positive".

Going for excellence

Dutch entrepreneur Adrie Reinders serves on a US university board and believes this is a good way to link business and higher education. The Netherlands and other European countries can learn from this: "you have to bring in experienced entrepreneurs in the educational system." (Adrie Reinders, EFactor). Vincent van de Poll also underscores the importance of strengthening the relationship between track record entrepreneurs and universities. But more needs to be done in his view. Based on his personal experience in the Dutch educational system he passionately pleads for raising the bar among students. Seeing the dedication and commitment of students in Silicon Valley, he feels that Dutch (and European) students need to do a much better job. A student culture of excellence and entrepreneurship must be developed. "Our standards are too low, it is easy for students to get away with a mediocre performance. The grading system is terrible."

Silicon Valley universities may also serve as an example, according to Dutch entrepreneurs, in the way they are involved in innovative startup activities and intellectual property issues. Serial entrepreneur Arthur van Hoff: "The problem with innovation in the Netherlands is that universities own the intellectual property of whatever you have invented. Here universities tell you well, while here you invent something you start a company and they say I have a right to invest, I've a right to give you more money." (Arthur van Hoff, Jaunt). Entrepreneur Pieter Bas Leezenberg had a different experience: "You know what, I remember when I went to Stanford I had to sign a little pink paper stating that whatever I invent there is the property of Stanford University." (Pieter Bas Leezenberg, SkyGeo). Van Hoff, however, claims that the reason it works in Silicon Valley is "that it is not an endless battle of who owns what. The university basically just says let me give you some money so that we can share in your success." It is a fundamental cross-continental difference in framing the role of universities in supporting startups. It makes Ronald Mannak think of the way some university-based incubators operate in the Netherlands: "startups have to pay the incubator to be part of their system. So they don't invest in companies but companies have to pay. It will not work." (Ronald Mannak, JumpCam). Band of Angel investor and VC startup funder Cees Jan Koomen is less pessimistic, at least as regards certain concerns. "My own experience is that Dutch universities are really good, you get good talent, and that good talent wants to go to

Silicon Valley. They already made up their mind." But the university curriculum should be much more organized around "practical innovations based on faculty research and on how to build some business out of it. Real startup companies, with real numbers, real cases. We have to create the best learning experience. The university has to be very eager to build an ecosystem, so that their PhD students and graduates have an easy entrance into the startup business. Of course they still have to do the heavy lifting. But the road to entrepreneurship needs to be made more smoothly. I think that is the way to do it."

9. Government

Demystifying the role of government

By way of an opening statement: the idea that the US government did and does not interfere in innovation policy is a myth and needs serious debunking. It is a myth that is both cherished by European observers and American entrepreneurs alike, though from different perspectives. European observers typically think that the US government leaves innovation policy to free market forces, whereas American entrepreneurs routinely believe that government as a rule should (and does) stay out of business and innovation. Reality, however, is quite different. The stereotyped vision of a passive government that only indirectly supports innovation and innovative startups should be discredited. US federal policies focusing on the development of advanced technologies actually made a substantial difference.

   In Chapter Two it was demonstrated that the US government played a proactive and highly significant role through its massive funding of defense and space research. Particularly during both World Wars and the Cold War period. Moreover, the American government was a driving force behind the development of the Internet, and invested considerably in health technology and nanotechnology. The 1981 R&D tax credit law was an important policy instrument that facilitated and enhanced investments by companies in basic research and development activities. The previous chapter on the role of universities in creating Silicon Valley's advanced ecosystem showed the great historic impact of federal funding of basic research by these renowned both public and private institutes of higher learning and by independent research laboratories. Which is still true today. As the Bay Area Science & Innovation Consortium Report concludes: "No other region in the United States or in the world has more federally funded research centers and laboratories."[1] Stanford University, a world class private university, gets over 80% of its more than 5,300 externally sponsored projects (totaling $1.33 billion in 2014-2015) funded through federal money.[2] Mariana Mazzucato, professor in the economics of innovation, University of Sussex, is quite accurate in her conclusion that "despite the perception of the US as the epitome of private sector-led wealth creation, in reality it is the State that has been engaged on a massive scale in entrepreneurial risk taking to spur innovation". (...) "The insight gained is that other than being an entrepreneurial society, a place where it is culturally natural to start and grow a business, the US is also a place where the State plays an entrepreneurial role, by making investments in radical new areas."[3] Mazzucato, a leading thinker on innovation, shows how Apple – the acclaimed champion of free market technology that revolutionized the computer industry – clearly benefited from federally funded technological developments. The iPhone, she argues, would not have been possible without the integration of state-funded technologies. She also adds that the algorithm underlying Google's search machines was funded by a National Science Foundation (NSF) grant. Apple and Google may not be the contemporary giants of innovation without the initial catalyst function of the government. Silicon Valley, so it seems, is less of a shining example of free market capitalism than the technology debate wants us to believe. Reality is more complex. As Harvard professor Josh Lerner concludes: "The public sector did play a key role in shaping the evolution of Silicon Valley." (...) "...far from a creation of unfettered capitalism."[4] But the pushing role of federal government should not mask the fact that public innovation policies were sometimes badly designed and lacked implementation effectiveness. Lerner's challenging book *Boulevard of Broken Dreams* provides a rich insight in ill-conceived and non-effective government programs in many nations around the globe aiming at stimulating innovation and entrepreneurship. Failing government intervention is firstly due to not understanding venture capital and entrepreneurial markets: bad timing (short-run orientation), bad program sizing (too small or too large incentives), and lack of flexibility (coping with uncertainty); and secondly due to pursuing a top-down approach which alienates venture capitalists and entrepreneurs from taking their place in the innovation process. Lerner's examples illustrate the vital importance of effective incentive schemes, well-designed program implementation, and rigorous evaluations of government venturing programs.

New laws, new programs, new roles

The role of US government in accelerating technological development, however, was not restricted to funding basic research and providing innovation incentives and subsidies. Government also acted as a law and rule maker, launching customer, stimulator of small business participation, and visa supplier, in stimulating innovative entrepreneurship, and in securing the collective innovation agenda.[5] A specifically stimulating law was the Bayh-Dole Act of 1980, which regulated the transfer of property rights of federally funded research to the university or the research laboratory.[6] The new act designed a uniform federal patent policy which greatly motivated and stimulated universities and other institutes (including nonprofits and small businesses) to commercialize innovations, inventions, and knowledge they developed in government-funded projects and programs. Through the new property rights system, the law shifted the incentive structure of bringing patented innovations and inventions to the market rather than to keep them on the dusty shelves in the public domain. The new bill intended to address the extensive under-utilization of public patents and innovations. As Senator Birch Bayh said in his introductory remarks: "A wealth of scientific talent at American colleges and universities – talent responsible for the development of numerous innovative scientific breakthroughs each year – is going to waste as a result of bureaucratic red tape and illogical government regulation."[7] The idea, so Senator Bayh claimed, was to make the billions of public dollars spend on government-supported research more productive and to diffuse its innovative outcomes faster and more widespread. According to the *Economist*, the Bayh-Dole Act was "possibly the most inspired piece of legislation to be enacted in America over the past half-century", a piece of legislation that "more than anything (...) helped to reverse America's precipitous slide into industrial irrelevance".[8] It reinforced commercial technology transfer based on a substantial increase of patented academic research. It led universities to streamline its patent policies, through its Technology Transfer Office (TTO), and paved the way to professionalize its management of commercial research spinoffs.

Almost by way of definition, new venture startups need to bridge the so-called "Valley of Death", i.e. the period in the innovation cycle of technology development between the time of technology creation and its early commercialization, between concept and prototype.[9] In this transition period new ventures face the urgent problem of survival because the new product or service is not bringing in real revenues from real customers. Cash flows are negative, the financial runway is short, resources are limited, and tend to dry up quickly. Raising money without sales is a tricky concept. Running out of funds is the ultimate cause of early startup death. Angel investors and VC's need a proof-of-concept in order to invest; a business model that is, or seems to be, sound and can be scaled. Surviving the Valley of Death indicates the creativity, the navigation competencies, and the entrepreneurial skills of the startup founder and his or her team. In order to cross the Valley of Death and to make the US economy more competitive and growth promoting, the US federal government in 1982 launched the Small Business Innovation Research (SBIR) program. The new initiative was (and is) directed to help small businesses to qualify for early-stage funding and to support them in establishing technological merit and commercial potential of its innovation activities.[10] The program is funded, with around $2.5 billion annually, through the eleven federal agencies that run SBIR.[11] Phase I of the program qualifies small businesses (less than 500 employees) to apply for funding up to $150,000 for a six-month period, to assess the feasibility and market prospective of the proposed idea. Phase II enables small businesses on the basis of favorable Phase I outcomes, to apply for additional funding (up to $1,000,000) for two years of further technological development. Between 1983 and 2006 almost 100,000 awards were granted by SBIR (70% to Phase 1 projects) with almost $20 billion distributed to small companies.[12]

SBIR is a good example of a successful government program directed towards supporting startups and existing small businesses through the demanding first stages of the innovation cycle. To help them bridge the Valley of Death when financial constraints really matter. The program has been evaluated systematically and in-depth, and the conclusions are quite robust: "the SBIR has made a key and unequivocal contribution to the innovative performance of the United States, especially in terms of technological innovation".[13] SBIR firms were more innovative, more growth oriented, better suited for survival, the program generated more technology-based startups, resulted in greater commercialization of firms' innovations and inventions, and increased the number of entrepreneurs.[14] But there are concerns too, such as the classic argument that firms would have undertaken innovation activities anyway, despite the SBIR funding. This concern, however, needs to be balanced with the finding that a significant number of small businesses and new ventures would not have started without the SBIR awards. The program helped startups to cross the dreaded Valley of Death and sharpened the commercial potential of their ideas and concepts.

The US federal government also acted and acts as the overarching agency that "sets the table" for the startup innovation game. It defines the rules, protects a level playing field, and secures (regional) distributive justice. It seeks to address competitive demands by the various parties involved. A clear example is the delicate business of issuing visa quotas to immigrant and non-immigrant startup founders and employees. Many of these new ventures depend on employing highly skilled scientists and engineers, often from abroad. Human capital after all is the main resource of innovative and competitive startups and existing businesses. The government acts as the national referee in determining these quotas. The Immigration and Naturalization Act of 1965, also known as the Hart-Celler Act, defined these quota based on immigrants' labor skills and family relationships with US residents, abolishing existing nation-of-origin restrictions, and criteria based on race and ancestry.[15] The law captured immigration quotas at 170,000 per year and assigned immigration visas on a first come, first served basis. Moreover, the Hart-Celler Act stipulated that immigrants will not replace a worker in the United States nor adversely affect the wages and working conditions of similarly employed individuals in the United States. The new immigration bill opened the US labor market to immigrants from Asia, Africa, the Middle East, and later from Latin America. It radically ended a period of non-inclusive and restricted immigration policies which particularly favored immigrants from Northern Europe. In the thirty years after the ratification of the new immigration law over 18 million legal immigrants entered the United States, more than three times the number that was allowed in the preceding thirty years. The law still remains intact today. It dramatically changed America's demographic profile, including its demographic business profile. Silicon Valley is a case in point with its large share of highly skilled immigrants and immigrant entrepreneurs.

A number of visa arrangements are relevant to startup founders, though the process of acquiring a visa can be a long and frustrating process. For startup founders and employees the H-1B visa is especially relevant as it permits foreign scientists with a "specialty occupation" for a prearranged professional job to stay in the United States for up to three years, with a possible extension to six years. The United States Citizenship and Immigration Services (USCIS) determines whether the employment constitutes a specialty occupation. H-1B is subject to a quota which starts on the first of April each year. Demand greatly exceeds supply, and small business entrepreneurs have to compete with large corporations to get access to the available pool. This leads toward much dissatisfaction as the interviews, with our sample of startup founders reported below, will indicate. Almost 60% of immigrant company founders indicated in a recent survey that their projects had been delayed because of a lack of H-1B visas; three-quarters of these companies agrees that current US immigration laws for skilled professionals harm American competitiveness.[16] The trouble with H-1B visas and green cards is in the top three of business concerns in Silicon Valley according to the 2014 CEP Business Climate Survey.[17]

The L1 visa is a temporary work permit for intra-company international employee transfers from companies that have both an office in the US and abroad. Persons with extraordinary ability in the sciences, arts, education, business, and athletics may qualify for an O1 visa. An E2 visa, finally, allows entrepreneurs to start a new venture in the United States, given certain investment criteria ($100,000 to 200,000). The general feeling among Silicon Valley new venture entrepreneurs and business stakeholders, according to the

Bay Area Council Economic Institute, is that "in addition to more H-1Bs, the US needs a visa category specifically tailored for entrepreneurs from overseas that would allow for more extended stays and increase the likelihood of their attracting investment and establishing permanent roots in the US".[18]

These four examples (the Bayh-Dole Act, the R&D tax credit law, the SBIR program, and the Hart-Celler Act) mirror the role of active US government intervention in the innovation market. Its strength, so we believe, lies in the long term stability and continuation of the government policies. Even in view of critical points raised by the business community, its persistent implementation creates permanency, predictability, and with the exception of some of the visa arrangements: certainty. Values that are generally saluted in the business profession.

A final but much more recent example of government innovation is the JOBS (Jumpstart Our Business Startups) Act of the Obama administration which passed Congress with large bipartisan support and was signed into law in 2012.[19] The new omnibus law enables startups to raise funding among the general public and not just among accredited investors. Every American now has access to invest in new ventures and small business and share in their revenues. Non-accredited investors will be able to start investing, e.g. through equity crowd funding, in early stage startups. The JOBS Act also provides a simpler regulatory trajectory for growing companies for successful IPOs. If properly implemented, the JOBS Act could be a game-changing law.[20] It shows, according to *New York Times* columnist and historian Randall Stross, "that startups, as a category, had become darlings in Washington".[21]

Entrepreneurs on government

Government intervention: Contrasting paradigms

As in the previous chapter, this section will also include beliefs of Silicon Valley stakeholders. How do Dutch startup entrepreneurs think about the role of government in advocating innovation and new ventures? How do they compare US and Dutch policies in this respect? Jan Grotenbreg (SiliconValleyLink) is very explicit: "No. I don't think there's any government role in Silicon Valley. No not at all. That's the US paradigm. I mean the government should stay out of business. I don't see it feasible because it's not the American vision. The idea in the US is that government impact should be minimized." VC investor Cees Jan Koomen sees some common ground. There is a role for government in stimulating a resilient a competitive startup economy. Non-interventionism does not necessarily equal passivity. "Silicon Valley has less government interference. Keep the government out, but that is not a negative statement. It means you need to give those new companies freedom. The government comes in by providing the support network. Could be subsidies, could be advisors, could be anything. Things that a company need at that point of their development. I think the government can facilitate that supportive network very well as it is happening in Silicon Valley. The Netherlands should not be any different in that aspect. It should be, as I said, supportive." (Cees Jan Koomen). The Netherlands, according to hightech entrepreneur Ronald Mannak, should make bigger steps. It not only has "a risk aversive culture but also risk aversive institutions and legislations. And that is a big difference with the United States. If it was up to me, I would definitely start changing the institutions and laws." (Ronald Mannak, JumpCam).

How do Silicon Valley stakeholders and political representatives view the role and task of government in advancing an innovative and competitive startup policy? How do they evaluate the role of federal and state government in building and maintaining the Silicon Valley ecosystem? We spoke extensively with Sean Randolph (President of the Bay Area Council Economic Institute) and Edwin Tan (District Director, US Congressman Mike Honda) on this topic. Here are their analyses. Sean Randolph points at the important role of federal research funding in the Bay Area and Silicon Valley since the beginning of the 20th century. A funding role that is still omnipresent today. "The biggest flow of research money comes from the federal government: the National Science Foundation, Department of Energy, and National Institutes of Health. A disproportionally large share of federal research money comes to this region, because of its universities and all the federal research labs. So there never has been a government plan or policy behind Silicon Valley, but a case can be made that things would look very different if there wasn't a large ongoing flow of federal research funding coming here. And then there is the State of California. The state didn't design or plan what happened in Silicon Valley, but what it did create one of the world's leading public institutions of higher education system in the University of California. Lately there have been funding issues and severe budget cuts, which raises issues, but historically this has been a critical investment by the state in California's intellectual capital and talent pools." The role of government, in short, has been decisive in funding innovation research (federal level) and in supporting the intellectual and talent infrastructure through funding the higher education system (state level). The government did not enter in the innovation arena at a late stage, but has rather taken a major role in building the Silicon Valley ecosystem, primarily through funding research and development.

Mike Honda is a well-known US Congressman, representing Silicon Valley in Congress since 2000.[22] Among many other accomplishments, he co-authored the Nanotechnology Research and Development Act, which was enacted in 2003. The Act enabled federal investment of up to $3.7 billion (over four years) in nanotechnology R&D. His District Director Edwin Tan: "I think that the government has played a critical role through funding initial investments – especially in nanotechnology. The federal government has provided a great deal of the basic research funding that allows for the creation of numerous innovations here today. And that is the part I think that does not get as much recognition, that a substantial part of the basic research was funded through government grants. Then much of that basic research gets translated and applied into an innovative product." Edwin Tan also points at other topics Congressman Honda is emphasizing on how government impacts entrepreneurship and innovation. "He wants to bring the private sector expertise to the government, because obviously the government has a few things to learn from the private sector. So he would create centers where entrepreneurs with a proven track record would voluntarily – and many would like to – go in and work with government agencies and see how they can streamline their operations."

Immigration is a next topic that needs support. Immigrants add to the entrepreneurial climate in Silicon Valley, have the right spirit, and are highly skilled. "Immigrants that come here are very hard working, very driven, very disciplined, highly educated, and they have some great ideas. There are also more specific concerns that need to be addressed by government, especially in its role of guaranteeing a level playing field. Another thing the federal government getting into is the whole issue of patent trolling. And companies filing patent suits where larger companies sue smaller companies. This is where the federal government is trying to speak into the area, to create the protection for the people." Environmental protection is another high priority issue in California, given its vulnerable environmental conditions (water scarcity, air pollution, earthquakes threats, traffic congestion). "So there is always the debate about environmental regulations at the California state level. There has been a tension between businesses and the state with respect to protecting the environment, while also encouraging manufacturing. Those who want a smaller role of the government are arguing that it is overregulated, that the government is overstepping its role. But then in other ways these regulations drives innovation, it creates new markets for clean energy, clean technology." (Edwin Tan, District Director, Congressman Mike Honda).

Redefining the role of Dutch government

Harm TenHoff is very outspoken on the role of Dutch government. It should define the main challenges the country is facing, the economic direction it will be taking in the next ten to twenty years given the global competition of countries such as the United States, China, and India. Innovation and hightech startup entrepreneurship should be linked. In this sense, the Dutch government has to redefine its core innovation policy, including the implementation of subsidy instruments. "Government also has its cultural peculiarities and its very rigid structures. You have to get out of the subsidizing mode without accountability and create more effective subsidizing modes. There is room I think for the government to do something, but I see it mostly in the very early stage, if there is an invention. We don't want government to invest in just any idea that is not yet an invention. The entrepreneur must be serious about commercialization. Pursuing at least a provisional patent application may show that intent. There needs to be push to get a patent, to go to the market. So, to help setting up these propositions on a path of potential success I can see a role for government, but as soon as you go to the next stage, as soon as you have let's say basic feasibility, there should not be a need to invest public money anymore, provided there is a good private investment climate." The current Dutch innovation subsidy trajectory, so the argument goes, is without entrepreneur risk and is weak on accountability. Entrepreneurs take the subsidy very willingly, but they will develop stuff that in most cases ends upon the shelf because in the end they are not responsible to get it to market. As Vincent van de Poll (GROM) states: "Here in Silicon Valley they call it dead capital." Jan Grotenbreg underlines this conclusion: "That's certainly dead capital and there is a lot of it in Holland."

Harm TenHoff's advice to the Dutch government is to streamline their regional Silicon Valley approaches and activities. "There are delegations from all over the Netherlands all the time passing by the same places. As a country you have to brand and manage a more centralized image, you have to compete with other countries, and figure out your own way of dividing the cookies internally."

Bankruptcy

Most startup entrepreneurs point at basic liability differences between the United States and the Netherlands. Bankruptcy in particular is a widely shared concern. Entrepreneurs feel that the present Dutch bankruptcy laws are a major barrier for startup founders. If their new venture fails they may be held personally liable which can haunt them (and their families) for a long period. "In the Netherlands you are making a big mistake depending on funding arrangements that may get you into bankruptcy. Because as soon as you then fail you make enemies because people don't get paid. Here in the United States it is as soon as you see that you fail – meaning you're working on something that the market doesn't want anymore – you pay the last bill, and you pull the plug. You let everybody go home so you don't have people waiting for money, you don't make enemies. A place like Silicon Valley would not exist without this common policy because nobody would cater to the startups, because not all of them are going to make it so you can't have them all go bankrupt and leave corpses." (Harm TenHoff, BayLink). Entrepreneur Ronald Mannak had to pay a high price for being personally liable for his failing startup some years ago in the Netherlands. He basically had to escape his home country. "We couldn't raise money from VCs or investors, the few there are in Holland, so we end up filing for bankruptcy. I was personally liable for part of the loan and I couldn't pay it back, so actually I had to leave the country and I have never been back to Netherlands." (Ronald Mannak, JumpCam). The liability situation in the United States is quite different and much better suited to startup needs as Ronald argues. "You can fail here. If as a startup founder you end up with insurmountable personal debts you can declare bankruptcy and start all over again from scratch. And it's relatively easy to do that. While in Holland, I speak out of experience, there is no way to get rid of it. It stays with you personally for 20 years or so; it's strange." These consequences are of course dramatic but Ronald seem to have found a new balance in his new career as a new startup founder in Silicon Valley. But it hurts. "There is no way I can ever go back to The Netherlands, so the better part of my life is just gone. Just fine, I'm fine with that."

Visa, visa, visa

One of the biggest problems for our sample of startup entrepreneurs was getting a visa to start and grow their new venture in Silicon Valley. For themselves but also for employing highly qualified foreign (Dutch or European) software engineers or filling internships for students. All entrepreneurs view the visa problem as a high priority challenge that needs urgent attention and diplomatic action from the Dutch government. Dirk de Kok (Mobtest) arrived on a B1-visa, which is valid for six months, and provides very limited business maneuverability. No US employment is permitted, raising VC money is a problem, which meant that Dirk essentially had no income for one and a half years. "I didn't know that I was going to be around for another few months so actually I didn't re-try to raise money." (...) "I was in limbo, I didn't know if I was going to stay here or go back. I lived on my savings and on money from my parents." In the end Dirk managed to get an O1-visa for persons with extraordinary ability, in his case in sciences and business. He hired a specialized organization that took care of all the paperwork, the credentials, the evidence. A 400-page file that the applicant needs to submit. Good relationships matter too. Ronald Mannak also succeeded in obtaining an O-1 visa. Back in the Netherlands he got his PhD, wrote scientific papers and published articles. His startup in Holland also was an advantage: "Steve Wozniak [Apple's co-founder, PE/AM] was a user of one of our products, he helped me with a cover letter for a visa, so for me it was pretty easy." Eric-Jan van Leeuwen (Login VSI) applied for an L2-visa (intra-company transfer) which was refused however. With the help of a specialized Silicon Valley visa lawyer, Eric-Jan and his startup colleagues managed to get an E2 Treaty Investor Visa. "Which means that we needed to show the plan why we wanted to start a business in the US, how many US personnel we are going to hire. And we needed to put $150,000 in an American account to show that we have serious interest in building up a business. That whole process took about six months and we received a visa for five years."

Preparation is absolutely crucial. Marieke van der Poel (Proef Trend Forecasting) is a good example. "I was very prepared for a lot of things, I arranged my own visa, and I made sure that all the legal setups were correct. So I got all the licenses and I did all of that work for both me and my husband. I also had negotiated our Green Card and paid for all that. I set up everything correctly, fill out the market and I have to say, that's really useful because if you are waiting for a visa you can already start talking to people. So the moment I got the visa I already had clients."

The quota based H-1B visa for skilled and professional workers causes much concern among our startup founders. Serial entrepreneur Arthur van Hoff is very outspoken on this subject. "Sun Microsystems offered good support for getting my Green Card. Nowadays just to get an H-1B visa can take, you know, six to eighteen months. It is limited by quota and you have to get in the queue for the visa in April for a start date the following October. That's absolutely ridiculous and it's hard to hire anybody this way. Many applicants are shut out. There are simply not enough visas available." The lack of visas, according to Arthur, is "the biggest pain that exists. The thing that I found to work over the years was internships, bring in kids from colleges in Holland and then have them for six months because they are smart, practical, well educated, and speak English. When they go back they are real entrepreneurs. I mean it is like night and day, they really catch the bug so that does work but the visas have to be arranged in Europe because it's so complicated to even get a student visa. The Dutch government needs to work with the American government to fix the visa problem." Eric-Jan van Leeuwen has a concrete suggestion. "It would be very helpful, just to have a sort of an office where you could go to and explain what kind of visas you can get, do an assessment on what kind of company you are, what visa is most likely to succeed." Getting the right visa on time, so much is clear, is a major barrier for foreign entrepreneurs to launch their startup in the US and to hire highly specialized non-US employees. It is a source of frustration and blocks entrepreneurship. For Vish Mishra, Venture Director at Clearstone and well-known Silicon Valley entrepreneur, the basic choice is a simple one: "Either you bring the work outside, or the talent inside."

10.   Network Support System

The art of networking: Trust and social capital

Networking is the core of the Silicon Valley spirit. The Valley's entrepreneurial psyche is deeply rooted in a professional system of social and business networks. An advanced system that links startups, corporations, venture capitalists, lawyers, accountants, consultants, political actors, and interest groups. In combination these agencies constitute a specialized network support system that is highly beneficial to startups and new venture formation. It gives them access to capital, resources, partners, and counseling. Networking, consequently, is an essential feature of our 'Silicon Valley Innovation & Startup Model' both at the meso-level (organizations) and at the individual level (startup teams). It builds and strengthens commercial relationships between startups and established companies, investors, talent, potential clients, and stakeholders. Through networking new opportunities arise that startups may take in order to open new markets and to meet new business partners. Networking, so to speak, transforms startups from outsiders to insiders. A vital network mirrors strong social and geographic relationships and indicates active startup community involvement. It builds and maintains interactive network systems and ties the participating actors and firms.

Networks, innovation, and entrepreneurship are interconnected. Innovation knowledge diffuses through effective networks.[1] As Emilio Castilla and his co-authors argue: "Innovation is so central to high technology industry that it is not an exaggeration to say that effective social networks determine a firm's chance for survival."[2] It enables collective learning, exchange of innovation experiences, diffusion of market information, mobilization of resources, communication and cooperation, joint projects, and creates bonds between startups and other organizations (e.g. universities, government). Castilla *et al.* made an interesting attempt to map the particular Silicon Valley institutional configuration. Their network analysis shows how actors in the regional economic infrastructure are interrelated and how these connections affect, in their case, IPO deals.[3]

Networking also has a fundamental cultural dimension: it reflects social trust and the amount of social capital within a community, including a business community. Mutual social trust among actors is assumed to create community bonds, to positively affect the functioning of social institutions, and to generate a cultural climate in which cooperation is sought. High trust societies appear to be economically more prosperous, politically more effective, and institutionally more stable than low trust societies, as the former are rooted in cultures of reciprocity, shared values, and community responsibility.[4] Trust is a prerequisite of social order, it is the touchstone of social capital. It facilitates social integration and solidarity, reinforces collaboration, diminishes social dilemmas, stabilizes social interactions, and cultivates face-to-face relationships.

Trust and social capital in Silicon Valley are important dimensions of its business community but not in the classic sociological sense of civic engagement, of civil society. As Stephen Cohen and Gay Fields, Berkeley University, state: "Silicon Valley is notoriously a world of strangers; nobody knows anybody else's mother there." But as they continue: "Silicon Valley is, however, an economic space built on social capital." (...) which "can be understood in terms of the collaborative partnerships that emerged in the region owing to the pursuit by economic and institutional actors of objectives related specifically to innovation and competitiveness. It is the networks resulting from the collaborations that form the threads of social capital as it exists in Silicon Valley."[5] Corporations, VC firms, law firms, incubators and accelerators, Chambers of Commerce, interest groups, government and political agencies, universities, research labs, business stakeholders, etc. all add to the collaborative Silicon Valley network system. The same holds for common organizations such as Joint Venture Silicon Valley which brings together leaders from business, government, and academia in addressing economic issues facing the Valley and in working on innovative and pragmatic consensus-based solutions.[6]

Trust and social capital in Silicon Valley are primarily performance-based and networking is a chief mechanism in securing these basic ecosystem features. Networking, as we said, is of utmost importance to startups. And there is a wealth of networking events that startup founders and CEOs can attend. From business meetings to lectures by seasoned serial entrepreneurs, from hackathons to startup presentations, from pitching events to investor meetings, from startup weekends to startup boot camps, from demo nights to prototype exhibits, from startup contests to startup happy hours, from technology forums to startup founder runs, from coding seminars to startup counseling, etc.

Networking, as we mentioned, operates both at the meso-level and the individual level. In the first part of this chapter, we especially focus on the intermediate level of organizations and institutions. More specifically, we will outline the role of law firms and next of incubators and accelerators as the most influential startup agencies in Silicon Valley's professional network support system.

Law firms as business counselors

Law firms play a major role in Silicon Valley in getting new ventures started. Not just in the sense of offering necessary legal advice, but particularly in helping ventures to get started by opening the firms' networks and disclosing its startup business experience. Given their prominent position in Silicon Valley's business community networks, they are well suited to help startups in their early-stage development. Law firms have strong and sustainable local networks and are well equipped to bring startups in contact with investors and to make introductions to relevant corporate partners and business stakeholders. Craig Johnson, the founder of the Venture Law Group and Virtual Law Partners, located in Menlo Park, states that: "Lawyers are better positioned than other professionals to provide the kind of business advice and contacts beginning entrepreneurs need."[7] Silicon Valley lawyers, of course, do support startups in getting the necessary documents ready but their role goes beyond the mere legal technicalities as they are dealing with beginning entrepreneurs who often lack a business track record. Lawyers help startup entrepreneurs with advice on how to set up their business, how to form a team, how to find the right investor(s), how to divide stock ownership, how to define and if needed redefine their business concept and strategy, how to select board members, and how to solve patent issues. Lawyers assist startup founders to avoid typical early-stage mistakes, to coach them through the starting phase, and help them to do things in the right sequence. Lawyers, in short, play a much broader role than providing legal advice. They are general business counselors and add credibility to the new startup venture. In this capacity, Silicon Valley lawyers need to excel in combining distinct roles. As Brown University sociologist Mark Suchman concludes about the Silicon Valley law practice: "Most local attorneys have, at one time or another, served as dealmakers, as counselors, as gatekeepers, as proselytizers, and as matchmakers."[8] Curtis Mo, lawyer and Partner at DLA Piper, confirms this. He adds that selecting the right startups is a tedious process: "you have to kiss a lot of frogs".

Silicon Valley law firms developed a multifaceted startup practice based on multiple roles in counseling new ventures. A situation that is quite different from the classic European law practice that is still predominantly directed towards providing legal advice to startups.

The active involvement of lawyers in launching startups may also lead them to postpone their billings to startups they advise until revenues come in or to take stock ownership positions. Traditional fee-based payments become less common. Some law firms even permit their attorneys to invest in startups they take on. Curtis Mo puts it this way: "I'm not spending money, I'm spending firm resources." Lawyers, so the conclusion holds, become entrepreneurs. As Suchman reasons: "Silicon Valley business lawyers often have unique access to all the pieces necessary to start a company around an idea. They have credibility with and access to a variety of funding sources. They know how to structure financings and corporate partnerships. They have experience with a large number of similar companies and can help with proper sequencing. So it's not surprising that more and more lawyers are becoming entrepreneurs themselves."[9] Lawyers, like all other professionals in Silicon Valley, depend on their network and referrals. "Good deals find me", says Curtis Mo.

Lawyers and law firms are key agencies in Silicon Valley's habitat. They represent focal assets to the region's startup community in counseling inexperienced new ventures. They help startups to grow, share an entrepreneurial attitude, and are at the core of the network support system which is at the basis of our 'Silicon Valley Innovation & Startup Model'. The explosion of the Internet makes it easier to start new ventures, even for entrepreneurs without a technology background, forcing laws firms to become more selective in accepting new startup clients. Alerting Craig Johnson to the statement that "At the Venture Law Group we have even been approached by high school students wanting to start companies!"[10]

Startup schools: Incubators & accelerators

An elementary part of the 'Silicon Valley Innovation & Startup Model' is the support offered by a wide variety of incubators and accelerators that help startups in their early development stage in raising funding, in focusing their concept, in assisting them to grow, and in providing high level mentorship.[11] These startup schools are generally very selective and equally competitive, and being accepted is a strong push in the right direction for a new venture. There are many excellent incubators and accelerators in the Bay Area.[12] Good examples in San Francisco include Greenstart, AngelPad, RocketSpace, and Parisoma. Prime names in Silicon Valley are Y Combinator, Plug & Play Tech Center, The Founder's Institute, and 500 Startups. To really get a feeling for how startup schools operate, we will have a closer look at two incubator examples: RocketSpace and Y Combinator. Furthermore, we will give an example how one of the VC's, Trinity Ventures, goes about in helping their startups blossom.

RocketSpace, launched in 2011, is a leading incubator for San Francisco startups.[13] Located in the iconic former Standard Oil Company Building in the city's downtown district. A hightech campus of 70,000 square feet, housing over 175 startups who already secured some seed money. An energetic yet concentrated atmosphere. One feels the dynamics but also the seemingly tranquility of hard-working software programmers developing a new app. The one killer-app that will disruptively change the digital world and that will bring in the big money. An open market place where startups work together with established companies and where everything is about fast growth. The collaboration with existing companies guarantees a go-to-market strategy with immediate product visibility. The power of innovation combined with the power of reputation. A smart formula brought up by Duncan Logan, founder and CEO of RocketSpace. Some high-profile companies begun as a startup in RocketSpace: Spotify, Uber, Supercell USA. The success of RocketSpace is ultimately determined by the success of its startups. In accordance with good American custom, RocketSpace does not shun big words, its mission is nothing less than "Bringing the future to the market". But a little self-overestimation can do no harm: euphoria and optimism are an intrinsic part of the Silicon Valley startup culture. Walking through the open RocketSpace "office" spaces gives you a feel for these cultural dynamics. The startups themselves only occupy one or two office desks in what looks at first sight as a poorly organized environment. Often it is not directly obvious who belongs to which startup.

RocketSpace is not a shared office building as known in Europe. The idea goes much further and reflects a much better entrepreneurial concept. It is a micro-ecosystem of its own where everything is dominated by rapid 'hightech growth'. In bringing innovative startups together and in creating conditions that enhance their success ("by tech entrepreneurs, for tech entrepreneurs"). To, for instance, provide them with legal support or marketing advice. To take off entrepreneurs and entrepreneurship to a higher level. There are RocketSpace labs, flexible work spaces, studios, developer bootcamps, pitches, and lectures. A nice example are the Rocket-Studios, "a dedicated event space" of more than 6,000 square feet. Here one finds a varied series of master classes by renowned serial entrepreneurs, panels, lectures, fireside chats, meetups, pitching events, hackathons, and presentations by RocketU grads. All based on the guiding principle that "isolation is not an option". The innovative power of RocketSpace lies in its associative and bonding capability. Between startups themselves and between startups and reputed businesses. Samsung, Amazon, Lufthansa, Tata, and British Airways are celebrated partners in the RocketSpace incubator model. RocketSpace is selective. You have to show that your startup is based on a smart idea with market potential; you need to have raised seed funding or beyond. Your startup must also have demonstrable added value for the other RocketSpace startups. And that makes the formula so powerful: highly motivated start-uppers who want but also have to make the difference. But always, in RocketSpace's self-description: "fiercely independent".

Y Combinator (YC) is a seed accelerator started in 2005 by Paul Graham, former CEO of Viaweb (sold to Yahoo in 1998 for about $50 million in stock), based in Mountain View. Each startup that is selected to partici- pate in YC receives an investment of $11,000 plus $3,000 for each team member in exchange for usually 6-7% equity. *Wired* has called YC "the most prestigious program for budding digital entrepreneurs".[14] *Forbes* has named YC as its top incubator and accelerator.[15] Two remarkably success- ful YC startups are Dropbox and Airbnb. Some other big exits include 280 North, Heroku, OMGPOP, Loopt, Cloudkick, Zecter, Wufoo, and Reddit. The general idea underlying the YC startup program is "to get you to the point where you've built something impressive enough to raise money on a larger scale".[16] The program itself has two three-month batches per year, one in summer and one in winter. Three months may sound like a short period but YC's mantra is: "launch fast". To move as quickly as possible from the initial startup idea to a minimum viable product.[17]

Awarded applicants are required to move to the Bay Area region to maximally profit from its vibrant entrepreneurial culture and mindset. Selected startups are moreover obliged to have at least two founders. YC strongly believes in the power of startup *teams*. Having no co-founder(s) is a sign of lacking confidence of the founder's friends, so the argument goes. A startup founder needs others or as Paul Graham clarifies: "colleagues to brainstorm with, to talk you out of stupid decisions, and to cheer you up when things go wrong".[18] YC invites less than 10% of the about 2,000 startup teams that apply for each batch. Around 3% will be finally chosen to take part in the YC program, which shows its selectivity. The YC cycle of winter 2014, for example, resulted in 75 startups that received funding. Decisions are all based on face-to-face interviews with applicants. Do they need to submit business plans? The answer is painfully clear: "Not for us. We love demos, but we never read business plans."[19] What about the success rate? YC believes that if 4 out of 10 participating startups succeed, their formula is functioning well. During the three-month program period, startups work on their product, a prototype or demo, on their fund raising pitch, are in touch with YC advisors, attend weekly YC dinners aiming at mutual interaction and exchange of experiences, listen to successful startup speakers, and network with YC alumni. Moreover, startup participants have free access to YC legal advisors who help them with basic legal and paper work (e.g. intellectual property rights, patents) to set up their startup. YC partaking startup founders are also offered business advice by the 15 full-time and 11 part-time partners (August 2015) to calibrate their business idea, to solve urgent problems, but also to define the big vision for the company. Most startups do not enter the YC program with a more encompassing grand perspective. "Helping founders come up with these big visions is one of our strengths, because we've explored so much of the space of startup ideas that we know what's over each hill."[20] The YC cycle culminates in Demo Day, an invitation-only event, on which all startups pitch their product or service for an expert audience of about 450 angel and VC investors. The purpose of this critical event is to match startup founders with investors to help grow the business beyond YC early-stage funding. To make them financially ready for the big jump.

Over the years YC has developed a very successful incubator and accelerator program. *Forbes* has calculated that "when taking into account the 172 companies that have been acquired, shut down or raised funding, the total value is $7.78 billion, for an average of $45.2 million per company".[21] If we look at all 800 startups that were funded by Y Combinator since 2005 – representing a community of some 1,600 founders – we arrive at a combined valuation of $30 billion.[22] A truly remarkable performance.

Trinity Ventures is an early stage venture capital firm. They have invested over $325M in 130 companies, and they have realized eight IPOs and 49 acquisitions.[23] If you want to have contact as a startup with Trinity, "[t]he most effective way (...) is to reach out through a common acquaintance".[24] Didn't we say networking was important? They claim on their website that "entrepreneurs are our passion", and try to make that work: Trinity Ventures has hired a space on Valencia Street in the heart of the Mission District for their startups. Trinity helps their startups the Silicon Valley way. That means, not only are their startups funded by them, but they also help with refining the concept, with the market introduction, with HR, with hiring new people, and also with all kinds of technical services. Trinity Ventures makes a point of getting their startups to network with each other. To facilitate that, they have so-called Friday Talks, where a seasoned entrepreneur, a partner of Trinity or a starting entrepreneur is invited to talk about his or her business. The Trinity startups can then freely ask any question, off-the-record, so to speak.

Entrepreneurs on network support system

Two main themes return in our entrepreneur interviews on how the Silicon Valley innovation and startup backing model affects new ventures: the strong support system of incubators and lawyers, and the vital role of networking. In combination, the support and networking system are decisive in the critical early stage of startup development. Successful new ventures know how to utilize this system of intermediaries and excel in effective goal-oriented networking. It also becomes clear that working with these intermediary agencies and engaging in networking is a rather smooth operation as the Silicon Valley ecosystem is fully fitted up in doing so. In fact, it is part of the Silicon Valley genius.

Incubators & lawyers

Incubators are important for startups. They teach them how to run a beginning business, how to scale their business model, help them with pivoting, offer startups some funding, and provide them with mentoring by experienced (often serial) entrepreneurs. RocketSpace, as we saw, is a fine example of a well-functioning incubator. Duncan Logan, founder and CEO of RocketSpace, describes the place as "co-working on steroids". The concept is, he adds, "co-working with a selection process at the gate", shortly described as "office-as-a-service". An office may sound old-fashioned, but Duncan believes that it serves a purpose: "as opposed to working virtually, an office gives the chance of exchanging infectious knowledge". Remarkably, RocketSpace does not want equity in their startups. As Duncan explains: "if we would ask for equity, the best startups wouldn't come here", referring to companies such as Uber and Spotify. With such successes, it takes a lot of determination to stick to your beliefs.

Marco ten Vaanholt, managing partner at BootUp Ventures, explains that BootUp goes much further than other accelerators. They have basically set up their own ecosystem. "We work with the 5A's," Marco says, and explains: "Access to partners, funding, knowledge, talent, and customers." BootUp has a nice venue in Menlo Park, and offers office space to their startups. By providing the 5A's, Marco says, "BootUp makes up for a service ecosystem, a five-star Ritz-Carlton." Next to these hard provisions, BootUp also takes care of genuine Dutch coziness (*gezelligheid*): there is a very big garden where one can sit and have a coffee or a drink, there is a bar. Events are very regularly organized to strengthen the informal network of prime Silicon Valley entrepreneurs.

500 Startups takes a different approach says Elizabeth Yin, startup investor and partner. This accelerator provides coaching regarding two critical startup qualities: fundraising and customer acquisition. Every startup is paired with a customer acquisition coach and a fundraising coach. 500 Startups has a staff of approximately 100 people to do that. The coaching is very detailed, Elizabeth explains, giving as an example the coaching of customer acquisition: "On day one we say: 'Tell me every detail about how you get a customer'", this ranges from elaborating how you find customers, what you tell them, how you follow up, etc. The whole sales funnel is scrutinized. By doing this, 500 Startups "help optimize the existing customer acquisition process".

Arthur van Hoff is a mentor advising RocketSpace new venture founders, and his experience is that teaching founders to think bigger is a major test of their entrepreneurial skills also because the funding provided by RocketSpace is limited. "You need to have a big idea and get really excited about it. Then you get lots of money. You can't be successful by thinking small, or thinking within your means. You got to think outside the box." (Arthur van Hoff, Jaunt).[25] Duncan Logan adds: "It takes a very unique individual to get money for a very uncertain idea, and to get personnel to work for them on this very uncertain idea". Dirk de Kok wanted to participate in the program of the incubator AngelPad, located in both San Francisco and New York City. "The most famous incubator here is Y Combinator but that's very, very hard to get into." Dirk learned a hard lesson. He was applying to enter AngelPad as a single startup founder. The first question that was raised in the application session was about his team of cofounders. "I answered, well it's just going to be me. Then the AngelPad executive said, thank you very much and good luck. Just cut it off. It was kind of tough." (Dirk de Kok, Mobtest). Later Dirk was accepted by Founder Institute.

JumpCam has been funded by Google Ventures and Trinity Ventures, $2.7M in total. Ronald Mannak explains that the setup of Trinity at Valencia Street, as described before, worked very well. Although he left JumpCam at the moment of writing, he is still very enthusiastic about Trinity's approach: "we had very regular contact, they helped us on numerous occasions". The networking worked as well: "we work together with three or four other Trinity startups. We use their technical products in our own product" (Ronald Mannak, JumpCam).

Come to think of it, only the best startups end up in an incubator or accelerator. Duncan Logan compares it with soccer: "This is Real Madrid. It is all about training and getting the last 1% right." The procedure is as follows, Duncan clarifies: only the best and most ambitious people from a country will leave everything behind to pursue their dream in the Valley. They have to go through a lot of hassle, not in the least for getting a visa. Then from all these ambitious people, only a small percentage get some sort of funding. The second gate. Then, from this small percentage, RocketSpace selects the most promising; the third selection.

Finding a good law firm is also essential for startups. Not only because of their legal expertise but also, as we saw, for their general business know how and advice. Moreover, as we outlined, legal firms are willing to postpone billing the startup until the stage that revenues are coming in. Of course, the idea is that the bill should be paid sooner or later, and will only be acquitted in case of bankruptcy. Deferred payment is a major advantage to startups, quite unlike the situation in the Netherlands and Europe. "In Europe it is unthinkable to have a lawyer working for you pro bono or with a delayed payment, simply based on the hope that you will succeed." (Neil Blaak, ZappoTV). As law firms are part of the Silicon Valley ecosystem, they are able to optimize their role as intermediate support agencies; they know the right people; they know the organizations that matter; they know the rules. Neil continues: "I make it a point to reach out to my legal counselor and give him updates. They love to hear about developments, about what we are doing. They brought us in touch with a couple of potential investors; they have their eyes and ears open in this entire Silicon Valley ecosystem." Salar al Khafaji also italicizes the positive role of Silicon Valley lawyers. "They are very different from Dutch lawyers, much more proactive and risk taking. They have their own contacts and networks. If I sit down with a Dutch lawyer he will just explain what the contract means and what they can do. Here lawyers think at a higher level, they help you with negotiations. They have an entrepreneurial mindset. I guess that for a startup the lawyer is the closest counterpart to the VC." (Salar al Khafaji, Silk). Valley lawyers, so is Salar's experience, give you solid feedback on your startup plans. "When they decide to work with you and help you around, there is always the risk that it is not going to happen. They might put in hours and not get paid for it, so they also kind of think as investors in a way. Our lawyer basically started billing but we did not have to pay. He would just add it up and we would only pay him if the deal was done." The deferred billing system, of course, is not based on philanthropic or altruistic considerations. If a startup gets really big, the participating law firm (and the lawyer himself) is going to become very successful. There is an advantage on both parts; startups benefit and so do law firms. And this is probably exactly why the system works.

The Silicon Valley network support system goes beyond incubators and law firms. It also includes stakeholder organizations such as the Chambers of Commerce and the Bay Area Council. These agencies play an elementary role in the ecosystem. "Everything these days is about social networking. Our Chamber has monthly meetings where entrepreneurs socialize and interact with each other. Even with the abundance of virtual networking, face-to-face meetings are still important." (Ken Rosenberg, Mountain View Chamber of Commerce. Sean Randolph of the Bay Area Council closely studied the ecosystem and its support agencies. "There is a deep network of professional service organizations, lawyers, and accountants that is not often recognized. People who have experience with venture capital, IPO's, copyright protection, for bio-tech companies working with the Food and Drug Administration (FDA), and other fields that are critical to the technology and startup world. Those special business support services, that are tailored for those communities, have a unique density here. " And the interesting thing is that all these professional service organizations actively work together: "We map of these companies and institutions, institutional competitors, incubators, accelerators, lawyers, investors, universities, federal labs, independent labs, and others. When we've asked them 'who do you collaborate with', it turns out that everybody was collaborating with almost everybody. What that means is that the institutional barriers to the movement of people and ideas within the region are very low, and this means people and organizations can be more innovative and go to market faster."

The need for networking

Being an enthusiastic networker is a required quality of a good startup entrepreneur. Networking is in Silicon Valley's DNA. The professional support system depends on active networking, on outgoing engagement, on community participation. The system demands and offers network involvement. The importance of networking is widely shared by our entrepreneurs, they all accentuate the essential role of building social capital and utilize the network for advancing their startup activities. And networking is rather simple in Silicon Valley, it is a very accessible community. Two telling anecdotes to illustrate the effectiveness and strength of networking. "It's being able to grab a coffee. I got coffee with Tony Fadell, the founder of Nest, when I just came over from the Netherlands in my first year here. I just called him and we had coffee; that's very amazing. This would be impossible in Holland. I could never have coffee with the CEO of TomTom or Philips." (Robert Mannak, JumpCam). Here's the second anecdote, told by Arthur van Hoff. "One of the reasons people actually are very willing to help each other, is because you never know if somebody is going to be successful. When I got here, I went to a Stanford party at Anna Patterson's house and talked to some nerds who told me they were going to compete with Yahoo's AltaVista search machine.[26] Those nerds were Larry Page and Sergey Brin, the founders of Google. That's why everybody here believes in karma, you never know if the guy you are talking to might be the next billionaire." (Arthur van Hoff, Jaunt).

"Talking startup" is the most common network conversation topic in Silicon Valley. "You can go to any coffee shop and literally everyone around you will be talking about their startup, the idea they are working on." (Faruk Ateş, Presentate). Knowing people is of utmost relevance for startup entrepreneurs. Your conversation partner might know some people you would like to come in contact with. "You might know people, I might learn something, or you might learn something. It is mysterious in a way, but networking is very important." (Jan Grotenbreg, SiliconValleyLink). And as Jan adds, it is easy to network in Silicon Valley. "There is a whole variety of events where you can go to and you talk to as many people as possible. You always get an opportunity to talk, you always get an opportunity to explain what you are working on (…) and everybody grants you their five minutes."

Ronald Mannak still likes to attend hackathons, if not for business then certainly for fun. "I did a hackathon a couple of weeks ago. I met a group of people, we all seemed to get along and I said let's work together on something completely different and just hack it out in the weekend. And that's what we did. Afterwards we stayed in touch but we are not going to work on that idea anymore. It was just for the fun of making something and that's fine. I mean, you get to know a lot of people; you get to work on interesting technology." Sharing is basic in the networking game. Some entrepreneurs fear that networking in the Netherlands is harder, not only because of the scale of network events but also because "Dutch people are not very eager to share their thoughts or try to meet new people. Here that is actually very easy and you can quickly build a network with a lot of people. But you need to find out which people you can trust and which people you can actually use." (Valentin Smirnoff, Wells Fargo).

11.   The Downside of the Valley

Increasing social inequality

Silicon Valley has much to offer. It is an Eldorado of innovation and entrepreneurship, a vibrant startup culture. The Valley is an environment that
brings out the best in yourself, the cultural climate is alluring, and the
climate – often an underestimated factor in understanding the dynamics
of entrepreneurship – is more than pleasant. San Francisco is a cultural
melting pot celebrating diversity, an invigorating bohemian city that since
many decades has been a very appealing place for younger generations to
work and live in. It is a hightech hotspot but also a cultural hotspot. Good
vibrations. Silicon Valley, somehow, is an area that easily seduces one to
aggrandize its (many) economic, cultural, and entrepreneurial plusses.
Nevertheless, a sound shot of critical reluctance is needed in praising the
Valley and the neighboring city of San Francisco. There are some obvious
downsides. The roads are congested, the infrastructure is far from ideal.
In 2014, the Silicon Valley Business Journal ran a series on Silicon Valley
transportation. They opened with the qualifying remark: "Sitting in traffic
do you get the feeling that for all Silicon Valley's rhetoric about innovation,
the region is stuck in another era?"[1] San Jose Mercury News adds: "The
Bay Area's long-neglected, crumbling streets will get a desperately needed
face-lift, much to the relief of motorists who have been dodging jarring
potholes for decades and shelling out big bucks for auto repairs when they
can't steer clear." They state that "[c]ity and county governments would need
to spend close to $875 million a year through 2040, to meet the Bay Area's
road maintenance needs -- over three times more than the current $285
million spent across the region".[2] Oscar Garcia (Mountain View Chamber
of Commerce) adds that the CoC did a poll among its members: "We polled
our members, and the three top issues were transportation, housing, and
workforce development." The problem is clearly recognized, but solving the
issue seems harder than the usual innovative challenges businesses face.

The number of homeless is upsetting. In 2013, the count was 6,436
homeless people in San Francisco.[3] The cost of living is exorbitant, housing
prices become prohibitive, and the materialism of the *nouveau riches* takes
extravagant proportions. What matters the most is the blatant inequality. This particularly strikes European observers raised with the much
cherished ideal of egalitarianism. The enormous wealth that is generated
in Silicon Valley is very unevenly distributed. And social inequality is on

the rise, also between population groups. The number of billionaires is stunning. According to the *Forbes* 2013 list, 34 billionaires live in Silicon Valley (Woodside, Palo Alto, Atherton) and 20 billionaires reside in San Francisco.[4] Silicon Valley's billionaires are worth over $300 billion, approaching the GDP of Malaysia. In comparison: the Hispanic population in Silicon Valley is close to 30%, and their per capita income is below $21,000. Wealth polarization is painful. Three out of ten Valley households are not self-sufficient, i.e. do not make enough money to meet their basic needs without public or informal assistance; 7.6% of households live below the poverty line.[5] Data indicate that the gap between the highest and lower incomes, between the "haves" and "have-nots", has widened significantly. According to the 2015 Silicon Valley Index, average real per capita income in Silicon Valley has continued to rise since 2009 to about $75,000 in 2013, much higher than in the rest of the US ($45,500).[6] The share of households in the Valley with incomes over $100,000 continues to increase, whereas the percentage of households earning between $35,000 and $99,000 steadily decreases. Since a decade the share of middle incomes has declined in Silicon Valley, a trend that is observable in the rest of California and the US as well. Russell Hancock, president of the Joint Venture Silicon Valley, states: "The wage distribution gap is actually growing. We are losing our middle class in Silicon Valley." Data for Santa Clara County, located in the heart of Silicon Valley, are even more pronounced. The county has the highest yearly median household income in the US: $93,500. Over 45% of households have incomes above $100,000. A clear sign of the disappearing middle class is that only 13% of the county's households are in the $50,000 to $74,000 per year income range.[7] The economy of Silicon Valley is "sizzling" but its benefits are unequally divided. African Americans and Hispanics in particular hardly profit from the Valley's economic success story.[8] Per capita incomes increased the most across white and Asian groups and decreased for African Americans and Hispanics. Moreover, Silicon Valley shows a substantial and growing gender wage gap.[9] According to George Packer, staff writer for *The New Yorker*, "Silicon Valley is one of the most unequal places in America."[10] The meritocracy that Silicon Valley claims to be, is not inclusive. Its economic blessings are quite selective. "A space of contradiction" as anthropologist Elsa Davidson concludes.[11] A split society: the glossy Valley culture of the techno-entrepreneurs versus the culture of survival of the less fortunate lower class.

Immigrant participation in Silicon Valley's startup economy is a much applauded phenomenon. The number of startups founded by first generation immigrants is truly impressive. But this – as we described earlier – primarily holds for Indian and Chinese immigrants. Not for African American and Hispanic groups. The former are typically highly educated graduates with much sought engineering backgrounds, whereas the latter are on average much less educated with jobs at the lower end of the labor market. Ethnic participation, consequently, is highly education specific. Its impact differs markedly across ethnic groups and is among others related to differential group composition effects and to unconscious biases in the workplace. The call for greater diversity among the ranks of the major hightech companies in the Valley became louder in the last two years, also with respect to gender representation.[12] The pressure to include more African Americans, Hispanics, and women in its predominantly white, Asian, and male ranks is widely felt by these companies. Apple's CEO Tim Cook publicly stated that the company needs to do a better job in advancing diversity. Google teamed up with Startup Grind to help diversify its workforce beyond the usual male, white suspects.[13] Civil rights activist Jesse Jackson called the need for greater diversity in the Valley's hightech industry "the next step in the civil rights movement".

Tech boom gentrification

Middle and lower income households face serious economic hardship in Silicon Valley and its main city San Francisco. These households can hardly meet the cost of living. A major factor is the rigid housing market dominated by excessive prices. Median San Francisco house sales prices increased from $665,000 in early 2012 to $1,125,000 in late 2014, an incredible post-recession raise of 70%![14] The city is now among America's least affordable home-buying markets. In Silicon Valley the median home sales price was almost 760,000 (California: slightly below $400,000).[15] The growing demand for highly educated hightech employees leads to a steady influx of well-paid workers. This, in turn, has an upward effect on housing prices in both rentals and home sales. Renting or buying a nice house in a good neighborhood on a middle income (let alone on a lower income) is not an option anymore. It has broken the iconic American dream of owning your own house. Sooner or later this subject enters the conversation here. For lower socioeconomic classes it is hardly possible to live in the heart of the Valley or the city. Commuting is their fate. But also the middle class pays a high price for Silicon Valley's success. They are unable to compete on the housing market. "Moving out" is their forced coping strategy. They too commute over ever longer distances.

The increasing social inequality in Silicon Valley evokes societal unrest and resistance. This was bound to happen. Protest activities take harsher forms, especially with respect to the situation on the housing market. Many young well-paid Google, Apple, LinkedIn, and Facebook employees prefer to live in sexy San Francisco over somewhat indolent places in the Valley such as Sunnyvale or Cupertino. Especially the Mission district – of old a Hispanic neighborhood – is highly sought after. As a consequence this traditional neighborhood became victim of "tech boom gentrification" and rapid demographic changes.[16] This is a typical American phenomenon by the way.[17] The result is that housing prices and rents increased dramatically, even exploded in some neighborhoods, with predictable negative consequences for the original residents many of whom live on modest incomes. A recent study by Priceonomics shows that as of the end of June 2014, the median monthly rental price of a one-bedroom apartment in San Francisco was $3,120, almost 11% percent higher than the year before.[18] Between 2011 and 2014, the median rent of a one-bedroom apartment in the Mission district rose from $1,900 to $3,250, an increase of 71%. The historically low-rent downtown and surrounding neighborhoods (SOMA, Civic Center, Castro) now rank among the most expensive places. For lower but also for middle income earners the cost of living in San Francisco has rocketed sky-high. Affordable housing is among the most pressing problems in the city. In comparison: the average Silicon Valley rental rate in 2013 was $2,127 per month (California: $1,578).

How does the hightech army that settled in the Mission district, SOMA, and elsewhere travel to their workplace in the Valley? This is partly by Caltrain which connects San Francisco with the main Valley towns. But the commuting needs also led to alternative transportation services. Loads of hightech employees are transported daily by hundreds of unmarked luxury company shuttle coaches (dark-tinted windows, comfort chairs, aircon, fridge, WiFi) between San Francisco and Silicon Valley. For free. With compliments of the company: Google, LinkedIn, Apple, Facebook, Yahoo. These corporate shuttles allow their employees to live in San Francisco.[19] These private company coaches make use (at no cost) of San Francisco's public bus stops. In a short time these buses have become *the* symbol of anger and inequality, of exploding housing prices and outrageous rent costs. And of bitterness and protest. These "gated communities on wheels", as writer, historian, and activist Rebecca Solnit described the corporate coaches, inspired a revolt against how tech giants price out ordinary citizens from the housing market.[20] Here is how one protest flyer directed at tech workers frames the issue: "You are not innocent victims (...) You live your comfortable lives surrounded by poverty, homelessness and death, seemingly oblivious to everything around you, lost in the big bucks and success."[21] Recently some protesters smashed the windows of a Google bus.[22] Tim Draper, a well-known venture capitalist, suggested making Silicon Valley a separate US state. The conclusion that inequality has become a most troubling social issue in the Bay Area is inevitable. We believe that – besides our fascination with Silicon Valley – this message needs to be voiced loud and clear too. The Valley is not paradise, especially not when you are living on the 'wrong side of the tracks' as they say in Palo Alto.

Entrepreneurs on social inequality and social problems

What are the beliefs and feelings of our sample of startup entrepreneurs on the issue of social inequality and other social concerns in the Valley? Do they share common attitudes and values regarding those problems? Entrepreneurs, so it appears, clearly have an antenna for the big differences between how the US and Europe approach social issues. In their minds this has primarily to do with contrasting perspectives on the role of government, the role of the individual, and the underlying rationale of collective responsibility. Dirk de Kok (Mobtest) states the European position as follows: "we like to take care of our needy people and even if we can't help them at least we want to have them some kind of a decent life. Here it's free for all, you have to find your own way." Eric-Jan van Leeuwen (Login VSI) adds: "If you just walk a couple of blocks in San Francisco, you are not getting very happy because the poverty is so much on the streets, so much visible." Serial entrepreneur and longtime Silicon Valley resident Arthur van Hoff (Jaunt) summarizes his feelings as follows: "America is great for people that are healthy, young, and rich; if you are none of these, then you shouldn't be here." Arthur is truly upset by the way the US treats its Vietnam veterans: "they are being dropped by society, they are being dropped by the health care system, and are being forced to beg on the street. It is unforgivable how they do that to their own people." Pieter Noordam (RFIsoft) fears that "the American dream is becoming more privileged. There is an undercurrent among many people that they cannot make it anymore." Ronald Mannak (JumpCam) states that "nowhere is the difference between rich and poor as big as here. It's nicer to be in a country where things like health care and other forms of basic care are well organized, where you don't have to live on the street." Quirijn Kleppe, student Business at SJSU, states that "life in the Valley is good for millennials, but not when you're raising a family", alluding to the differences between rich and poor. Philipp Schubert, student Physics at SJSU, adds another related element to the equation: "I can't imagine to live here for a longer time. It's too dense, too vivid, here."

Worries about the lacking Valley infrastructure are widely shared. This issue too is related to a divergent view on collective role-taking. In the words of Pieter Bas Leezenberg (SkyGeo): "The holes in the road. You sit and cry. (...) There is hardly any public transport here and it's pretty run down. This country does not like to spend money on infrastructure or anything collective." Rip Pruisken (Rip van Wafels) also points at the need for more centralized responsibility. Gentrification and infrastructural problems "really need a municipal standpoint. The city needs to take responsibility. (...) Ultimately a city is a city of many people and should be a livable place for all." Harm TenHoff (BayLink) explains that it all comes down for a price. "And the price is that many things collective and public in this place suck. They have created this big and richest place in the world and they can't get their priorities straight and put the money together out of public funding to even keep up the infrastructure." And what about diversity in the Valley? Faruk Ateş (Presentate) believes that the Valley "should not miss out on people with great ideas who are not young and white. Female startups, for example, have much higher success rates than their male counterparts. Moreover, they develop products that are catering to real people' needs." Engineer Maarten Sierhuis (Ejenta) thinks that "having diversity in terms of gender helps in the innovation process. Females are better bosses and better managers. Unfortunately it's a male-dominated engineering society. "Marieke van der Poel (Proef Trend Forecasting) points at the very gender-specific and traditional roles that men and women need to play in corporate America. "Women are supposed to act like women, and men like men. It is a very different interaction. How do you as a business person stay professional in such an environment? It was easier to get a black president than a female president!" Education, finally, is another concern. It tends to reproduce social inequality. Arthur van Hoff sharply expresses his view: "The schools are financed through local real estate tax which means rich areas having good schools and poor areas having bad schools. It's just reinforcing the status quo."

Overall it can be concluded that our sample of entrepreneurs is quite sensitive to the pressing issue of growing social inequality in Silicon Valley. Comparing the situation to Europe and the Netherlands they all relate this to divergent social and political values and to different basic views on the role of collective responsibility and solidarity. In short: to differences on what the good society is.

Winners & losers

Silicon Valley has a privileged class of extremely successful entrepreneurs and groups at the other end of the socioeconomic ladder that hardly share in the Valley's success story. Solidarity is weakly developed and mainly functions through charity. The winners are those entrepreneurs who sold their company for big money or cashed substantially at an IPO. In the eyes of Europeans, CEOs in the Bay Area earn unlikely high salaries. But also a beginning software engineer, fresh from college, has a generous income. In many cases those well-paid employees are less fortunate than appears at first sight. Dismissal rules for the workforce are minimal. Job security is zero. If for some reason the stock exchange value of a renowned hightech company plummets, management will not hesitate to directly call for massive redundancies. Highly educated employees therefore need to cope too with uncertainty. Some of them can handle this perfectly, other feel gnawing worries that their job can be over soon.

Silicon Valley, so much is clear, pays a price for its success: awkward social inequality. There seem to be two parallel Valleys: one for the haves, and one for the have-nots. The question arises whether this price is too high. For losers the answer is a straightforward "yes", but also many winners are not so sure any more of their initial "no".

12. Silicon Valley's Secret Sauce: (Ecosystem x Culture)[2]

The Silicon Valley innovation puzzle

Sooner or later discussions about Silicon Valley raise the question whether other countries or regions can learn from this innovation miracle. What is its secret? Or as they say in the Valley: "what's the secret sauce?" What is so special about it? What do you need to become and remain an innovative top region? How can we solve the Silicon Valley innovation puzzle? In order to answer this basic issue, we bring together the conclusions from our interviews with startup entrepreneurs and stakeholders with literature research and our own observations. Two questions are leading: what are the main pieces of the innovation puzzle and what are the pieces missing in Europe and the Netherlands?

As argued throughout this book, the various parts that make up the innovation miracle in Silicon Valley constitute a remarkable and highly developed "Innovation & Startup Model". The different parts reinforce one another, and as John Seeley-Brown, former Chief Scientist of Xerox, argues, make for a "perpetual innovation machine".[1] A well-oiled knowledge ecology that encourages the creation of a stream of new firms and stimulates the fast growth of existing companies. An ecology that has led to pioneering companies and pioneering products. Companies and products that are often inspired by disruptive thinking and disruptive technologies. An ecology that is rooted in high trust (openness, sharing) and solid social capital (networks, community) and that is welcoming to outsiders. The core of the 'Silicon Valley Innovation & Startup Model' is that all parts are indispensable, stripping the value chain is not an option.

The Silicon Valley story shows that innovative regions have an innovation history. It started with already present electronic giants such as Fairchild Semiconductor, and spin-offs like Varian Associates, Hewlett-Packard, and Intel. The acceleration of its development came later. There was, in other words, a favorable breeding ground for innovation, for R&D, and for the commercialization of new products. The Valley did not start from scratch. The implication is evident: innovation regions are unlikely to flourish in the middle of nowhere. There needs to be some sort of a common innovation history, of early technological pioneers, that provided the right conditions for new innovation initiatives to reap the benefits.

Furthermore, innovation regions need a mega pool of highly educated talent. With top universities such as Stanford and Berkeley, with thousands of graduate students, Silicon Valley has access to a highly qualified workforce. Talent with the right education, especially software engineers and computer scientists. But being talented alone is not sufficient. Startups and established firms demand entrepreneurial and competitive employees, who are passionate about the innovative projects they work on, who feel challenged by the enormous opportunities that the Valley offers, and who want to perform. Talent with the right combination of hard and soft skills. A combination that is in high demand in the Valley, and one that earns handsomely.

Universities and colleges are prime knowledge agencies in successful innovation regions. Silicon Valley is a fine example. Outstanding public and private universities as well as excellent research labs focused on practical applications of scientific innovations and breakthroughs. And these learned centers of higher education have been doing so for many decades. Leading research institutions that attract the best scientists in their fields and who educate exceptional students. Institutions with a long track record in applied innovations and in launching numerous highly successful startups.

Silicon Valley has a somewhat peculiar relationship with government. It is sharply against government intervention, but gladly accepts its significant R&D investments, its military patronage, and its role as launching customer. These three roles, so Silicon Valley's history illustrates, have a substantial impact on innovation development. Government interference should therefore not be underestimated or played down. European countries, as we will see, explicitly stress the importance of a more leading role of government in the field of innovation and startups. This is particularly a facilitating role in promoting innovation and in creating the necessary infrastructure. But also with respect to removing institutional barriers, e.g. more liberal visa policies for highly talented global startup entrepreneurs.

Access to ample venture capital is a next crucial precondition for regions to become and remain top innovation regions. This is one of the strongest points of Silicon Valley. Almost half of US venture capital is invested in Silicon Valley. A concentration of funding and capital that is hard to grasp. But funding becomes only available for winning teams with innovative products with huge market potential. Not for business as usual. "Think Big, Aim High" is the leading motto.

What finally helps is a professional infrastructure of supporting intermediaries: lawyers, attorneys, financial experts, property rights and patent specialists, startup counselors. The remarkably high concentration of legal firms specialized in helping startups is a striking feature of Silicon Valley. This is not only with traditional legal advice but also with more general business counseling and deal-making. Interestingly, their business model is often on a risk basis: startups pay their legal counselors when they are making money or offer stock in lieu of payment.

These rudimentary ingredients are distinctive characteristics of the 'Silicon Valley Innovation & Startup Model': innovation history, highly qualified talent pool, excellent universities and private laboratories, plentiful venture capital, selective and cooperative government, and a sophisticated support infrastructure. But this advanced ecosystem does not tell the whole story. The most important feature of the Valley, of the Bay Area, is the omnipresent startup mentality. Over 20,000 startups can be found in an area that an average Dutch person crosses by bike in a day. It is the cultural factor that makes the difference: pro-innovation attitude, competitive and open minded, dynamic and interactive, willing to share, strong in networking, and achievement oriented. A culture that underlines perseverance, a robust work ethic, risk proneness, and is relatively free of the fear of failure syndrome. It is a truly enterprising culture which dares to go beyond its own comfort zone; a culture that gives ample room to immigrant entrepreneurs and acknowledges their accomplishments, skills, and talents. Without such an entrepreneurial culture, without this startup mentality, building innovation valleys is doomed to fail.[2] This combination of institutional and cultural characteristics is the nucleus of Silicon Valley's anatomy, the basis of its innovation architecture. In the words of Cees Jan Koomen, eminent Dutch-American angel investor: "It is the kind of an environment that feeds on itself in the positive sense. It enhances, explores, and explodes. In a nutshell, that's the key to success."

The uniqueness of the 'Silicon Valley Innovation & Startup Model' was recently confirmed in an in depth study by Startup Genome that compared eight institutional ecosystem and cultural indices (startup output, funding, startup performance, talent, support infrastructure, entrepreneurial mindset, trendsetting, and differentiation from Silicon Valley) for over 50,000 startups in the top 20 global startup cities (Silicon Valley, Tel Aviv, Los Angeles, Seattle, New York City, Boston, London, Toronto, Vancouver, Chicago, Paris, Sydney, Sao Paulo, Moscow, Berlin, Waterloo, Singapore, Melbourne, Bangalore, and Santiago).[3] It turned out that Silicon Valley ranks highest on *all* eight indices simultaneously, confirming the point that its success depends on both ecosystem and cultural factors. And this is exactly why Silicon Valley, in the words of the late Bay Area economist Tapan Munroe, is "the mother of all innovative regions in the world."[4]

What does this all mean for public policies aiming to stimulate regional clusters of innovative entrepreneurship with the Silicon Valley model in mind? Some of the learning lessons have been documented in a cross-national research project by Timothy Bresnahan, Alfonso Gambardella and AnnaLee Saxenian: "Direct, top-down policies are most likely to fail." They need to focus instead "on the enabling conditions like the creation of suitable demand and markets (including formation of standards), openness, competition for encouraging the success of skilled people and people with entrepreneurial ambitions, and on education in the first place".[5]

The European context

Many European countries closely monitor the Silicon Valley innovation saga and many of them took initiatives to realign and to reinvest in their national innovation ecosystems. Research shows that EU member states can be classified on the basis of its innovation performances in roughly four groups: innovation leaders (Denmark, Germany, Finland, and Sweden), innovation followers (Austria, Belgium, Cyprus, Estonia, France, Ireland, Luxemburg, Netherlands, Slovenia, and United Kingdom), moderate innovators (Croatia, Czech Republic, Greece, Hungary, Italy, Lithuania, Malta, Poland, Portugal, Slovakia, and Spain), and modest innovators (Bulgaria, Latvia, and Romania).[6] It turns out that the most innovative countries score highest on all innovation input and output performance indicators. Specifically on the level of regions and cities, cross-national research on ICT poles of excellence in Europe has indicated that Munich, London, and Paris are in the first tier. Dutch cities Eindhoven (rank nine), Amsterdam (rank ten) are in the second tier, and Delft (rank 18) in the third tier.[7] The study by the Joint Research Centre of the European Commission tracks R&D investments, innovation, and business; while looking at the agglomeration of tech, internationalization and networking. Results show that ICT excellence is concentrated in a relatively small number of regions (and cities) in Europe. A recent investigation by the European Patent Office indicates that Germany ranks first on the European list of patent fillings, France ranks second, and the Netherlands changed places with Swiss as number three on the list.[8] The Netherlands are particularly good in biotechnology and medical technology patent fillings. Philips is the Dutch number one and European number two applicant.

The most sizeable innovation efforts can be seen at the level of the European community. The European Union recently launched its comprehensive "Horizon 2020 program" which is the Union's leading research & innovation program. With nearly €80 billion in funding available, the Horizon 2020 initiative aims at securing Europe's global competitiveness, driving sustainable economic growth, and creating jobs. By strategically investing in the coupling of research and innovation, "the goal is to ensure Europe produces world-class science, removes barriers to innovation and makes it easier for the public and private sectors to work together in delivering innovation".[9] The main focus is on excellent science (meeting the needs of the scientific community, talent development and mobility, research infrastructures), industrial leadership (e.g. ICT, nanotechnologies, space, innovation in SMEs, access to risk funding), and societal challenges (health, food security, clean energy, climate action, resources efficiency, inclusion & innovation, and securing societies).

Investing in R&D is important, but it is not enough. Europe's innovation competitiveness also depends on the strength of its entrepreneurial mindset, on creating a vigorous startup culture. No innovation without entrepreneurship. Creativity and risk-taking are fundamental cultural dimensions of both innovation and entrepreneurship. The EU has a specific "Entrepreneurship 2020 Action Plan" which focuses on "entrepreneurial educational and training to support growth and business creation; removing existing administrative barriers and supporting entrepreneurs in crucial phases of the business lifecycle; reigniting the culture of entrepreneurship in Europe and nurturing the new generation of entrepreneurs."[10] Europe, so the underlying idea states, needs to unleash its entrepreneurial deficit, it must revolutionize its culture of entrepreneurship. Having the right culture is key. "Culture eats strategy for breakfast", a brilliant quote attributed to famous management theorist Peter Drucker.

Advancing the entrepreneurial spirit as reflected by a strong startup-state-of-mind is imperative for an effective and competitive European innovation policy. In essence, this calls for profound cultural change. Fortunately, Europe – at least at Commission level – is aware of the need for such a paradigm shift: "there is (…) a widespread culture that does not recognize or reward entrepreneurial endeavors enough and does not celebrate successful entrepreneurs, as role models who create jobs and income. To make entrepreneurship the growth engine of our economy Europe needs a thorough, far-reaching cultural change."[11] Vint Gerf, inventor (with Bob Kahn) of the TCP/IP-protocol, the core fundament of the Internet, and presently Google's Chief Internet Evangelist, argues that Europe should simply become more competitive and more tolerant towards failure. "When a company fails in Europe, the entrepreneur is stigmatized and is not supported by investors anymore. This hampers innovation. Silicon Valley values failure. If a startup goes bankrupt, it is framed as an experience. Which is a major advantage! This is very different in Europe. Europe must develop more of an appetite for risk."[12] As Mathilde Collin, co-founder and CEO of social email app maker Front, concludes on differences between raising startup capital in the US compared to Europe: "US funds invest in case your company succeeds, whereas in Europe, they invest because your company succeeded."[13] A significant difference indeed. European VCs need to be less risk-aversive when it comes to investing in early stage startups.[14]

Ambition is another defining feature and basic success parameter of Silicon Valley's thriving entrepreneurship and startup culture. Recently the Netherlands presented a new policy agenda to empower ambitious Dutch startup entrepreneurs.[15] More ambitious entrepreneurship, so the underlying policy assumption holds, is needed to find and market innovative solutions to key social challenges such as e.g. care for the elderly, the transition to sustainable energy, and clean drinking water for the growing world population. The agenda both aims at strengthening startups in its initial phase as well as at helping startup entrepreneurs with explicit growth aspirations.

One of the issues with Dutch entrepreneurship is the almost exploding number of self-employed freelancers in the last decade. This trend drastically changed the Dutch labor market. Partly as a response to the economic crisis and companies' outsource policies, partly as a reaction to the broader cultural need for personal flexibility and individual self-direction, self-employment now adds up to more than ten percent of the Dutch workforce.[16] Startup growth paths could be more ambitious, however. It turns out that after two years of its foundation on average only less than 3.5% of starting businesses hires employees. The vast majority of self-employed freelancers apparently is quite content with their one-person businesses or is unable to grow. The new policy aims at improving the general climate for entrepreneurship, creating better financial conditions and access to capital, improving fiscal arrangements for startups, reducing bureaucracy and red tape for beginning and growing enterprises, entrepreneurship education, and facilitation of incubator and accelerator programs. This cocktail of economic, financial, social, educational, and legal incentives should boost innovative and competitive entrepreneurship in the Netherlands. And above all: it should stimulate ambitious higher growth businesses. Research has shown that growth, ambition, startup skills, and making innovative products are relatively weak points of Dutch entrepreneurs.[17] The new policy reflects an attempt to improve the Dutch startup ecosystem to bring it on par with the international competition.[18] The self-defined government target of strengthening the growth ambition of Dutch startup entrepreneurs is a structural top-five position in the OECD rankings as of 2020 (now at place 22).

The Netherlands, so we would argue, will not realize this hard ball objective by merely polishing its innovation and entrepreneurial ecosystem. However important the redesign of the ecosystem is, we need to learn from Silicon Valley that this must be accompanied by a vibrating and dynamic pro-innovation culture. A culture that pushes big ideas, emphasizes openness and sharing, that is averse to a nine-to-five mentality, and encourages competition, risk-taking, and growth. An interesting Dutch initiative in this context that was launched in early 2015 is "StartupDelta: the place where entrepreneurs stand up, start up, and scale up".[19] StartupDelta is founded by leading serial entrepreneurs and governmental bodies, located in Amsterdam (because of its cosmopolitan atmosphere and culture), and led by former Dutch EC commissioner Neelie Kroes. Startups from around the globe are invited to grow fast at StartupDelta. This new initiative could gratefully profit from the recent (2015) change of Dutch immigration law which created a separate startup visa track for innovative international entrepreneurs.[20] This law change permits global startup founders easier access to the Netherlands, a lesson clearly learned from Silicon Valley's struggles with restrictive visa procedures for non-US talents.[21] By connecting over ten innovation hubs across the Netherlands, StartupDelta aims at becoming the largest startup ecosystem in Europe.[22] From our view on innovation this initiative is interesting because it seeks to operate in the very niche between ecosystem and culture. We strongly argue that creating this niche is a focal issue, not only for the Netherlands but for Europe as well. Ecosystems may be copied, cultures cannot.

Realizing an ambitious entrepreneurial culture is probably the greatest business challenge for Europe and its single countries. One thing we know for sure: cultures do not change overnight. Europe needs to re-address its innovation ecosystem (and is working hard on this) but it must also reinvent its entrepreneurial spirit. The fundamental lesson from Silicon Valley is that the innovation ecosystem must be embedded in a culture that celebrates entrepreneurship and that excels in total commitment. Creating this embedding, in our opinion, is the essential challenge for Europe to become a truly competitive player in the global arena of innovation, entrepreneurship, and startups. Other economies are eager to learn from Silicon Valley as well. Japan's Prime Minister Shinzo Abe recently visited the Bay Area and publicly stated that it is imperative for Japan to adopt the Silicon Valley model as a challenging cultural environment that boosts entrepreneurship, risk-taking, and innovation. As a way to regain its position as a worldwide leading hightech economy. "We would love to capture the dynamism of Silicon Valley and to bring it to Japan."[23]

Entrepreneurs on lessons to be learned from Silicon Valley

We asked our group of startup founders and CEOs what European and Dutch entrepreneurs could learn from Silicon Valley's impressive innovation history. What in their minds are the most striking advantages of the Silicon Valley experience and how can we work on that on the European continent? As it turns out their thoughts are particularly related to cultural differences and to a balanced innovation ecosystem. Arthur van Hoff (Jaunt) kicks off by stating "you can't get anywhere without having a big idea and get really excited (...) you can't be successful by thinking small, or thinking within your means." Neil Blaak agrees: "people here think big. I don't want to sound too negative about the Netherlands but I feel people there think small." David Mayer (RENDLE) adds that we have to "change our mindset, part of the Dutch culture is to be modest and not take too much risk". And Dirk de Kok (Mobtest) feels that "the biggest pro in America is always looking on the bright side of things. And if you fail, just pick up yourself and try it again." Harm TenHoff (Baylink) also points at differences in mentality: "here in Silicon Valley everybody is going for gold. In Holland that's not true." And Vincent van de Poll (GROM), "proud to be Dutch", applauds the fact that in Silicon Valley "you are way more free to do crazy things, your only goal is to become the number one in the world". Think bigger and be more ambitious, that seems to be the main message to their continental co-entrepreneurs. What about learning from the Valley's innovation track record? Harm TenHoff is very clear: "a good part of the Dutch economic growth in the coming decades will come from innovation. If that is a given you need to be very much in sync with Silicon Valley: the innovation spot number one in the world." Eric-Jan van Leeuwen (Login VSI) agrees and adds: "there should be a firm bridge between Silicon Valley and the Netherlands, especially from the larger companies, they should have a local office here in the Valley just to be at the point on what's going on from an innovation perspective." Innovation is key. Maarten Sierhuis (Ejenta) is very outspoken on this subject: "I left Holland because it irritated the hell out of me that companies never wanted to spend a dime on innovation."

Entrepreneurs also come up with specific suggestions. Ronald Mannak (JumpCam) strongly pleas for changing bankruptcy laws, laws on personal liability that primarily block entrepreneurship. "In America you can declare bankruptcy and start all over again. It's even relatively easy to do that." Fighting bureaucracy is another issue. As Vincent van de Poll argues: "what they should do in the Netherlands, I think, is to make sure they don't have to be as far away from the entrepreneurs and startups as possible, but they should make sure that startups can keep away as far as possible from government. So making rules a lot simpler for startups." Harm TenHoff points at a fundamental difference between Silicon Valley and the Netherlands when it comes to building a business in terms of ownership. "The Dutch business model is based on a company's autonomous growth and that the company will be there until your retirement. Companies hesitate to extract external funding and dilute equity and power. It is your baby and stays your baby. In Silicon Valley you build value, you go for the exit of your company. You know that from day one. Growth is accelerated by external funding and everyone has to share in the company's created value. This also explains the whole idea of stock options in the early stage of a startup."

Another interesting business practice suggestion is made by Eric-Jan van Leeuwen: "what is quite normal here in Silicon Valley, and quite abnormal in the Netherlands, is that with very large enterprise customers you may ask your customer to become an advisor to your company. I never heard that but I think it makes a lot of sense. It is not just building a relationship, it's also building a formal network." It is important for the Netherlands and for Europe to not copy the 'Silicon Valley Innovation & Startup Model'. Adrie Reinders is very outspoken on this issue. "You cannot copy a culture, so we have to find our own culture when it comes to entrepreneurship and how it fits into our society. Everybody is looking for replicating Silicon Valley but I don't think that's the answer. You cannot copy Silicon Valley, so you have to find your own way." (Adrie Reinders, EFactor). Ruben Daniëls (Cloud9 IDE), finally, is quite optimistic about startup developments in Europe: "I think over time we are going to see – with the right changes in laws and things like that – the Silicon Valley idea happening in Europe. But it will be different, it will be different culture, different ways of doing things. I'm actually very positive that we will see a lot more entrepreneurship and a lot more risk taking in Europe. Amsterdam is on the rise. But you need a couple of things to make that happen: you need to have money, you need to have entrepreneurs, you need to have culture, and you need to have a support system." It all comes down, so it seems, to the right blending of culture, regulations, and stimulation.

Boosting the European startup spirit

What can Europe do to reset and recharge its entrepreneurial culture over and beyond advancing its innovation ecosystem? We have developed a Startup Stimulation Model (see figure, which incorporates the most important lessons that we have learned. It encompasses three different market players that all can contribute to a thriving entrepreneurial startup culture: education, business, and government. Although the lessons have been distilled out of Silicon Valley, this model can be applied irrespective of country, region or city.

The Startup Stimulation Model

EDUCATION	BUSINESS	GOVERNMENT
Learn to think big Invoke open, sharing culture Enhance competitive skills Teach & practice teamwork skills	Close collaboration with students/teachers Share experience (e.g. give master classes) Enabletraineeships	Targeted subsidies Enable visa for startups Make filing for bankruptcy easier Loosen up compensation possibilities Enable investors

ENTREPRENEURIAL STARTUP CULTURE

Education

We think that investing in the right entrepreneurial startup mentality should begin with the youngest generation. Not exclusively, but in terms of focus and priority. They are the new cultural carriers, they are open to cultural change, and their ranks will bring forth the new generation of new entrepreneurs. That's why the educational system is so important in motivating young people to become entrepreneurs, in teaching startup skills. And startup skills are mainly skills, not just knowledge. Of course, the young generation should learn theories, models etc. But what we have seen in the Valley, and what we hear from all entrepreneurs, is that knowledge in itself does not make for a good entrepreneur. It should be accompanied by analytical, social, presentation, and collaborative skills, to name but a few. It is these skills that will make the difference between a skilled employee and a successful entrepreneur. We cannot emphasize the role of education enough in promoting an innovative, challenging, and entrepreneurial culture. A creative culture, in which students learn to Think Big, be competitive, but also to share experiences and be open about their dreams and projects. A culture that raises the bar and emphasizes distinction, where students learn to make the difference but also how to cooperate effectively in teams, and cope with diversity. Where they learn to realize their goals and be committed. Where students learn how to present themselves in a convincing way and work on sharpening their talents. Education, so we hold, is the key factor. But it is also the biggest challenge, the biggest wake up call. Education and entrepreneurship are not the closest friends, to put it mildly. They are more like separate worlds. The educational system should look in the mirror and hold itself against the light. It should much more open up and be inviting to the corporate world. From personal experience we know that there is still a lot of ground to cover.

Business

But redefining the educational system is not enough. More needs to be done. The business community should take responsibility too. It is a double-edged sword. In bringing in their business know how and practices, in sharing their business stories with students and their professors, in helping to upgrade and target educational materials, and in facilitating work placement, traineeships, and business case competitions. Gifted entrepreneurs and successful startup founders should volunteer to give master classes at universities and colleges. The business community should knock more forcefully at the doors of the educational system. We meet with many entrepreneurs who would like to do just this, but who run up against a sometimes impenetrable educational culture. A system that still is very much inner-oriented. Everything seems to be about formats, teaching loads, and bureaucracy. This, evidently, is not the entrepreneur's world, not the mental frame of reference of a startup founder. And equally important: not the student's future world either. Diminishing the gap between education and business is paramount in order to promote an entrepreneurial culture, a culture with the right set of attitudes, skills, and ambitions.

Government

What about government? It is obvious that its role in Europe differs markedly from the US and Silicon Valley. Still, European governments can do more and do better in facilitating innovative startup initiatives. In creating the right conditions for startups to stand out and grow. Access to funding is of course decisive. It is observed that much government innovation funding flows to larger companies, though they should be able to free their own resources. This so-called "Matthew-effect" (government benefits go to groups who already benefit disproportionally) is a major barrier for smaller and starting innovative businesses to get funding. Innovation tax benefits on profits, for example, are only interesting if your company is actually making a profit. And this is exactly the problem of many startups in its initial stage: they lose rather than make money. Regulations should be more entrepreneur-friendly. Bankruptcy should not result in an almost life-long debt, giving stock options instead of a salary to early startup employees, should be stimulated rather than fiscally unattractive.

Furthermore, it is important that experienced entrepreneurs, e.g. serial startup founders, have a seat on government funding agencies. They know what it means to start a business, they know the pitfalls, and they know what it takes to be successful or to fail. Funding in Silicon Valley signifies much more than money alone: it brings networks and expertise, it brings mentorship and feedback, it brings social and intellectual capital. Such mixed funding board representation would greatly help European innovation policy as well, also with respect to single European countries.

What Europe – and for that matter the Netherlands as well – needs is a full-fledged agenda for ambitious entrepreneurship. An agenda that is based on the conviction that the strength of our economy depends on the strength of our startup culture, on how successful we are in founding new and innovative businesses. This can only be realized through the right combination of institutional reform of our innovation ecosystem and a process of cultural change. It is at this fundamental hinge point that Silicon Valley teaches us wise lessons.

13. Go West, Young (Wo)Man, Go West?

European innovation regions and ambitious European entrepreneurs share a keen eye for how Silicon Valley succeeded in becoming the world capital of innovation, entrepreneurship, and hightech startups. European trade missions to Silicon Valley come and go. They all want to understand and learn from the "secret" of this most successful technological and economic region in the United States. Many of them are entrepreneurs who want to make the difference with a long cherished business dream of settling in Silicon Valley. Of becoming part of the world's leading innovative hub that fosters high growth startups, nurtures a competitive entrepreneurial spirit, and celebrates a vibrant culture of talent, seizing opportunity, and distinctiveness. But is this a smart dream? Should they stay or should they go? Imagine a student with startup plans or a beginning entrepreneur. Is going to Silicon Valley a wise and feasible option? What should be the main drivers of the cross-Atlantic migration decision calculus? What are the determining success or failure factors? Based on our study of the Silicon Valley entrepreneurial mindset and the anatomy of the region's innovation and startup system, we come up with twelve practical guiding principles that may facilitate this complicated and far reaching decision-making process. Or perhaps more accurately: preconditions that are crucial for a successful business transition to the Valley. These guiding principles have to do with psychological framing, entrepreneurial thinking, venture capital, self-presentation and personal branding, team building, strategic learning and business redefinition, perseverance and hard work, networking, and last but not least the ability to enjoy all the nice things Silicon Valley has to offer. The practical guiding principles should help entrepreneurs in deciding whether or not to move their business to the Valley.

1. Passion, Passion, Passion

One thing is crystal clear: without being deeply passionate about your business and product there is nothing to gain from going to Silicon Valley. Your passion determines whether you qualify for venture capital, whether talented and scarce employees want to work for you, whether you excel in networking and leadership, and whether the right people want to team up with you. And we're talking real passion, real commitment: an almost obsessive drive to be successful. And an almost fanatical determination to outrival the competition. The need for passion is a central message of this book. In short: no passion, no glory. No business success without business passion. Passion is a chief correlate of business achievement and separates winners from laggards.

2.   Think Big

There is no sense at all in going to Silicon Valley if you are satisfied with a modest one-person business without any growth potential or growth ambition. Essential for the Silicon Valley state of mind is to think in tens of millions of dollars or better in hundreds of millions. If this mental horizon is beyond your psychological comfort zone, stay in Europe. Silicon Valley is all about growth and about fast growth in particular. You need to think BIG if you want to raise venture capital for your startup. Silicon Valley venture capitalists – unlike European banks – are not interested in going from 100K to say 400K but from 2M to 200M. In Valley jargon: venture capitalists go for The Next Big Thing. So should you.

3.   Cash is King

In order to survive as a startup founder in Silicon Valley you need sufficient resources. Do not underestimate this. The Valley is a very expensive area in terms of cost of living. It may easily take two years before your product or service is ready to go to market, before you have your first customers, before you are making some money. It takes time to build a track record. Venture capitalists and business angels need to see a solid demo or a successful pilot before they consider investing in your business. They are likely to wait and see how your startup and personal leadership develop. The burn rate of your capital is high, extremely high, in Silicon Valley. You simply need cash to help you through the first years of your startup. Or put more dramatically: to simply survive.

4.   Perfect Pitch

Make sure your pitch is perfect. Shorten your business proposal to one minute: "what is the pain & what is your solution?" What are the unique features of your business to realize this solution (product development) and who will pay for it (sales)? Polish your pitch continuously and first rehearse your pitch at investors who actually are not on top of your list. Your first pitch will fail anyway and you need to frame this as a great learning experience. Do not approach your favorite investor unless your pitch is impeccable.

5. Personal Branding

Networking is a pure must for everyone who wants to be successful in Silicon Valley. Go to network events – there are many of them – show yourself, be proactive and don't be modest. Call yourself CEO, even if you are on your own. Present your business idea as groundbreaking, revolutionary even. Point out the phenomenal market potential of your startup. Be aware of the opportunities that come along, seize your chances. Think of yourself as a quality brand and act accordingly. One of the nice things about Silicon Valley is that people are willing to talk to you. From big hightech hotshots to the lesser gods. Not for an hour but certainly for a couple of minutes. Make sure you outshine yourself in those critical minutes.

6. Work Hard & Hard Work

One thing is painfully clear: you need to be willing to work extremely hard in Silicon Valley in order to be successful. A nine-to-five mentality is disastrous and predictably leads to a sudden death of your career as startup founder. Perseverance is absolutely essential. If your business fails: do it quickly. "Aim high, fail fast" and "failing forward" are totally normal and accepted concepts. It is widely understood that mistakes are made. You may fail as an entrepreneur, as a startup founder. Unlike in Europe, this is not held against you. Decisive is that you get up and start again. The Valley is full of stories of serial entrepreneurs whose business career is marked by great successes and deep failures.

7. Serious Stuff

Beginning a startup in Silicon Valley is no small thing. It turns your life upside down. It totally dominates your micro-cosmos and state-of-mind.

Be prepared, read books on Silicon Valley, and talk to entrepreneurs that crossed the ocean. This, at least, is the official opinion of startup founders on this issue. Some entrepreneurs confess that they hardly knew what their move to the Valley implicated with respect to all kinds of practical business challenges. This becomes less dramatic the more financial resources one has. Lacking preparation means that more needs to be learned and organized after the initial move which leads to an unnecessary higher burning rate of your startup capital.

8.   Super Team

Having the right team is priceless. Don't start a business with your best friend simply because he (or she) is your best friend. Choose your business partners with the greatest care. Who brings what and how important is this input for the business? If you are not highly selective in picking your team members, your investor will do that for you. Countless stories circulate of startup founders being fired by venture capitalists because their leadership failed or because their team performance part was deficient. By long experience VCs know the vital significance of team skills and competencies, of team appeal and credibility, of team energy and decisiveness. Another factor to consider is having the right team balance with respect to diversity (ethnic groups, gender). Diversity and innovation are closely linked in the startup history of Silicon Valley.

9.   Pivot!

It is almost self-evident that your initial business idea, product or service or your target group are far from perfect. Business reality and market logic are complex phenomena and there is no single road to business success. This means by implication that startup founders need to be willing to change the course of their business. Redefinition, sharpening, and adjustment are indispensable qualities of sound strategic judgment. This is particularly true under conditions of extreme uncertainty. Validated learning is basic to continuously test and modify one's business vision. Timely adaptation and adjustment are elementary strategic issues in this process of policy change and product reorientation. To pivot or not to pivot, that is the question.

10.   "If you're going to San Francisco...."

The basic question every startup founder who considers moving to Silicon Valley has to answer is: what exactly do you seek in this extremely competitive hotspot of hightech innovation? How does it benefit you and your startup? And vice versa: what does your business has to offer to Silicon Valley? How innovative is your product? Is your startup a fine example of disruptive innovation? Can you explain this to yourself and your social environment in plain, clear, and convincing language? If not: stay on the European side of the Atlantic Ocean.

11.   Help!

We met some of the nicest Dutch and other European entrepreneurs in Silicon Valley. But they choose to live in this part of the globe. Their willingness to help other entrepreneurs from the old continent is striking. Status, class and track record are irrelevant. Thinking along and sharing are defining features of the Valley's culture. Do not hesitate to ask for help to improve your business idea. Be open about your ideas and share your thoughts. Benefit from this remarkable culture of openness. Accept help, accept advice. Several European consulates in San Francisco offer practical assistance on how to do business in Silicon Valley. The Dutch consulate is a fine example. Each year the consulate organizes the "Holland in the Valley Startup Bootcamp". A unique experience that also teaches you the dos and don'ts of the Valley's business culture. Participate, it will make you stronger.

12.   Have Fun

All preceding eleven guiding principles are basic. No doubt about it. But going to Silicon Valley is not only about doing business. It is also about all the beautiful things that the Bay Area and California have to offer: climate, nature, culture. Teach yourself to relax and to enjoy the niceties of this part of the world.

The woman-machine interaction: making technology sexy
Interview with Jonna van Dungen, founder and CEO of StyleScript, planning to move to Silicon Valley

Guiding principles are only relevant when the persons who *could* use them, actually *do* use them. Therefore we discussed our twelve guiding principles with a Dutch female entrepreneur who is on the brink of leaving the Netherlands to conquer Silicon Valley with her new startup StyleScript (www.stylescript.com).

Jonna van den Dungen is a passionate and energetic entrepreneur. For more than seven years, she's been focusing on the next level of digital interaction. And she and her investors feel that now, in autumn 2015, the moment of truth is arriving. After years of working in 's Hertogenbosch, a beautiful city in the middle of the Netherlands, the move to Silicon Valley is about to be made. Jonna has a burning sense of urgency to cross the ocean and to convince the Valley of her vision of integrating technology, lifestyle, and the human touch.

What Jonna wants is to make technology both understandable and personal. And she means *really* personal. Her idea is disruptive: let consumers handle their own hard and soft data to have offered products and services to their liking. Consumer data must not only include age, previous purchases, and website visits, but especially personal tastes, favorite atmosphere, preferable shapes and colors, and emotional needs. A fashion buyer will know what Jonna is talking about, but will not be able to describe all products in that way. One could label jeans as informal and dresses as suited for parties, but Jonna wants to go much further. A party dress may suit one woman, but be abhorred by another. There are personal differences that cannot be captured by general product specifications. All products should be tagged so that consumers can find what they want, or better: be offered what they like. Indeed, consumers should only be offered those products and services that fit their own lifestyle preferences. Jonna has developed and programmed a special universal lifestyle language for that, the StyleScript. It has taken her several years to develop this solution. She works closely together with technologists, lifestyle experts, data scientists, and psychologists.

An essential part of StyleScript is that consumers fill in a Style Intake. This needs to be done once, and takes about five minutes. From that moment, a consumer can decide which websites are allowed to use the data from her personal StyleWallet. Each company that uses StyleScript can then offer really personal and personalized items or services. The consumer does not pay for this service. More precisely, she "pays" with personal information. Jonna claims that "privacy is dead; however, you should be able to decide what you share with whom". Who then is paying for this service?

The companies are, in two ways. First of all, they pay for the Style Intake of a consumer, which can be personalized per company. Second, all products of the company should be tagged in order to be matched with consumers. For this tagging, a company pays once for each product in its assortment.

At the start of the development, Jonna pitched her idea at the Dutch version of Dragon's Den. Interestingly, from the 11 winners that have come out of two seasons of the Dutch Dragon's Den, only Jonna eventually closed the deal. Her investors, successful entrepreneurs Arjen de Koning and Annemarie van Gaal, have supported her during the last years. She needed those investors, since the market was absolutely not ready for StyleSript. Where Jonna was busy thinking about making technology personal, she states, "most brands were still in the phase of Google Adwords". At parties, people were asking whether she was "still" working on this new concept. At some point, she reveals, "I just said to people that I have a marketing agency". This goes to show that the Netherlands is sometimes an uncomfortable place to be for a disruptive entrepreneur.

Jonna is seriously considering to move to Silicon Valley and is mentally preparing herself for this life changing event. On an earlier trip to the Valley, she felt people understood her immediately, grasping the big idea within seconds. Her mission in Silicon Valley is not so much to seek extra funding, but to make her idea become BIG. It is her assessment, and that of her investors and advisors, that the launching customer should be a major American retailer. If one or two big retailers adopt her StyleScript next-generation application, the rest of the market will follow. It won't work the other way around: if a Dutch retailer would start, it would mean nothing in the USA. And "time is of the essence", as Jonna puts it. She is driven by a strong sense of urgency. Leading companies are trying to make their websites and products more personal. Facebook is testing its virtual assistant Moneypenny, Bill Gates' Microsoft is already reviving personal assistant Cortana, and Apple already has three years of experience with the more seasoned assistant Siri. Fortunately for Jonna, these companies start reasoning from a mere technological point of view. Jonna wants to combine technology and lifestyle by introducing a new language to translate technology into lifestyle and vice versa. Hence to help technology talk with and work for "normal" people. Not in a technological, computer language like IBM Watson, but in a lifestyle language. Jonna starts from the other side with StyleScript. Using consumer language to let products fit the consumer. "Communication should not be about the brand or the product, but about the consumer," Jonna states. In the end it is all about emancipating the consumer, in realizing consumer autonomy and self-direction. That is the new marketing.

The move to Silicon Valley has, in Jonna's mind, almost no negatives. The one big negative is that she will see much less of her parents, and her parents much less of their grandchildren. Apart from that, Jonna only sees exciting opportunities. When she says that, her eyes are shining. An entrepreneur, driven to the max. Jonna is an excellent sparring partner to test our guiding principles. One of a kind.

– Passion, Passion, Passion
  Jonna immediately recognizes this principle. Passion is her natural state of being. At the same time, she believes that "you should not always be too enthusiastic, too passionate. It sometimes pays to limit myself in order to convey the message better." That, we admit, is a very relevant addition: one can lose the audience, if it only gets your passion but not your message.

– Think Big
  Again, Jonna instantly underlines this principle, but also in this case she wants to share a second thought: "Thinking big is very important, but you also need focus. I have a mission to accomplish. There are many areas that I could easily extend to, such as personal health, personal recruitment, etc. But first I need to make StyleScript a success."

– Cash is King
  Jonna is very positive about her current investors. That is not only because they invested in her company, but much more so because they are her first and foremost advisors and believe in her business mission. It is "smart money" (see also Chapter 6): sometimes the advice of the investor is more important than the money (s)he brings. So yes, cash is king, but smart cash rules.

– Perfect Pitch
  Jonna totally agrees on the necessity of a strong and convincing pitch. Very important. She polished her pitch to perfection with a keen eye for the subtleties needed for getting one's vision and message across. Network interaction to Jonna is a recurring opportunity to present her business idea in less than two minutes.

–   Personal Branding
    "Reading this principle in your book made me realize that I should pay
    more attention to my personal branding," Jonna says. She explains that
    it is so non-Dutch to care about your personal brand, so she too easily
    forgets about it. For her upcoming trip to Silicon Valley (a few weeks
    after our interview), she went buys clothes some clothes that are very
    much Jonna, but are also tactfully fitting with the Silicon Valley dress
    codes. So yes, personal branding and, Jonna adds: great storytelling!

–   Work Hard & Hard Work
    Simply a no-brainer for Jonna. "Working is the best thing there is. It
    has nothing to do with 'having to work', it is my intrinsic and utter
    motivation." Jonna is not driven by the desire to get rich. She is driven
    by wanting to make a difference, in both business and the world at large.

–   Serious Stuff
    This principle is plainly obvious to Jonna. One could argue that in fact
    she has already been preparing for five years to go to Silicon Valley.
    "Sometimes," she says, "it is a great benefit to make a mess of everything.
    You will arise even better from it. If they knock me down, I'll be stronger
    when I get up again." Jonna's move to the Valley may cause a big change
    in the things she is doing, also in her personal life, but the time is now.
    And Jonna is ready.

–   Super Team
    A crucial asset of any company that wants to make it. Jonna uses
    Insights Discovery (based on Jung's ideas) to create an excellent team.
    She recruits her staff on the basis that they must fit the company and
    its mission and really complement the team. Next to her own role as
    CIO (i.e. Social Innovation), the team consists of a CTO with, obviously
    technological responsibility and a Commercial Manager, responsible
    for lead generation.

–   Pivot!
    Very recognizable. Jonna has made a quite significant shift from B2C
    to B2B. This enabled her to speak to companies rather than consumers,
    and has been the best choice she made. The leverage is much bigger,
    and other companies don't see her as a competitor. Jonna admits that "I
    can imagine we will go back to B2C later in the process", which would
    be another pivot.

–   "If you're going to San Francisco…"
    It's clear that the Valley will bring Jonna what she is looking for: a
    stimulating, inspiring, and dynamic environment, and people able
    and willing to help her to make StyleScript a success. But what does she
    bring to the Valley? Jonna is very outspoken: "I'm a female, they need
    more female entrepreneurs over there! Moreover I am European, which
    brings in a different flavor." Next to that, she wants to bring change to
    the Valley: "with StyleScript we will translate big data into personal
    relevancy again. I can make technology sexy!". Now, that is a mission.

–   Help!
    Jonna immediately highlights this principle. The collaborative at-
    mosphere of openness and sharing has already brought her a lot of
    inspiration during previous trips. "Here in the Netherlands, especially
    in retail, secretaries are door bitches, trained to keep you outside. It is
    so much different in the Valley, where you will always get at least one
    chance to speak to someone."

–   Have Fun
    Stating the obvious. Work is fun. Meeting inspiring people is fun. Self-
    actualization is fun. Challenging yourself is fun. The Valley is fun. That
    sums it up, really.

Notes

1.   Introduction: The Silicon Valley Saga

1.   In several cases our unit of analysis will be the greater Bay Area. This nine-county Bay Area embraces San Francisco, Marin, Napa, Sonoma, Solano, Contra Costa, Alameda, Santa Clara and San Mateo Counties, and includes the cities of San Francisco, Oakland and San Jose, as well as the high technology center of Silicon Valley and the heart of Northern California's wine country.

2.   Piero Scaruffi, who wrote a history of Silicon Valley, is very outspoken and harsh: "Unlike the other high-tech regions of the world, the (boring, nondescript) urban landscape of Silicon Valley looks like the epitome of no creativity, no originality, no personality, nor style. It is difficult to find another region and time in history that witnessed an extraordinary economic boom without producing a single building worthy of becoming a historical monument." Piero Scaruffi, *A history of Silicon Valley, 1900-2014*. Self-published. Silicon Valley, 2014: 380.

3.   *The 2014 Silicon Valley index*. Joint Venture Silicon Valley/Silicon Valley Community Foundation.

4.   *The Bay Area innovation system*. How the San Francisco Bay Area became the world's leading innovation hub and what will be necessary to secure its future. Bay Area Council Economic Institute. San Francisco, 2012.

5.   See: http://www.siliconvalley.com/sv150.

6.   *The 2014 Silicon Valley index*. Joint Venture Silicon Valley/Silicon Valley Community Foundation.

7.   See: http://www.strategyand.pwc.com/innovation1000.

8.   http://siliconvalleyindicators.org/snapshot/.

9.   Organization for International Investment, Washington, DC. *Foreign investments in the United States*. 2013 report. http://www.ofii.org/sites/default/files/FDIUS_2013_Report.pdf. Cumulative Foreign Direct Investments in the United States amounted to $2.65 trillion: $475 billion from the United Kingdom, $308 billion from Japan, and $275 billion (over 10 percent) from The Netherlands. See also Fintan van Berkel, 'Foreign direct investments', in: *Internationalisation Monitor 2013*. Statistics Netherlands, The Hague, 2013.

10.   See: http://www.bea.gov/scb/pdf/2014/07%20July/0714_direct_investment_positions.pdf.

11.   *Europe and the Bay Area: Investing in each other*. Bay Area Council Economic Institute. San Francisco, 2014. Philips Lumileds in San Jose is one of the biggest Dutch firms in the Bay Area, employing 600 people, including 400 in R&D (among which 100 with PhDs). There are no data on the Netherlands' share of total European investment in the Bay Area. In the 2009-2012 period, European investments grew from 19 to 49 percent of total foreign inflows, amounting to $4.05 billion. The Bay Area investment in Europe is also quite

strong: flows to Europe reached \$3.3 billion in 2012 out of a total of \$6.0 billion Bay Area oversees investment.

12. *Economic ties between the USA and the Netherlands*. Infographic. Economicties.org. The state of Texas ranks first with 94,000 jobs supported by NL-USA trade and investments, and \$9.6 billion export to the Netherlands.

13. See for the underlying principles of research method triangulation: Norman K. Denzin (ed.), *Sociological methods: A sourcebook*. Chicago Aldine Atherton, 2006. 5th edition and Paulette Rothbauer (2008). 'Triangulation'. In: Lisa Given (ed.), *Sage encyclopedia of qualitative research methods*. Sage Publications.

14. Cf. Rowland Atkinson and John Flint, 'Snowball sampling', in Michael S. Lewis-Bech, Alan Bryman, and Tim Futing Lia (eds.), *Sage encyclopedia of social science research methods*, 2004.

2.   The Silicon Valley Innovation & Startup Model

1.   See Timothy Bresnahan, Alfonso Gambardella and AnneLee Saxenian, "'Old economy" for "New Economy" outcomes: Cluster formation in the New Silicon Valleys', in: *Industrial and Corporate Change* (2001): 835-860.

2.   Dana Stangler, *Path-dependent startup hubs. Comparing metropolitan performance: High-tech and ICT startup density*. Ewing Marion Kauffman Foundation, 2013.

3.   Christophe Lécuyer, *Making Silicon Valley. Innovation and the growth of high tech, 1930-1970*. Cambridge: MIT Press, 2007: 1.

4.   Piero Scaruffi, *A history of Silicon Valley, 1900-2014*, 2014: 21.

5.   Via the so-called "Poulsen arc", developed by Danish engineer Valdemar Poulsen and improved by FTC engineer Lee DeForest.

6.   E.g. Magnafox (1910), Single-dial radio tuner (1925), Fisher Research Laboratories (1928), Litton Industries (1940).

7.   See Timothy Sturgeon, 'How Silicon Valley came to be'. In: Martin Kenney (ed.), *Understanding Silicon Valley. The anatomy of an entrepreneurial region*. Stanford: Stanford University Press, 2000: 23.

8.   See Lécuyer, *Making Silicon Valley*: 13-51.

9.   Stewart Gillmor, *Fred Terman at Stanford: Building a discipline, a university, and Silicon Valley*. Stanford: Stanford University Press, 2004.

10. Particularly in the Boston area.

11. Ibid.: 97-100.

12. See David Packard, *The HP way: How Bill Hewlett and I built our company*. New York: Harper-Collins, 2013.

13. Walter Isaacson, *The innovators*, London: Simon & Schuster, 2014.

14. W. Isaacson (2014).

15. Lécuyer, *Making Silicon Valley*: 77.

16. Later to be followed by the Applied Electronics Laboratory (AEL) which conducted (largely secret) research for the military sector.

17. See Thomas Heinrich, 'Cold War armory: Military contracting in Silicon Valley', in: *Enterprise & Society* 3 (2002): 247-274.

18. The original name was ARPA. See for a current overview of DARPA's military and security innovation and technology program and projects: http://www.darpa.mil/default.aspx.

19. Stuart W. Leslie, 'The biggest "Angel" of them all: The military and the making of Silicon Valley'. In: Martin Kenney (ed.), *Understanding Silicon Valley*, 2000: 48-67.

20. Ibid.: 49.

21. Terman shared this nickname with William Shockley, co-inventor of the transistor.

22. Jon Sandelin, 'The story of the Stanford Industrial/Research Park', Paper prepared for the International Forum of University Science Park, China (2004).

23. Stewart Gillmor, *Fred Terman at Stanford*, 2004: 255.

24. Cf. S.B. Adams, 'Stanford and Silicon Valley: Lessons on becoming a high-tech region', in: *California Management Review*, 2005, 48 (1): 29–51.

25. The name "Silicon Valley" was coined by reporter Dan Hoefler, reporter for the *Electronic News* in a series of articles on the semiconductor industry in the Santa Clara Valley.

26. E. Floyd Kvamme, 'Life in Silicon Valley. A first-hand view of the region's growth'. In: Chong-Moon Lee, William F. Miller, Marguerite Gong Hancock, and Henry S. Rowen (eds.), *The Silicon Valley edge. A habitat for innovation and entrepreneurship*. Stanford: Stanford University Press, 2000: 61.

27. See Lécuyer, *Making Silicon Valley*: 148-159.

28. Martin Kenny and Urs von Burg, 'Institutions and economies: Creating Silicon Valley'. In: Martin Kenney (ed.), *Understanding Silicon Valley*, 2000: 230.

29. Dado P. Banato and Kevin A. Fong, 'The valley of deals. How venture capital helped shape the region'. In: Chong-Moon Lee *et al.* (eds.), *The Silicon Valley edge*, 2000: 297.

30. Lécuyer, *Making Silicon Valley*: 167.

31. Walter Isaacson. *The innovators*. London: Simon & Schuster, 2014.

32. William John Martin Jr. and Ralph J. Moore Jr., 'The Small Business Investment Act of 1958', in: *California Law Review* 47 (1959): 144-170.

33. Martin Kenney and Richard Florida, 'Venture capital in Silicon Valley: Fueling new form formation'. In: Martin Kenney (ed.), *Understanding Silicon Valley*, 2000: 122.

34. Mark Suchman, 'Dealmakers and counselors: Law firms as intermediaries in the development of Silicon Valley'. In: Martin Kenney (ed.), *Understanding Silicon Valley*, 2000: 79.

35. Charles Duhigg and Steve Lohr. *The patent, used as a sword. The New York Times*, Oct. 7, 2012.

36. Annalee Saxenian, 'Networks of immigrant entrepreneurs'. In: Chong-Moon Lee *et al.* (eds.), *The Silicon Valley edge*, 2000: 252.

37. See e.g. Theodore Roszak, *The making of a counterculture*. New York, Doubleday Books, 1969.

38. See Scaruffi, *A history of Silicon Valley, 1900-2014*, 2014: 9.

39. Eva de Valk, *Silicon Valley. Waar de toekomst wordt gemaakt*. [Silicon Valley. Where the future is being made.] Amsterdam: Lebowski Publishers, 2014.

40. Michael Lewis, *The new new thing. A Silicon Valley story*. New York: W.W. Norton & Company, 2000: 66.

41. Tapan Munroe (with Mark Westwind), *What makes Silicon Valley tick? The ecology of innovation at work*. Nova Vista Publishing, 2009.

42. Munroe, ibid.: adds quality of life as a discriminating factor in his Silicon Valley ecosystem model. Quality of life is undoubtedly important but its direct impact on innovation is difficult to measure.

3. Product: Innovation Silicon Valley Style

1.   See David Rosenberg, *Cloning Silicon Valley: The next generation of high-tech hotspots*. London: Reuters, 2001.

2.   Michael Lewis, *The new new thing. A Silicon Valley story*. New York: W.W. Norton & Company, 2000: 15.

3.   See e.g. Michael S. Malone, 'The purpose of Silicon Valley', in: *MIT Technology Review*, January 20, 2015. http://www.technologyreview.com/review/534581/the-purpose-of-silicon-valley/.

4.   http://www.cnet.com/news/zuckerberg-in-10-years-folks-will-share-1000-times-what-they-do-now/.

5.   http://www.inc.com/eric-markowitz/big-ideas/investors-influence-entrepreneurs-big-ideas.html.

6.   http://www.foundersfund.com/.

7.   Idem. Peter Thiel furthermore states that: "We believe that the shift away from backing transformational technologies and toward more cynical, incrementalist investments broke venture capital."

8.   http://www.claytonchristensen.com/key-concepts/.

9.   Clayton M. Christensen, *The innovator's dilemma: When new technologies cause great firms to fail*. Boston: Harvard Business School Press, 1997: 15.

10. Ibid.

11. http://www.innosight.com/innovation-resources/upload/Disruptive_Innovation_Overview_Final.pdf.

12. See e.g. http://techcrunch.com/event-type/disrupt/. And: https://www.thinkdif.co/.

13. See e.g. Max Nisen, 'How "disrupt" got turned into an oversized buzzword', in: *Business Insider*, September 28, 2013. http://www.businessinsider.com/how-silicon-valley-killed-disruption-2013-9?IR=T.

14. Jill Lepore, 'The disruption machine. What the gospel of innovation gets wrong', in: *The New Yorker*, June 23, 2014. http://www.newyorker.com/magazine/2014/06/23/the-disruption-machine.

15. Ibid. See for Christensen's response to Lepore's essay: http://www.bloomberg.com/bw/articles/2014-06-20/clayton-christensen-responds-to-new-yorker-takedown-of-disruptive-innovation.

16. See also: Constantinos Markides, 'Disruptive innovation: In need of a better theory', in: *Journal of Product Innovation Management,* 2006 (23): 19-25.

17. Guy Kawasaki, *The art of the start 2.0.* New York: Portfolio, 2015.

18. Guy Bauwen, *Innovation compass. How to develop a market and build a successful business.* Puurs: ShopmyBook, 2012 and Guy Bauwen, *Growth through innovation.* Brussels: Academic and Scientific Publishers (ASP), 2013.

19. *The culture of innovation.* What makes the San Francisco Bay Area companies different? A Bay Area Council Economic Institute and Booz & Company joint report. San Francisco, 2012.

20. Ibid.: 12.

21. Ibid.

22. Ibid.

23. Ibid.: 11. As Booz & Company researchers conclude: "The 44 percent of companies who reported that their innovation strategies are clearly aligned with their business goals – and that their cultures strongly support those innovation goals – delivered 33 percent higher enterprise value growth and 17 percent higher profit on five-years measures than those lacking such tight alignment."

24. Ibid, 19. Note that the number of Bay Area firms is 28, hence these percentages should be interpreted with care.

25. Ibid.

26. http://www.siliconvalleyhistorical.org/nxp-semiconductors-history/.

27. *Hotel California* by The Eagles: "Relax," said the night man, "We are programmed to receive. You can check-out any time you like, but you can never leave!"

4. Market: Pivot and Perseverance

1. Clayton M. Christensen, *The innovator's dilemma: When new technologies cause great firms to fail.* Boston: Harvard Business School Press, 1997.

2. W. Chan Kim and Renée Mauborgne. *Blue ocean strategy. How to create uncontested market space and make the competition irrelevant.* Boston: Harvard Business School Press, 2005.

3. http://www.ey.com/GL/en/Industries/Consumer-Products/Eleven-risks-for-consumer-products-companies---3--Speed-and-success-of-innovation#1

4. Guy Bauwen, *Innovation compass. How to develop a market and build a successful business.* www.innovationcompass.eu, 2012.

5. Eric Ries. *The lean startup. How constant innovation creates radically successful business.* London: Penguin Books, 2011: 111.

6. Ibid.: 49.

7. Ibid.: 77.

8. Ibid.: 120.

9.   Ibid.: 161.

10.   Ibid.: 169.

11.   The main pivot question runs as follows: "For the startup that you are telling us more about, please answer the following. Is your business currently similar to your initial idea/plans or vision in the very beginning? We're interested in whether the business, customers, technology, distribution/sales channels are similar to the initial plan. [If the business is no longer in operation, was there aspect of the initial plan or idea that you would change as a result of your experience?]." Answer categories: changed 5% or less, changed 25%, changed 75%, changed completely. (Stanford Innovation Survey Questionnaire).

12.   Charles E. Eesley and William F. Miller, *Impact: Stanford University's economic impact via innovation and leadership*. Stanford University, 2012.

13.   Everett M Rogers. *Diffusion of innovations*. New York: Free Press, 1962.

14.   Geoffrey A. Moore. *Crossing the chasm. Marketing and selling disruptive products to mainstream consumers* (3rd Ed.). New York: HarperCollins Publishers, 2014.

15.   Marieke de Mooij. *Global marketing and advertising. Understanding cultural paradoxes* (2nd Ed.). Thousand Oaks: Sage, 2005.

16.   Geoffrey A. Moore, *Crossing the chasm*, 2014.

17.   Ibid.: 6.

18.   Ibid.: 69-71.

19.   Ibid.: 71.

20.   http://www.bizjournals.com/sanjose/subscriber-only/2013/08/16/the-list-silicon-valleys-largest.html

21.   Walter Isaacson. *Steve Jobs*. London: Little, Brown, 2011.

22.   Jeff Sutherland. *Scrum. The art of doing twice the work in half the time.* New York: CrownBusiness, 2014.

23.   Joe Pulizzi and Newt Barrett. *Get content, get customers. Turn prospects into buyers with content marketing.* New York: McGraw-Hill, 2009: xv.

24.   https://www.youtube.com/watch?v=-8r6PoHiPwU

25.   https://www.youtube.com/watch?v=qgqsgXSJ7g8

26.   Gerrita van der Veen, Arne Maas, Anne-Marie Delfgaauw, and Han Gerrits. *We didn't start the fire. Social media? Social business!* Assen: Koninklijke Van Gorcum, 2015.

27.   Companies generally will ask money for premium versions of its apps.

28.   Chris Anderson. *The long tail. Why the future of business is selling less of more.* New York: Hyperion, 2006.

29.   Quote from https://www.zuora.com/academy/guides/is-freemium-right-business-model/, visited 15/06/29.

30.   Joe Pulizzi and Newt Barrett. *Get content, get customers.*, 2009.

31.   https://www.palantir.com/, visited 15/06/24.

32.   Fundraising values Palantir at $20B. http://www.cnbc.com/id/102783212, visited 15/06/25.

33.   J.R.R. Tolkien. *The lord of the rings*. London: HarperCollins Publishers, 1995.

34. Klaus Fog, Christian Budtz, Philip Munch, and Stephen Blanchette. *Storytelling. Branding in practice.* (2nd Ed.). Berlin: Springer Verlag, 2010: 22.
35. http://tomtunguz.com/bill-macaitis-talk/, visited 15/06/23.
36. https://www.youtube.com/watch?v=RrhkxfhRNDg.
37. https://www.youtube.com/watch?v=VtvjbmoDx-I.
38. https://www.youtube.com/watch?v=DZSBWbnmGrE.

5. Team and Talent

1. Robert Cressy, 'Determinants of small firm survival and growth'. In: Marc Casson, Bernard Yeung, Anuradha Basu and Nigel Wadeson (eds.), *The Oxford handbook of entrepreneurship.* Oxford: Oxford University Press, 2009: 161-193.
2. Randall Stross, *The launch pad. Inside Y Combinator. Silicon Valley's most exclusive school for startups.* London: Portfolio Penguin, 2012: 161.
3. Ibid. The rule is less strict now but Y Combinator states in its FAQ's that the odds of getting funded are lower for single startup founders as "a startup is too much work for one person".
4. John R. Katzenbach and Douglas K. Smith, *Harvard Business Review* (March, April) 1993: 112. See also their book *The wisdom of teams: Creating the high-performance organization.* Harvard, MA: Harvard Business School Press, 1993.
5. Ibid.: 112.
6. Thomas Lechler, 'Social interaction: A determinant of entrepreneurial team venture success', in: *Small Business Economics* (2001) 263-278.
7. *Innovative teams.* 20 minute Manager Series. Harvard, MA: Harvard Business Review Press, 2015.
8. http://www.fastcompany.com/3032548/hit-the-ground-running/the-only-6-people-you-need-on-your-founding-startup-team.
9. Ibid. Bernd Schoner, *The tech entrepreneur's survival guide. How to bootstrap your startup, lead through tough times, and cash in for success.* New York City: McGraw-Hill, 2014.
10. J. Richard Hackman, *Leading teams. Setting the stage for great performance.* Harvard, MA: Harvard Business Press, 2002.
11. Kevin C. Stagl, Eduardo Salas and C. Shawn Burke, C. S. 'Best practices in team leadership: What team leaders do to facilitate team effectiveness'. In: Jay Conger and Ronald Riggio (eds.), *The practice of leadership: Developing the next generation of leaders.* San Francisco: Jossey-Bass, 2007: 172-198. Also see: https://www.psychologytoday.com/blog/cutting-edge-leadership/201108/10-rules-high-performing-teams.
12. David Audretsch and Erik Monsen, 'Entrepreneurship capital: a regional, organizational, team and individual phenomenon'. In: Rowena Barrett and Susan Mayson (eds.), *International handbook of entrepreneurship and hrm.* Cheltenham: Edward Elgar, 2008: 47-70.
13. http://steveblank.com/2013/07/29/building-great-founding-teams/.
14. Ibid.

15. Lynn M. Martin, Sheena Janjuha-Jivrai, Charlotte Carey and Srikanth Sursani Reddy, 'Formalizing relationships? Time, change and the psychological contract in team entrepreneurial companies'. In: Rowena Barrett and Susan Mayson (eds.), *International handbook of entrepreneurship and hrm,* 207.

16. Clem Molloy, *Talent is gold. Talent management for today's workforce.* Chatswood: Sage MicrOpay, 2008: 7.

17. NOVA Workforce Development and the Economic Advancement Research Institute (EARI), *Bridge to career success. A study of career mobility and advancement in the information and communication technologies workforce.* Sunnyvale, CA: 2014.

18. Cf. the OECD report on 21st century skills based on the Survey of Adult Skills (The International Assessment of Adult Competencies), http://skills.oecd.org/documents/SkillsOutlook_2013_Chapter1.pdf.

19. Ibid.: 16.

20. Laszlo Bock, *Work rules! Insights from inside Google that will transform how you live and lead.* New York City: Hachette Book Group, 2015: 99-101.

21. http://www.entrepreneur.com/article/243660.

22. See: Simon Barrow and Richard Mosley, *The employer brand: Bringing the best of brand management to people at work.* Hoboken, NJ: 2005.

23. https://www.google.com/about/careers/lifeatgoogle/benefits/.

24. See for an overview: Laszlo Bock, *Work Rules!*: 274. One of the side-projects that turned out to be greatly successful was Gmail, invented by Google engineer Paul Buchheit. Google's extrinsic (financial) rewards are based on four principles: pay unfairly; celebrate accomplishments, not compensation; make it easy to spread the love; and reward thoughtful failure (*idem.:* 231).

25. https://www.apple.com/jobs/us/corporate.html.

26. See: http://fortune.com/2014/10/02/apple-employee-perks/.

27. Quoted from http://fortune.com/2014/10/02/apple-employee-perks/.

28. https://www.apple.com/jobs/us/corporate.html.

29. See: Alan Hyde, *Working in Silicon Valley. Economic and legal analysis of a high-velocity labor market.* Armonk, NY.: M.E. Sharpe, 2003 and Chris Brenner, *Work in the new economy: Flexible markets in Silicon Valley.* Hoboken, NJ.: Wiley-Blackwell, 2002.

30. Bruce Fallick, Charles A. Fleischman, and James B. Rebitzer, *Job-hopping in Silicon Valley: The micro-foundation of a high technology cluster.* Cambridge, MA.: National Bureau of Economic Research, 2005. http://www.nber.org/papers/w11710.pdf.

31. See: Ronald Gilson, 'The legal infrastructure of high technology industrial districts: Silicon Valley, Route 128, and covenants not to compete', in: *New York University Law Review* 74 (1999): 575.

32. http://www.ppic.org/content/pubs/report/R_215HJR.pdf.

33. Silicon Valley Workforce Investment Boards, *Silicon Valley in transition. Economic and workforce implications in the age of iPads, Android Apps, and the social web.* 2011 Silicon Valley Innovation Study.

34.   http://www.ppic.org/content/pubs/report/R_215HJR.pdf: 1.
35.   Silicon Valley Workforce Investment Boards, 34.
36.   Ibid.: 30.
37.   http://rivierapartners.com/engineering-salaries-reviewed-2/.
38.   http://svlg.org/wp-content/uploads/2014/03/CEO_Survey_2014.pdf.
39.   Charles E. Eesley and William F. Miller, *Impact: Stanford University's economic impact via innovation and leadership.* Stanford University, 2012.
40.   Ibid.: 44.
41.   Ibid.: 20.
42.   Ibid.: 60.
43.   http://www.nytimes.com/2015/07/02/upshot/the-next-mark-zuckerberg-is-not-who-you-might-think.html?_r=1&abt=0002&abg=0
44.   Ibid.

6.   Funding

1.   https://www.crunchbase.com/organization/sequoia-capital. Visited August 10, 2015.
2.   http://techcrunch.com/2014/02/19/sequoia-and-jim-goetz-are-big-winners-in-facebooks-whatsapp-acquisition/
3.   Ibid. Sequoia's partner Jim Goetz led the investment. See for his reaction: http://sequoiacapital.tumblr.com/post/77211282835/four-numbers-that-explain-why-facebook-acquire.
4.   https://www.crunchbase.com/organization/kleiner-perkins-caufield-byers. Visiterd August 10, 2015.
5.   http://www.kpcb.com/companies.
6.   Santing estimates that Dutch pension funds invest over 1€ billion in Bay Area venture capital. Coos Santing, 'Op zoek naar financiering voor startende en snelgroeiende innovatieve ondernemingen. Lessen voor Nederland uit de San Francisco Bay Area.' [Looking for funding of starting and fast growing innovative ventures. Lessons for the Netherlands from the San Francisco Bay Area]. http://www.rvo.nl/sites/default/files/San%20Francisco%20starters%20en%20snelgroeiers.pdf.
7.   John C. Dean, 'Fueling the revolution. Commercial Bank Financing'. In: Chong-Moon Lee *et al.* (eds.), *The Silicon Valley edge*, 2000: 317. The reluctance of the big commercial banks to invest in new venture startups eventually led to the creation of the Silicon Valley Bank. Dean was the bank's CEO until 2001 and is now managing general partner of Startup Capital Ventures.
8.   Thomas Hellmann, 'Venture capitalists. The coaches of Silicon Valley'. In: Chong-Moon Lee *et al.* (eds.), *The Silicon Valley edge*, 2000: 276.
9.   Thomas Hellmann, 'Venture capitalists', 2000: 276.
10.   Tapan Munroe, *What makes Silicon Valley tick?*, 2009: 72.
11.   https://www.pwcmoneytree.com/Reports/FullArchive/National_2015-2.pdf.

12. *The Silicon Valley tech venture almanac*, CB Insights, New York City, 2013. Data cover the 2009-Q3 2013 period. www.cbinsights.com/research-reports/Silicon-Valley-Venture-Capital-Almanac.pdf.

13. PricewaterhouseCooper and National Venture Capital Association, *MoneyTree Report*, Q4 2014 – full-year 2014. PWC, 2015. See for a Q1-2015 update: *The Q1'15 US venture capital report. Financing and exit analysis*. CB Insights, New York City, 2015.

14. https://www.cbinsights.com/blog/largest-tech-deals-2014-silicon-valley-new-york-boston/#siliconvalley.

15. http://googleblog.blogspot.co.uk/2014/07/google-ventures-invests-in-europe.html?m=1.

16. The phenomenon of acqui-hire has become more popular in recent years. For many struggling startups being acquired for its teams of smart people is a nice exit alternative to bankruptcy. Companies like Facebook, Twitter, Yahoo have been quite active in acqui-hiring. See: CB Insights, 'The rise of the acqui-hire: Breaking down talent acquisitions.' New York City: January 9, 2014.

17. Q1 – Q3.

18. At the end of Q3 of 2014.

19. *The 2015 Silicon Valley index*. Joint Venture Silicon Valley/Silicon Valley Community Foundation.

20. http://www.kpcb.com/news/kpcb-launches-green-growth-fund. Recently, KPCB reviewed its green tech portfolio and refocused its investment strategy. Russ Garland, 'Lessons learned, Kleiner Perkins stays committed to green technology', in: *Wall Street Journal*, March 17, 2012.

21. Marc Philips, *Inside Silicon Valley. How the deals get done*. Melbourne: Melbourne Books, 2013: Section 2. Also see: http://blog.eladgil.com/2011/03/how-funding-rounds-differ-seed-series.html

22. Research shows that just over 1 percent of startups will eventually hit the unicorn mark of reaching a one billion-dollar evaluation. CB Insights, New York City, May 25, 2015: 'Your startup has a 1.25% of becoming a unicorn.'

23. Identifying unicorn startups – startups that exit over 1$ billion – in an early stage is a continuous challenge for VC funds. Analyses by CB Insights show that VC first investments in such highly profitable startups are generally not in the first funding rounds. CB Insights, 'The exceedingly rare unicorn VC'. In: *Analyzing venture capital performance. A data-driven look at 'unicorn' exits and VC*. New York City: November 21, 2013. See for their update of US unicorns: https://www.cbinsights.com/reports/KPMG-CB-Insights-unicorn-report.pdf.

24. Marc Philips, ibid.: 15.

25. Ibid.: 23.

26. Somewhat older (2004) research, cited by Tapan Munroe, *What makes Silicon Valley tick?* (2009: 75-76), by the Center for Venture Research of the University of New Hampshire, observed that angels investors are mostly male, over 60 years old, annual incomes between $100,000 and $250,000, selecting startups that market high technologies they are familiar with and understand, prefer-

ring an active advisory role, and willing to co-invest with other angels, investing in 2-3 deals per year (roughly between $25,000 and $50,000 per deal).

27.   www.cbinsights.com/reports/Halo-Report-2013.pdf.

28.   https://paulcollege.unh.edu/sites/paulcollege.unh.edu/files/2013%20Analy-
      sis%20Report%20FINAL.pdf.

29.   See *The Silicon Valley tech venture almanac*, 2013.

30.   *The 2014 Silicon Valley index*. Joint Venture Silicon Valley/Silicon Valley Com-
      munity Foundation. 2014: 26-27.

31.   Bruce Booth, 'Data insight: Venture capital returns and loss rates.' *Forbes*
      (July 10, 2012).

32.   See: https://www.cbinsights.com/research-reports/2014-Tech-Exits-Report.
      pdf?utm_source=Global+Tech+Exits+2014&utm_campaign=a718c1b2c1-
      global_tech_exits_2014&utm_medium=email&utm_term=0_e9dbb0a3a7-
      a718c1b2c1-86682169.

33.   Unfortunately the study has not been published. We have to rely on a recon-
      struction of the main outcomes by Bruce Booth, *Forbes*, see note 31. See for
      additional research: Robert E. Hall and Susan E. Woodward, 'The incen-
      tives to start new companies: Evidence from venture capital. Cambridge:
      National Bureau of Economic Research, 2007; Henry Chen, Paul Gompers,
      Anna Kovner, and Josh Lerner, 'Buy local? The geography of successful and
      unsuccessful venture capital expansion'. Cambridge: National Bureau of
      Economic Research, 2009.

34.   Data by CB Insights for 2014 indicate that unicorn exits represent only 1.1%
      of all exits. Moreover, three quarters of exiting companies had not raised
      institutional (VC, private equity, growth equity) funding prior to exit. Half
      of the exits were of Internet companies but mobile company exits are one
      the rise with taken 20% of the deals. CB Insights, *The 2014 global tech exits
      report*. New York, 2015.

35.   Josh Lerner, *Boulevard of broken dreams. Why public efforts to boost entrepre-
      neurship and venture capital have failed – and what to do about it*. Princeton:
      Princeton University Press, 2009: 52.

36.   Martin Kenny and Urs von Burg, 'Institutions and economies: Creating Sili-
      con Valley'. In: Martin Kenney (ed.), *Understanding Silicon Valley*, 2000: 237.

37.   The Band, incidentally, was founded by Dutchman Hans Severiens, a former
      nuclear physicist, Wall Street analyst, and later entrepreneur and venture
      capitalist in California and Silicon Valley.

38.   See website Band of Angels: http://www.bandangels.com/.

39.   Amos Tversky & Daniel Kahneman, 'Judgment under uncertainty: Heuris-
      tics and biases', in: *Science*, (185), 1974: 1124-1131.

40.   Marc Philips, *Inside Silicon Valley. How the deals get done*. Melbourne: Mel-
      bourne Books, 2013: 84-85.

41.   David Beckett. *Three minute presentation*. Netherlands: DJB Pubs BV, 2012.

7.   Culture

1.   Parts of this section have been adopted from Peter Ester and Pieter van Ni-
      spen tot Pannerden, 'Foreign policy and the cultural factor. A research and
      education agenda.' Malta: Mediterranean Academy of Diplomatic Studies
      (MEDAC), 2013.
2.   UNESCO Universal Declaration on Cultural Diversity, Paris: 2001.
3.   Geert Hofstede, *Cultures and organizations*. Intercultural cooperation and
      its importance for survival. London: HarperCollinsBusiness, 1994: 5.
4.   See Amir N. Licht and Jordan I. Siegel, 'The social dimensions of entre-
      preneurship'. In: Marc Casson, Bernard Yeung, Anuradha Basu, and Nigel
      Wadeson (eds.), *The Oxford handbook of entrepreneurship*. Oxford: Oxford
      University Press, 2009: 516-521.
5.   http://geert-hofstede.com/countries.html.
6.   Loek Halman, *The European Values Study: A third wave. Source book of the
      1999/2000 European Values Study Surveys*, EVS, WORC, Tilburg University: 2001.
7.   Niklas Luhmann, 'Soziologie als Theorie sozialer Systeme', in: *Kölner
      Zeitschrift für Soziologie und Sozialpsychologie*, IX (1967): 615-644.
8.   Charles K. Kluckhohn, 'Values and value orientations in: the theory of
      action'. In: Talcott Parsons and Edward E. Shils E. (eds.) *Toward a general
      theory of action*. Cambridge, MA, Harvard University Press, 1951: 395.
      Harry Triandis, 'Dimensions of culture beyond Hofstede'. In: Henk Vinken,
      Joseph Soeters and Peter Ester (eds.), *Comparing Cultures. Dimensions of
      culture in a comparative perspective*. Leiden & Boston: Brill, 2004: 28-42.
9.   Chong-Moon Lee, William F. Miller, Marguerite Gong Hancock, and Henry
      S. Rowen, 'The Silicon Valley habitat'. In: Chong-Moon Lee, William F.
      Miller, Marguerite Gong Hancock, and Henry S. Rowen (eds.), *The Silicon
      Valley edge. A habitat for innovation and entrepreneurship*. Stanford: Stan-
      ford University Press, 2000: 6.
10.   http://www.teslamotors.com/blog/all-our-patent-are-belong-you.
11.   http://www.mercurynews.com/breaking-news/ci_15363242.
12.   http://geert-hofstede.com/countries.html.
13.   Randall Stross, *The launch pad. Inside Y Combinator. Silicon Valley's most
      exclusive school for startups*. London: Portfolio Penguin, 2012: 116.
14.   http://www.city-journal.org/html/11_1_ecstatic_capitalisms.html.
15.   http://www.forbes.com/sites/kevinkruse/2013/03/07/motivating-employ-
      ees/. See also Maynard Webb and Carlye Adler, *Rebooting work. Transform
      how you work in the age of entrepreneurship*. San Francisco: Jossey-Bas, 2013.
16.   See: http://www.forbes.com/sites/davidshaywitz/2012/10/08/silicon-valley-
      work-life-balance-is-for-losers-not-closers/.
17.   See: http://www.scmp.com/business/economy/article/1384057/group-
      wants-shun-silicon-valley-and-revive-40-hour-working-week.
18.   Andreas Rauch and Michael Frese. *Meta-Analysis as a tool for developing en-
      trepreneurship research and theory*. In: Jerome Katz and Andrew C. Corbett,

Advances in entrepreneurship, firm emergence and growth, Volume 9: Entrepreneurship: Frameworks and empirical investigations from forthcoming
leaders of European research, 2006.

19.   http://thefailcon.com/.

20.   Claire Martin, 'Wearing your failures on your sleeve', in: *The New York Times*
      (November 8, 2014).

21.   Rob Asghar, 'Why Silicon Valley's "Fail Fast" mantra is just a hype', in: *Forbes*
      (July 14, 214).

22.   Rory Carroll, 'Silicon Valley's culture of failure … and the "walking dead" it
      leaves behind', in: *The Guardian* (June 28, 2014).

23.   https://www.cbinsights.com/blog/startup-failure-reasons-top/. New York:
      CB Insights (October 7, 2014).

24.   Geert Hofstede, *Culture's consequences.*, Thousand Oaks: Sage, 2001: 148.

25.   http://images.forbes.com/forbesinsights/StudyPDFs/Innovation_Through_
      Diversity.pfd: 9.

26.   See e.g. Jawed Syed and Mustafa Ozbilgin (eds.), *Managing diversity and
      inclusion. An international perspective*. London: Sage, 2015.

27.   Günter Stahl, Martha Maznevski, Andreas Voigt, and Karsten Jonson, 'Unrave-
      ling the effects of cultural diversity in teams: A meta-analysis on multicultur-
      al work groups', in: *Journal of International Business Studies,* 41 (2010): 690-707.

28.   Katherine W. Philips and Charles A. O'Reilly, 'Demography and diversity in
      organizations: A review of 40 years of research'. In: Barry M. Staw & Larry L.
      Cummings (eds.)*, Research in organizational behavior*, 20. Greenwich, CT:
      JAI Press, 1998: 77-140.

29.   Henri Tajfel, 'The psychological structure of intergroup relations'. In: Henri
      Tajfel (ed.), *Differentiation between social groups: Studies in the social psy-
      chology of intergroup relations*. London: Academic Press, 1978.

30.   Geert Hofstede, *Culture's consequences.*, 2001.

31.   Ursula Brinkmann and Oscar van Weerdenburg, *Intercultural readiness. Four
      competences for working across cultures*. London: Palgrave Macmillan, 2014.

32.   See also Mike Noon, 'Managing equality and diversity'. In: Julie Beardwell
      and Tim Claydon (eds.), *Human resource management. A contemporary ap-
      proach*. Harlow: FT Prentice Hall, 2007: 225-253.

33.   Vivian Hunt, Dennis Layton, and Sara Prince, *Diversity matters*, Mc Kinsey
      and Company, February 2015.

34.   Ibid.: 1.

35.   Elsa Davidson, *The burdens of aspirations. Schools, youth, and success in the
      divided social worlds of Silicon Valley*. New York City: New York University
      Press, 2011: 9.

36.   http://wpusa.org/WPUSA_TechsDiversityProblem.pdf.

37.   http://www.nytimes.com/2014/12/27/opinion/joe-nocera-silicon-valleys-
      mirror-effect.html?_r=0.

38.   http://www.apple.com/diversity/.

39.   http://www.wired.com/2015/06/google-diversity-nancy-lee/.

40.   http://www.intel.com/content/www/us/en/diversity/message-from-brian-krzanich.html.

41.   http://www.wired.com/2015/06/vc-firms-arent-investing-diversity-bad-move/.

42.   http://uk.businessinsider.com/ben-horowitz-on-diversity-in-silicon-valley-2015-5?r=US.

43.   See for a more general empirical analysis of the contribution of immigrants to the US economy: Robert W. Fairlie and Magnus Lofstrom, *Immigration and entrepreneurship*, Bonn: Institute for the Study of Labor (IZA), Discussion paper no. 7669, 2013.

44.   Gary Gereffi, Ben Rissing, AnnaLee Saxenian, and Vivek Wadwha, *America's new immigrant entrepreneurs*, Duke University and Berkeley University, 2007.

45.   *American made 2.0. How immigrant entrepreneurs continue to contribute to the US economy*. Arlington: National Foundation for American Policy, 2013.

46.   Ibid.: 12.

47.   Ibid.: 5.

48.   *The 2015 Silicon Valley index*: 13-14.

49.   See The Economist (May 23, 2015): http://www.economist.com/news/special-report/21651331-india-should-make-more-valuable-asset-abroad-worldwide-web?fsrc=scn/tw/te/pe/ed/theworldwideweb. Based on an upcoming (2016) book by Sanjoy Chakravorty, Devesh Kapur and Nirvikar Singh, *The other one percent: Indians in America*.

50.   Both Stanford and Berkeley opened facilities in China, respectively in Beijing and Shanghai.

51.   http://icenter.stanford.edu/ and http://engineering.stanford.edu/about.

52.   It is estimated that about one-third of all foreign students in California – almost 37,000 – are from greater China. See: *Ties that bind*. 2014 Edition. The San Francisco Bay Area's economic links to greater China. Bay Area Council Economic Institute. San Francisco, 2014: 14.

53.   http://internationaloffice.berkeley.edu/students/current/enrollment_data.

54.   AnnaLee Saxenian, 'Networks of immigrant entrepreneurs'. In: Chong-Moon Lee *et al.* (eds.), *The Silicon Valley edge.* 2000: 251.

55.   Ibid.: 252.

56.   Ibid.: 255.

57.   Ibid.: 256-257.

58.   http://www.svcwireless.org/svcw/.

59.   See for a more general discussion of the role of ethnic resources, or social capital, in building business networks: Anuradha Basu, 'Ethnic minority entrepreneurship'. In: Mark Casson, Bernard Yeung, Anuradha Basu and Nigel Wadeson (eds.), *The Oxford handbook of entrepreneurship*. Oxford: Oxford University Press, 2009: 580-600.

60.   *Ties that bind*. 2014 Edition: 104-106.

61.   Geert Hofstede, *Culture's consequences,* 2001: 180.

62.   http://data.worldbank.org/indicator/IC.BUS.EASE.XQ/countries/1W?display=default

63. Stuart Anderson, *American made 2.0*, 2013: 16.

64. Marieke de Mooij. *Global marketing and advertising.* Understanding cultural paradoxes (2nd edition). Thousand Oaks: Sage, 2005.

65. Geert Hofstede, *Culture's consequences,* 2001.

8.   Universities and R&D Labs

1.   See http://www.topuniversities.com/university-rankings; http://www.timeshighereducation.co.uk/world-university-rankings/2014-15/world-ranking

2.   *The Bay Area innovation system.* How the San Francisco Bay Area became the world's leading innovation hub and what will be necessary to secure its future. Bay Area Council Economic Institute. San Francisco, 2012.

3.   Ibid.: 1.

4.   Emilio J. Castilla, Hokyu Hwang, Ellen Granovetter, and Mark Granovetter, 'Social networks in Silicon Valley'. In: Chong-Moon Lee *et al.*, (eds.), *The Silicon Valley edge*, 2000: 229.

5.   The student-to-faculty ratio signifies the number of students per teacher. Hence a low a ratio is considered to be better.

6.   Bay Area Council Economic Institute, 'UC Berkeley. Stimulating entrepreneurship in the Bay Area and Nationwide.' San Francisco, 2014: 5. Figures mentioned in this section on Berkeley are largely based on this source and on Berkeley's website.

7.   Ibid.: 7-8.

8.   See for a more complete list: http://ipira.berkeley.edu/partial-list-uc-berkeley-start-ups

9.   Bay Area Council Economic Institute, 'UC Berkeley. Stimulating entrepreneurship in the Bay Area and Nationwide'. San Francisco, 2014, Chapter 3.

10. Figures based on the IMPLAN model, ibid.: 45.

11. http://ipira.berkeley.edu/success-stories.

12. http://entrepreneurship.berkeley.edu/about-us/mission/.

13. http://funginstitute.berkeley.edu/.

14. http://ei.haas.berkeley.edu/C2M/; http://vcresearch.berkeley.edu/bio2market/overview.

15. http://vcresearch.berkeley.edu/bakarfellows/about.

16. http://qb3.org/about.

17. http://foundry.citris-uc.org/.

18. http://skydeck.berkeley.edu/.

19. Berkeley also features Free Ventures an independent startup launch pad by and for students. "We envision a world where Berkeley students spend less time on class projects and more time on building tools that create a positive impact on people's lives and the world. By connecting students with the right resources, motivation, and support, students can be empowered to build more, and do more." http://www.freeventures.org.

20. http://cet.berkeley.edu/.

21. http://bpep.berkeley.edu/.
22. http://bigideas.berkeley.edu/about/.
23. A translation of "Die Luft der Freiheit weht". The phrase is a quote from Ulrich von Hutten, a 16th-century humanist. See for a further explanation of this unofficial and rather peculiar motto: http://web.stanford.edu/dept/pres-provost/president/speeches/951005dieluft.html.
24. Charles E. Eesley and William F. Miller, *Impact: Stanford University's economic impact via innovation and leadership*. Stanford University, 2012. Most data on Stanford in this section are based on this study.
25. Ibid.: 6.
26. Ibid.: 7.
27. Ibid.: 17.
28. http://www.siliconvalley.com/SV150/ci_25548370/.
29. http://web.stanford.edu/group/wellspring/economic.html.
30. http://otl.stanford.edu/.
31. http://otl.stanford.edu/documents/otlar10.pdf: 5.
32. See: http://facts.stanford.edu/research/innovation.
33. Charles E. Eesley and William F. Miller, *Impact: Stanford University's economic impact via innovation and leadership*, 2012: 82.
34. https://www.cbinsights.com/blog/university-entrepreneurship-report/. Harvard University took second place.
35. Ibid.: 61.
36. http://stvp.stanford.edu/.
37. http://dschool.stanford.edu/launchpad-design-and-launch-your-product-or-service/.
38. http://ecorner.stanford.edu/index.html.
39. http://epicenter.stanford.edu/.
40. http://sen.stanford.edu/.
41. http://www.gsb.stanford.edu/ces.
42. http://www.gsb.stanford.edu/ces/students/venture-studio.
43. http://www.gsb.stanford.edu/programs/stanford-ignite.
44. https://seed.stanford.edu/.
45. http://biodesign.stanford.edu/bdn/index.jsp.
46. Some critics feel that a more independent position of Stanford vis-à-vis the business community would be preferable. See e.g. Ken Auletta, 'Get Rich U. There are no walls between Stanford and Silicon Valley. Should there be?', in: *The New Yorker*, April 30, 2012.
47. http://etl.stanford.edu/about/.
48. http://bases.stanford.edu/.
49. http://startx.stanford.edu/.
50. http://www.bizjournals.com/sanjose/print-edition/2014/12/19/a-startx-is-born-how-a-stanford-student-project.html.
51. http://www.sjsu.edu/about_sjsu/.
52. http://www.scu.edu/business/.

53. http://cms01.scu.edu/business/cie/upload/2015-CAPE-Flyer.pdf.
54. *The Bay Area innovation system*, 2012: 85-88.
55. See the Bay Area Council Economic Institute White Paper, 'Reforming California Public Higher Education for the 21st Century' which addresses the most pressing challenges. Bay Area Council Economic Institute. San Francisco, 2014.

9. Government

1. *The Bay Area innovation system*, 2012: 28.
2. http://facts.stanford.edu/research/.
3. Mariana Mazzucato, *The entrepreneurial state. Debunking public vs. private sector myths*. London: Anthem Press, 2014: 73.
4. Josh Lerner, *Boulevard of broken dreams*, 2009: 35: 41.
5. Henry S. Rowen, 'Serendipity or strategy. How technology and markets came to favor Silicon Valley'. In: Chong-Moon Lee *et al.*, (eds.), William F. Miller, *The Silicon Valley edge*, 2000: 189.
6. http://www.archive.org/stream/bayhdoleactrevieoounit/bayhdoleactre-vieoounit_djvu.txt.
7. Dennis Patrick Leyden and Albert N. Link, *Public sector entrepreneurship: US technology and innovation policy*. New York: Oxford University Press, 2015: 75.
8. http://www.economist.com/node/1476653.
9. See Eric Ries, Patrick Vlaskovits, and Brant Copper, *The lean entrepreneur: How visionaries create products, innovate with new ventures, and disrupt markets*. Hoboken: John Wiley & Sons, 2013: Chapter 8, 'The Valley of Death'.
10. Additional SBIR program goals include meeting the research and development needs of federal government and to increase the participation of minorities and disadvantaged people in innovation activities.
11. Federal agencies with budgets over $100 million are required to set 2.5% of its budget aside for SBIR.
12. http://www.nsf.gov/statistics/seind14/index.cfm/chapter-4/c4s8.htm.
13. *The development of US policies directed at stimulating innovation and entrepreneurship*, European Commission: Joint Research Centre. Report EUR 26518 EN, 2014: 20.
14. Ibid.: 21.
15. See: http://library.uwb.edu/guides/usimmigration/79%20stat%20911.pdf.
16. Stuart Anderson, *American made 2.0. How immigrant entrepreneurs continue to contribute to the US economy*. Arlington: National Foundation for American Policy, 2013: 18-19.
17. http://svlg.org/wp-content/uploads/2014/03/CEO_Survey_2014.pdf.
18. *Europe and the Bay Area: Investing in each other*. Bay Area Council Economic Institute. San Francisco, 2014: 58.
19. http://www.gpo.gov/fdsys/pkg/BILLS-112hr3606enr/pdf/BILLS-112hr3606enr.pdf.

20. The SEC (Securities and Exchange Commission), however, still did not publish regulations and rules that would allow the law going into effect. This meets with serious criticism. See: http://www.gpo.gov/fdsys/pkg/BILLS-112hr3606enr/pdf/BILLS-112hr3606enr.pdf.

21. Randall Stross, *The launch pad*, 2012: 205.

22. http://honda.house.gov/.

10.   Network Support System

1. See e.g. Maxine Robertson, Jacky Swan, and Sue Newell, 'The role of networks in the diffusion of technological innovations', in: *Journal of Management Studies*, 33 (1996) 333-354; Stefano Breschi and Franco Malerba (eds.), *Clusters, networks, and innovations*. Oxford: Oxford University Press, 2005; Thomas W. Valente, *Network models of the diffusion of innovations*. Cresskill, NJ: Hampton Press, 1995.

2. Castilla, *et al.*, 'Social networks in Silicon Valley'. In: Chong-Moon Lee *et al.*, *The Silicon Valley edge*, 2000: 222.

3. Ibid.: 241-245.

4. See Francis Fukuyama, *Trust*. The social virtues and the creation of prosperity. London: Penguin Books, 1995. Political scientist Ronald Inglehart found that interpersonal trust and similar cultural orientations are strongly associated with both economic development and democratic stability. Ronald Inglehart, *Culture shift in advanced industrial society*. Princeton: Princeton University Press, 1990, and Ronald Inglehart, M*odernization and post modernization*. Princeton: Princeton University Press, 1997.

5. Stephen S. Cohen and Gary Fields, 'Social capital and capital gains: An examination of social capital in Silicon Valley'. In: Martin Kenney (ed.), *Understanding Silicon Valley*, 2000: 191-192.

6. http://www.jointventure.org/.

7. Craig W. Johnson, 'Advising the New Economy: The role of lawyers'. In: Chong-Moon Lee *et al.*, (eds.), *The Silicon Valley edge*, 2000: 327.

8. Mark Suchman, 'Dealmakers and counselors: Law firms as intermediaries in the development of Silicon Valley'. In: Martin Kenney (ed.), *Understanding Silicon Valley*, 2000: 79.

9. Ibid.: 338.

10. Craig Johnson, 'Advising the New Economy', 2000: 332.

11. See for a conceptual and empirical framework of incubators: Anna Bergek and Charlotte Norman, 'Incubator best practice: A framework', in: *Technovation*, (28), 2008: 20-28.

12. See: http://uipalette.com/top-startup-incubators-in-the-sf-bay-area/.

13. http://rocketspace.com/.

14. http://www.wired.com/2011/05/ff_ycombinator/all/1.

15. http://www.forbes.com/sites/tomiogeron/2012/04/30/top-tech-incubators-as-ranked-by-forbes-y-combinator-tops-with-7-billion-in-value/.

16.   https://www.ycombinator.com/about/.

17.   Randall Stross, *The launch pad*, 2012: 77.

18.   Randall Stross, *The launch pad*, 2012: 161.

19.   https://www.ycombinator.com/faq/.

20.   http://www.ycombinator.com/atyc/.

21.   http://www.forbes.com/sites/tomiogeron/2012/04/30/top-tech-incubators-as-ranked-by-forbes-y-combinator-tops-with-7-billion-in-value/.

22.   https://en.wikipedia.org/wiki/Y_Combinator_(company). Visited August 10, 2015.

23.   https://www.crunchbase.com/organization/trinity-ventures#x, visited July 10, 2015.

24.   http://www.trinityventures.com/contact/.

25.   A similar observation is made by Randall Stross, *The launch pad*, 2012: 144.

26.   Anna Patterson is currently Google's vice-president of Engineering.

11.   The Downside of the Valley

1.   http://www.bizjournals.com/sanjose/silicon-valley-transit-all-the-coverage.html.

2.   http://www.mercurynews.com/bay-area-news/ci_27391607/bay-area-cities-will-see-millions-dollars-more.

3.   http://www.sfchronicle.com/archive/item/A-decade-of-homelessness-Thousands-in-S-F-30431.php.

4.   *Forbes* 2013 Billionaires List. See also Eric van Susteren, 'Silicon Valley tops San Francisco in resident billionaires', in: *Silicon Valley Business Journal*, March 12, 2014.

5.   2012 data; *The 2015 Silicon Valley index*. 21.9% of Silicon Valley households is below the self-sufficiency standard but above poverty and 7.6% is below poverty. Figures for California are 24.9% and 13.4%, respectively. Recent data about the Bay Area shows that in 2013, 11.3% (830,000 in absolute numbers) of its residents live in poverty. http://siliconvalleyindicators.org/special-reports/poverty-brief-march-2015/.

6.   *The 2015 Silicon Valley index*. Joint Venture Silicon Valley/Silicon Valley Community Foundation.

7.   George Avalos, 'Santa Clara County has highest median household income in nation, but wealth gap widens', in: *San Jose Mercury News,* August 11, 2014.

8.   See for a detailed account of how economic insecurity and inequality affect the aspirations of Silicon Valley's youth along lines of class and ethnicity: Elsa Davidson, *The burdens of aspirations. Schools, youth, and success in the divided social worlds of Silicon Valley*. New York City: New York University Press, 2011.

9.   Michelle Quinn, 'Is Silicon Valley's growing gender wage gap a booming byproduct?', in: *San Jose Mercury News*, February 8, 2015.

10.   George Packer, 'Change the world. Silicon Valley transfers its slogans – and its money to the realm of politics', in: *The New Yorker*, May 27, 2013. Reflecting

on his high school years in Palo Alto in the late seventies, Packer states: "The Valley was thoroughly middle class, egalitarian, pleasant, and a little boring."

11.   Elsa Davidson, *The burdens of aspirations*, 2011: 185.

12.   Jane Porter, 'Inside the movement that's trying to solve Silicon Valley's diversity problem'. www.fastcompany, October 29, 2014.

13.   Heather Somerville, 'Google, Startup Grind join forces on tech diversity', in: *Siliconbeat.com*, February 12, 2015.

14.   http://www.paragon-re.com/Market_overview/

15.   *The 2015 Silicon Valley index*.

16.   Joe Kloc, 'Tech boom forces a ruthless gentrification in San Francisco', in: *Newsweek*, April 15, 2014. Rory Carroll, 'Geek-driven gentrification threatens San Francisco's bohemian appeal', in: *The Guardian*, March 5, 2013.

17.   See e.g. Loretta Lees, Tom Slater, and Elvin K. Wyly, *Gentrification*. New York: Routledge/Taylor & Francis Group, 2008.

18.   http://priceonomics.com/the-san-francisco-rent-explosion-part-ii/.

19.   "Transportation is the new status symbol," said Chuck Darrah, chair of the anthropology department at San Jose State, who studies Silicon Valley. The hulking luxury buses complete with Wi-Fi and electricity outlets "signal that you have a job and that you have one with a firm that is forward-thinking and enlightened." Citation from Michelle Quinn, 'The shuttle effect and the commute that divides us', in: *San Jose Mercury News*, May 12, 2014.

20.   Rebecca Solnit, 'Diary: Google invades', in: *London Review of Books*, 35, no. 3, February 7, 2013. See also: Bard Wieners, 'Are the techno riche really ruining San Francisco? Yes, says Rebecca Solnit', in: *Bloomberg Businessweek*, December 31, 2013.

21.   Andrew Gumbel, 'San Francisco's guerilla protest at Google buses swells into revolt', in: *The Guardian*, January 25, 2014.

22.   Sean Hollister, 'Protesters block Silicon Valley shuttles, smash Google bus window', in: *The Verge*, December 20, 2013.

12.   Silicon Valley's Secret Sauce: (Ecosystem x Culture)[2]

1.   Foreword to Martin Kenney (ed.), *Understanding Silicon Valley*, 2000.

2.   Martin Obschonka, Michael Stuetzer, Samuel D. Gosling, Peter J. Rentfrow, Michael E. Lamb, Jeff Potter, and David B. Audretsch, Entrepreneurial regions: do macro-psychological cultural characteristics of regions solve the "knowledge paradox" of economics? Online at http://mpra.ub.uni-muenchen/65202/MPRA Paper no. 65202, posted June 25, 2015.

3.   *Startup Ecosystem Report 2012*, Startup Gnome. See: http://www.venturelab.ca/The-Startup-Ecosystem-Reports-2012-and-2014.

4.   Tapan Munroe, *What makes Silicon Valley tick*: 261.

5.   Timothy Bresnahan, Alfonso Gambardella and AnneLee Saxenian, '"Old economy" for "New Economy" outcomes: Cluster formation in the New Silicon Valleys', in: *Industrial and Corporate Change* (2001) 858.

6. *Regional innovation scoreboard 2014*, European Commission, Directorate-General for Enterprise and Industry, 2014. The eight indices are based on 50 variables. The results confirm that the "innovation paradox" is at work in Europe: "whereby less innovative regions with greater needs for investments in innovation and in solutions to structural problems have lower absorption capacity than performing regions and invest lower amounts of resources into supporting RTDI activities." (p. 36).

7. *Mapping the European ICT poles of excellence: The atlas of ICT activity in Europe. European Commission*, Joint Research Centre. Report EUR 26579 EN, 2014.

8. *Annual report 2014*, European Patent Office, Munich, 2015.

9. http://ec.europa.eu/programmes/horizon2020/en/what-horizon-2020.

10. http://ec.europa.eu/growth/smes/promoting-entrepreneurship/action-plan/index_en.htm.

11. http://eur-lex.europa.eu/LexUriServ/LexUriServ.do?uri=COM:2012:0795:FIN:EN:PDF: 4.

12. Interview in the Dutch daily *NRC*, April 25, 2015. Translation PE/AM.

13. http://startupjuncture.com/2015/04/17/a-founders-perspective-on-the-difference-between-early-stage-startup-funding-in-the-us-vs-europe/#more-8586.

14. There are some signs of a change in mentality among VCs, however. See for Dutch examples, Suzanne Blotenburg, 'Dutch VCs look to invest early stage for deals with "envy factor"', in: *StartupJuncture*, May 6, 2015.

15. *Ambitieus ondernemerschap. Een agenda voor startups en groeiers*. [Ambitious entrepreneurship. An agenda for startups and startup growth]. The Hague: Ministry of Economic Affairs, 2014.

16. *Achtergrondkenmerken en ontwikkelingen van zzp-ers in Nederland*. [Background characteristics and trends among self-employed freelancers in the Netherlands.] Statistics Netherlands, 2014.

17. Mirjam van Praag & Floor Kwik, *De stand van het ondernemerschap in Nederland. Een internationale vergelijking* [The state of entrepreneurship in the Netherlands. An international comparison]. Amsterdam Centre of Entrepreneurship, University of Amsterdam, 2011.

18. A recent report by the World Economic Forum and Global Entrepreneurship Monitor, *Leveraging entrepreneurial ambition and innovation. A global perspective on entrepreneurship, competitiveness and Development* (2015) ranked the Netherlands among the neutral economies: with average or lower levels of early-stage entrepreneurial activity, ambition, and innovative entrepreneurs.

19. See: www.startupdelta.com.

20. http://startupjuncture.com/2014/12/01/dutch-startup-visa-law/. The new law was first introduced in the Dutch Liberal Party's (VVD) 2013 startup manifesto. See: http://startupjuncture.com/2013/11/04/vvd-startup-agenda/. In March 2015 the first startup visa was presented to New Zealander Finn Hansen, founder of Med Canvas. *Forbes* (March 13, 2015) called the new Dutch startup visa program a "bright star of the global startup universe', and

'one of the smartest tactics yet" for generating economic growth. See also: http://startupjuncture.com/2015/05/12/how-to-dutch-startup-visa/.

21.   It has to be added, however, that the new startup visa only applies to founders, not to their employees.

22.   In 2014 Dutch startups managed to raise about €500 million in funding; startup investments in the first quarter of 2015 amounted to € 80 million. Top three startups were: WeTransfer (€22 million), AppMachine (€13 million), and Bottlenose (€12 million), all of them software companies. http://startupjuncture.com/2015/04/02/dutch-startups-raise-80-million/#more-8438.

23.   Jack Detsch, 'Can Shinzo Abe inspire Silicon Valley's dynamism in Japan?', *The Diplomat*, May 01, 2015.

Appendix 1: Interviewed Dutch Startup Founders & CEOs

Faruk Ateş, Presentate (www.presentate.com)
Neal Blaak, ZappoTV (www.zappotv.com)
Thijs Boekhoff, Ingen-Housz (www.ingen-housz.com)
Ruben Daniëls, Cloud9 IDE (www.c9.io)
Edial Dekker, Eventbrite (www.eventbrite.com)
Jonna van den Dungen, StyleScript (www.stylescript.com)
Jan Grotenbreg, SiliconValleyLink (www.siliconvalleylink.com)
Pieter Hoff, Groasis (www.groasis.com)
Arthur van Hoff, Jaunt (www.jauntvr.com)
Jurriaan Kamp,The Intelligent Optimist (www.theoptimist.com)
Salar al Khafaji, Silk (www.silk.co)
Dirk de Kok, Mobtest (www.mobtest.com)
Eric-Jan van Leeuwen, Login VSI (www.loginvsi.com)
Pieter Bas Leezenberg, SkyGeo (www.skygeo.com)
Ronald Mannak, JumpCam (www.jumpcam.com)
David Mayer, RENDLE (www.rendle.com)
Pieter Noordam, RFIsoft (www.rfisoft.com)
Marieke van der Poel, Proef (www.getproef.com)
Vincent van de Poll, GROM (www.getgrom.com)
Rip Pruisken, Rip van Wafels (www.ripvanwafels.com)
Adrie Reinders, EFactor (www.efactor.com)
Maarten Sierhuis, Ejenta (www.ejenta.com)
Valentin Smirnoff, Incubator Wells Fargo R&D (www.wellsfargo.com)
Harm TenHoff, BayLink (www.BayLink-llc.com)

Appendix 2: Interviewed Silicon Valley & Dutch stakeholders

Anuradha Basu, Director Silicon Valley Center for Entrepreneurship, Lucas Graduate School of Business, San Jose State University

Tom Beck, President, R2integrated (http://www.r2integrated.com/)

Allen Chiu, Congressional Aide, Congressman Mike Honda

Nathalie Delrue-McGuire, Honorary Consul Belgium

Oscar Garcia, Director Mountain View Chamber of Commerce

Eric Gabrys, Brussels Invest & Export

Alexandre Gallardo, student Business, San Jose State University

Scott Gardner, President and CEO, Liquid (http://www.liquidagency.com/)

Marguerite Gong Hancock, Associate Director Stanford Program on Regions of Innovation and Entrepreneurship (SPRIE)

Baudouin de Hemptinne, Belgian Trade Commission

Waad Jaradat, student Software Enigineering, San Jose State University

Quirijn Kleppe, student Business, San Jose State University

Steve Kwan, Associate Dean, Lucas Graduate School of Business, San Jose State University

Duncan Logan, Founder and CEO, RocketSpace, (https://rocketspace.com/)

Audra Martyn, Belgian Trade Commission

Vish Mishra, Venture Director, Clearstone, (http://www.clearstone.com/)

Curtis Mo, Partner at DLA Piper (https://www.dlapiper.com/)

Sean Randolph, President Bay Area Council Economic Institute (http://www.bayareaeconomy.org/)

Bill Reichert, Managing Director, Garage Technology Ventures (http://www.garage.com/)

Ken Rosenberg, Chair of the Mountain View Chamber of Commerce

Philipp Schubert, student Physics, San Jose State University

Ian Patrick Sobieski, Managing Director Band of Angels (https://www.bandangels.com/)

David Steele, Dean, Lucas Graduate School of Business, San Jose State University

Edwin Tan, Deputy District Director, Congressman Mike Honda

Marco ten Vaanholt, managing partner, BootUp Ventures (http://www.bootupworld.com/)

Elizabeth Yin, Startup Investor, 500 Startups (http://500.co/)

Interviewed Dutch stakeholders

Nora Dessing, Ministry of Foreign Affairs, The Hague

Cees Jan Koomen, Band of Angels, Venture Capitalist (Silicon Valley & High Tech Campus Eindhoven), Initiator of Point One Innovation Fund (Eindhoven)

Peter Laanen, Former International Trade Director of the Netherlands Business Support Office, Consulate-General of the Netherlands, San Francisco

Hugo van Meijenfeldt, Consul-General of the Netherlands, San Francisco

Bianca Oudshoff, Coos Santing, Pieter Waasdorp, Ministry of Economic Affairs, The Hague

Ard van der Vorst, Anne Donker, Jasper Smit and Robert Thijssen, Consulate-General of the Netherlands, San Francisco

Appendix 3: Questionnaire Personal Interviews Dutch startup Founders & CEOs in Silicon Valley

Name respondent:
Name startup:
Date of interview:

Coming to Silicon Valley
Q1.   When did you start your business here in Silicon Valley?
Q2.   Before coming to Silicon Valley: were you involved in business in the Netherlands?
Q3.   Could you tell us a little bit about your background in the Netherlands: upbringing, education, first jobs?
Q4.   How did you get the idea of going to Silicon Valley and begin a startup here?
Q5.   Why did you **not** start your business venture in the Netherlands?
Q6.   How did you prepare yourself for coming over to Silicon Valley?
Q7.   Did you know any people in Silicon Valley before coming here?
Q8.   What were your main worries in deciding to come over? And have they become true?
Q9.   Did you come alone or with your partner/wife/husband?
Q10.   Is this your first startup in the united states?

If no: what other startups did you found?
If no: are those startups still around?
If no: what was the main reason the startup(s) no longer exists or failed?

Strategy
Q11.   How do want your startup to develop say in the next two years?
Q12.   Do you have a growth strategy? If so, what are the plans?
Q13.   What is your exit strategy?

Team
Q14.   Are you the main founder or do you have a business partner?
Q15.   Did you have a mentor with who you could spar on your startup idea?

Q16. Do you have a role model for your startup venture?
Q17. How many people are presently employed by your startup?
Q18. What are the qualities you look for in your team?
Q19. Is it difficult to find the right people with the right skills?
Q20. What about salary levels compared to the Netherlands?

Market
Q21. What is the main product or service of your startup? What is your lead market?
Q22. How do you rate this product or service in terms of innovation?
Q23. How difficult was it to find the right balance between product development and sales in the first period?
Q24. How solid in your opinion was your business plan? What were the weak points?
Q25. Who did you see as your main customers? Who were the first customers?
Q26. What were the main features of your marketing strategy? Did it work?
Q27. If co-founder: what were the main commercial discussion points or controversies between you and your startup business partner?

Funding
Q28. How did you finance your startup business?
Q29. Was it difficult to get funding?
Q30. Any Silicon Valley venture or angel money involved?

Entrepreneur issues
Q31. What were the main challenges in your first year as a startup?
Q32. What were the main things going wrong in the first period?
Q33. What is your most painful experience as a startup entrepreneur?
Q34. Did you ever think of giving up and going back to the Netherlands?
Q35. Was there a turning point in the startup phase of your business?
Q36. All in all: did coming to Silicon Valley and founding your startup meet your expectations?
Q37. If you knew then what you know now: would you start your business again here in Silicon Valley?
　　　a. What would you do differently?
　　　b. And what would you certainly do again?

Q38. What, on balance, are the defining values of a succesful startup entrepreneur?

Q39. What is your main advice to dutch entrepreneurs who think of starting a business in Silicon Valley?

Collaboration & network

Q40. Do you collaborate with other dutch startups here in the valley or is your business network primarily American?

Q41. Do you work with other startups in Silicon Valley?

Q42. Any business relations with the big technology companies in Silicon Valley?

Impact of culture & change

Q43. In what respect is the culture in Silicon Valley truly pro-innovation & pro-startups? How did you experience that?

Q44. What is true of the magic of Silicon Valley to make startups flourish? Is there a secret?

Q45. Silicon valley is also witnessing a number of radical social and economic changes and challenges? What is your view on these developments?

Final questions

Q46. Any suggestions to the dutch consulate how they can better service dutch startups here in Silicon Valley?

Q47. The last question. What can the Netherlands learn from American entrepreneurship? What should we do differently?

Thank you very much for your time. We truly appreciate your collaboration!

Appendix 4: Questionnaire Group Interviews Dutch Startup Founders & CEOs in Silicon Valley

Name respondents:
Date of group interview:

Q1.   Before we begin: could you briefly introduce yourself?
(For the transcripter)

Coming to Silicon Valley

Q2.   How did you get the idea of going to Silicon Valley and to begin a startup here?
Q3.   Why did you **not** start your business venture in the Netherlands?
Q4.   How did you prepare yourself for coming over to Silicon Valley?
Q5.   What were your main worries in deciding to come over? And have they become true?

Team

Q6.   How do you select your people? What are the qualities you look for in your team?
Q7.   Is it difficult to find the right people with the right skills?

Funding

Q8.   How did you finance your startup business? Vc? Business angel?
Q9.   Was it difficult to get funding?

Entrepreneur issues

Q10.   What were the main challenges in your first year as a startup?
Q11.   What were the main things going wrong in the first period?
Q12.   What was surprisingly easy in the first period?
Q13.   What is your most painful experience as a startup entrepreneur?
Q14.   Did you ever think of giving up and going back to the Netherlands?
Q15.   All in all: did coming to Silicon Valley and founding your startup meet your expectations?
Q16.   If you knew then what you know now: would you start your business again here in Silicon Valley?

    a. What would you do differently?

    b. And what would you certainly do again?

Q17. What is your main advice to dutch entrepreneurs who consider starting a business in Silicon Valley?

Impact of culture & change

Q18. In what respect is the culture in Silicon Valley truly pro-innovation & pro-startups? How did you experience that?

Q19. Silicon valley is also witnessing a number of radical social and economic changes and challenges. What is your view on these developments?

Final questions

Q20. Any suggestions to the dutch consulate how they can better service dutch startups here in Silicon Valley?

Q21. The last question. What can the Netherlands learn from American entrepreneurship? What should we do differently?